BFF?

The truth about female friendship

Claire Cohen

PENGUIN BOOKS

TRANSWORLD PUBLISHERS
Penguin Random House, One Embassy Gardens,
8 Viaduct Gardens, London SW11 7BW
www.penguin.co.uk

Transworld is part of the Penguin Random House group of companies
whose addresses can be found at global.penguinrandomhouse.com

Penguin
Random House
UK

First published in Great Britain in 2022 by Bantam Press
an imprint of Transworld Publishers
Penguin paperback edition published 2023

Lyrics on p.191 from 'You've Got A Friend' written by Carole King.
Extract on p.227 from Series 3, Episode 1 of *Motherland*,
written by Holly Walsh, Helen Serafinowicz
and Barunka O'Shaughnessy.

Every effort has been made to obtain the necessary permissions with
reference to copyright material, both illustrative and quoted. We apologize
for any omissions in this respect and will be pleased to make the
appropriate acknowledgements in any future edition.

This book is a work of non-fiction based on the life, experiences and
recollections of the author. In some cases names of people, places, dates, sequences
and the detail of events have been changed to protect the privacy of others.

A CIP catalogue record for this book
is available from the British Library.

ISBN 9781529176032

Typeset in Bembo Std by Jouve (UK), Milton Keynes.
Printed and bound in Great Britain by Clays Ltd, Elcograf S.p.A.

The authorized representative in the EEA is Penguin Random House Ireland,
Morrison Chambers, 32 Nassau Street, Dublin D02 YH68.

Penguin Random House is committed to a sustainable
future for our business, our readers and our planet. This book
is made from Forest Stewardship Council® certified paper.

For my friends

BFF?

The truth about female friendship

Contents

Prologue

Most days, on the train to work, I sit beside the same group of women. They are in their thirties and forties, stylishly dressed and clearly confident in whatever it is they do. But that's not what fascinates me about them. It's their laughter and easy camaraderie that has me removing one earphone and straining to listen to their conversation. I've overheard them talking about work, offering advice that is sometimes brutally honest. When one woman had a broken phone, she was visibly touched when another offered her a spare: 'Take it, I don't need it!' Sometimes they just talk rubbish for half an hour.

These women jokingly call themselves the Mum Commute Club (told you I was eavesdropping), because their children go to the same school, but their bond clearly runs deeper than shared homework timetables. There's something about soaking up a little of their friendship each morning that puts me on the right track. And, if I'm being honest, intrigues me. Why? Because for years, I struggled to connect with other girls and women and I know how hard it is – at school, university and well into adulthood. I was never one of those people who seemed to be able to slide seamlessly into a squad, or find that perfect BFF. Perhaps you feel the same way. So many of us do and yet we tend not to vocalize it. Instead, we come through any tricky friendship experiences or look back at our younger selves, when we might have struggled to make friends, shrug and think, 'Phew, that was tough.' We can spend years silently consumed with self-doubt or licking our wounds. But does it have to be that way? Are we really destined to go through life not paying as much attention to our friendships as we do our romantic relationships? Or could we be having a different conversation?

It took me until my thirties to feel truly secure in my friendships – my female ones in particular. I firmly believe that if I'd had a book like this when I was younger, it would have fallen into place sooner. That I'd have been happier, more trusting and better able to deal with any bumps in the road. And we do need help. According to the Onward think tank[1] in July 2021, a fifth of adults under thirty-five say they have only one or no close friends – three times higher than a decade ago. We are in the grip of an 'epidemic of loneliness', as they put it.

According to the Office for National Statistics, 4.2 million British adults describe themselves as 'always or often lonely' compared to 2.6 million before the pandemic. Overall – including those who said they were 'sometimes lonely' – one in four adults in the UK said they were experiencing loneliness, and women more than men. The Campaign to End Loneliness takes it even further, estimating that almost half

(45 per cent) of adults in England feel 'occasionally, sometimes or often lonely'. And while social isolation is something that can disproportionately impact the unemployed, poor and migrant populations, none of us is immune – it can strike anyone, of any age. Indeed, a 2020 Children's Society report[2] found that British youngsters aged ten to fifteen are the unhappiest they have been for decades, with a lack of strong friendships specifically blamed. Which makes the fact that *Friends* is one of the most streamed series among Generation Z – who weren't even born when it started in 1994 – not so much interesting as sad. A new lonelier-than-ever generation is searching for aspirational depictions of friendship it can feel good about, because it's struggling to make and maintain its own.

When it comes to female friendships – which, as we will learn, are naturally more intense and intimate – that process can be even more fraught. Of course, a certain amount of friendship trial and error is all part of growing up, but I'm convinced that it doesn't have to be so hard. That's why it's more important than ever that we start being honest about what's going on behind closed doors. This is a moment to take stock. To think about who our friends really are. Because, when we get it right, there is nothing so nourishing as female friendship. And there are things we can do right now to change how we see them, how we define them – and how we celebrate them.

I believe this is the golden age of female friendship and it's only going to get brighter. We're entering a future where the women in our lives are just as important, if not more so, than anyone else. The conventional markers of femininity that have followed us around for centuries are shifting, and with that will come a recasting of our most significant relationships. It means that, for many of us, our female friendships are taking on a much higher level of visibility and importance.

It's already happening: we are marrying and having children later than ever, if at all. The roles we are expected to perform as women – thinking of ourselves first and foremost as romantic love interests, defined by the male gaze – are slowly starting to be questioned. Is that what we want? What other shape might our lives take? Friends are having children on their own, secure in the knowledge that they have a strong network around them to help make it work. Others are happy to say that they don't want a family, where they felt unable to just a few years ago, so strong was the sense that it was somehow 'unwomanly' not to give birth.

'The friendship tie is incredibly powerful and for women is going to become more and more important as we move through this century,' evolutionary anthropologist Dr Anna Machin of the University of Oxford tells me. 'Actually we need to reassess friendship because for an increasing number of women, that is going to be your "survival critical relationship" – the bond that is going to give you stability, give you that secure attachment, influence your life decisions and your health. If you don't want to be in a relationship, if you don't want children, then it's your friends who are going to be the ones that will carry you through.

Friendship is becoming more important for women than it has been in the past, and we need to recognize that.'

Isn't that exciting? The idea that we don't have to rely on finding a romantic partner to make our happily-ever-after come true? That it's a bonus if it happens – the cherry on the top of a big cake made entirely of female friendships – but not the be-all? I love the idea that female-friendship love is occupying the same space as romantic love in our lives. It's about time and I have a feeling that, if we talk about it as much as we do our relationships, it could be even bigger and better.

That's why I want us all to start telling the truth about female friendship. Because if I – raised in a house full of women, the product of two all-girls schools and the women's editor of a national newspaper – found it hard to trust and open up, and had convinced myself that female friends 'weren't for me', then you might not have it worked out either. It took me a long time to realize that the people who might seem like the 'right' friends on paper can be nothing of the sort. That humans are thrillingly unpredictable and that sometimes, the greatest friends are the ones you least expect.

That's not the narrative we're sold, though. From the time we start school, we are fed a diet of 'Best Friends Forever' – the idea that you should have a female soulmate to whom you tell all your secrets and who always has your back. But for most of us this is unachievable, so we spend years striving for a vision of female friendship that isn't realistic, instead of searching for what suits us best or appreciating what we've already got.

Well, you know what? I'm fed up with pretending that the 'perfect' female friendship exists.

It's a lie that every woman must have a cosy clique. It's a lie that the rest of the world is brunching like the *Sex and the City* gang, smoking fags like Bridget Jones and her mates, singing along to the car radio like the pals in *Waiting to Exhale*, having a hotel pyjama party like the 'Flossy Posse' in *Girls Trip*, or dissecting one another's love lives in kooky apartments straight out of *Girls*. Not that there's anything wrong with these models of female friendship, and they might ring true to you. But, in my experience, they're just as idealistic as the expectations of romantic love they're intended to free us from. And even if you do relate, I bet you've also had moments when you've sat at home feeling like you don't have anyone to call. It's also a lie that, if we're not BFFs, we're at one another's throats. Women are so 'tricky', 'overreact' and want to be 'queen bee' – I'd carry on, but you've probably heard all these stereotypes before.

Female-friendship stories might be starting to make themselves heard above those of romantic love, but they come with all their own cliches and myths. Those friendship tropes are just another version of the Madonna/whore complex, identified by psychoanalyst Sigmund Freud in the early twentieth century, that says women are either chaste and pure, or degraded. We're saints or sluts. Good girls or bad girls. BFFs or mean girls.

These myths stem from the same tradition that historically tried to hold women back and keep us in our place. To put us in boxes with neat little labels to make it easier for men to identify what 'kind' of woman we might be. It's why female friendship wasn't even seen as a socially acceptable concept until around two hundred years ago. We women might have been making friends for as long as we've walked the Earth, but our bonds weren't deemed legit until the eighteenth century. Nice.

'For a very long time, there was a kind of assumption that it was only men,' explains Professor Barbara Caine, a historian at the University of Sydney and editor of the book *Friendship: A History*. 'You need independence in order to have friendship and women lacked the power and the capacity in that way. Partly [women were seen as] not high minded enough; lacking the rationality that friendship was seen to require, as well as the independence.'

This only changed when Romanticism suddenly made having deep feelings fashionable, especially in letter-writing – something women were thought to be better at than men. Then, in the nineteenth century, women began to have friendships outside of the home, *doing* things together and gaining a sense of self. (Imagine!) They joined reform movements, political groups and became involved in suffrage. So while we continued to be legally beholden to men, our independent relationships began to flourish, too.

Barbara Caine sees Jane Austen as a major turning point in normalizing female friendship, putting the concept at the centre of the popular novels of the day.

The example she gives is from *Pride and Prejudice*, when Elizabeth Bennet's friend Charlotte marries the dreadful Mr Collins, a man Lizzie loathes, but we see their friendship survive despite that. 'You begin to see women's friendships existing within familiar constraints but being accorded a particular kind of significance and weight,' says Barbara.

The incredible female friendships I have encountered while researching this book make it seem impossible to me that the strength and ability of women to bond was ever in doubt. Some of the accounts that will stay with me are those from Holocaust survivors, who had their own word for female friendship, *lagerschwestern*, which means 'camp sisters' – used to describe the groups of unrelated women who tried to help one another to make the best of their tragic situation.

They taught one another recipes, passed around their lice combs and gave out precious pots of rouge, carefully hidden from the guards, before the 'selection' process – a matter of life and death, since the healthier you looked, the more likely you were to be given hard labour and not sent to the gas chambers. Incredibly, there was also a menstruation sisterhood: there are stories of older women befriending confused young girls who began their periods and didn't have their mothers to help them. In one astonishing tale, a woman lent another her bloodied underwear (many women's periods having stopped through malnutrition and stress) to help her avoid being raped by squeamish German guards. It worked.

When our past and present are filled with such

amazing and nuanced stories of female friendship, isn't it maddening that we're still trapped in those stereotypes? That we think it's impossible to have more than one 'best friend', that we can't make new ones later in life, that once a gap opens up in a friendship it's too late to close it.

The myths that we perpetuate around female friendship are poisonous, for both women and men. They hold us back, pit us against one another and see us give up too easily. And they have followed me around my entire life – making me feel inadequate, insecure and as if I didn't know where I stood. I'll bet you've been nodding your head at some of them, too.

Because that's the thing about friendship: on some level, everyone's an expert. By that I mean that we all have our own tales to tell: our own heartbreaks, dramas, love stories and the general ups and downs of the friendship-coaster. And whether we have one close friend, a scattered group from across our lives, or a circle of casual acquaintances, we are navigating those same grey areas every day. We need to start speaking about female friendship in this way: giving voice to the almost invisible things that go into making it the complex beast it is – so much more than the catchy labels suggest. Yes, we should be celebrating the good times and calling out the not-so-good ones. But it's those many small moments – the thoughtful card, the hand squeeze, the act of kindness, the unexpected apology – that are the oxygen of every female friendship, and deserve to be aired. Right now, we're often pretty bad at doing so and I'm no exception. It is only through my work, some soul-searching and a lot of painful personal experience that I have started to understand the true power of female friendship and how to talk about it more truthfully.

It's taken me more than three decades to realize who my friends really are and, importantly, what it takes to be a good friend myself. During that time, I had my faith in women blown to bits, and had to rebuild it slowly – in part while spending my days reporting on inspirational women doing inspirational stuff, with this mystical-sounding thing they referred to as a 'support network'. But despite outwardly being part of this Sisterhood, inside I felt like a total imposter who wasn't sure she even knew how to trust women – let alone love them.

Because female friendships are, at their core, love stories. For many women, they are the great romances of our lives. Think about it – what really separates our closest friends from our lovers? It's all there: loyalty, selflessness, kindness, generosity, companionship. The laughter and tears. The shared world view. In other words, all the things you look for in a relationship and which are ultimately far more important than sleeping in the same bed. And if a friendship breaks up? The pain can rival any heartbreak, and leave deeper wounds.

That's why, in these pages, I want to bring to life some of my own stories – and those from other women – for the purpose of discovering all the faces of female friendship, and so that we can better understand our own. I have interviewed women (and the odd man) aged nine to ninety-two, and had conversations with many, many more. I've picked the brains of psychologists, anthropologists, linguists, historians and coaches to identify trends in female friendship – unpredictable as they can be. Mostly, I'm humbled and hugely grateful to everyone who has shared with me their most intimate and painful friendship moments.

So many of the women I spoke to found it hard to put their female friendships under the spotlight – whether replying to my research email Q and A or during formal interviews in which they were forced to examine certain aspects in detail, often for the first time. But once they started to talk, most said it felt like a release. Even the experts I spoke to, once we were done talking about psychology or science, couldn't wait to tell me about their own friendships. This is something that is central to our lives – whether we have it, want it, or are seeking more from it – and every person's story begets another and another. Speaking about it is liberating. Even if, right now, you're feeling as though you don't have enough friends, you want to go deeper with someone in particular, or you feel fulfilled but there's a nagging doubt at the back of your mind about that old school pal . . . there will be so many other women who are going through the same thing, or have done so and have come through it understanding more about themselves and their friendships.

Through their words and mine, I want to offer hope; that despite not having a 'perfect' girl gang, or even one best friend – and despite it all feeling impossible at times – our friendships can be hilarious, joyful and mutual. And that any struggles along the way will be worth it. You might not recognize every single tale from your own life and the cast of characters will undoubtedly be different, but I'm certain that many of the scenarios and the emotions associated with them will be all too familiar. I hope to help you see your female friendships in a new light – hopefully for the better, leaving you with a renewed sense of security and pride in the women you know. This process might be challenging at times and demand honesty, from yourself and your friends – as it did from me.

Before I go on, perhaps I should explain why I'm not writing about male and female friendships. It's something you've probably had a conversation about at some point – the different ways in which men and women interact. Perhaps you find it easier to make friends with men, as I have done in the past. For a long time, I saw myself as 'one of the boys', and it was only on looking around at my wedding, three years ago, that I realized this was no longer true. But while I absolutely believe that men and women can have wonderful friendships – my male friends will no doubt be put out not to see themselves in these pages, and I know that for many women, their gay male friends are a crucial part of their circle – there's something about female friendship that meets our emotional needs in a way that friendships with men often can't. It's all that unspoken stuff about being a woman; the things you don't have to explain (or womansplain) to a female friend, and which can help press fast-forward on forming a bond. For me, the massive hole in the conversation is around women's friendships with other women. There's a female friendship gap in our lives and that's the one I want to begin to close.

A disclaimer here: not all my female friendships are easy, even now. Far from it. They are, and will always be, works in progress, defined by intimacies shared, effort maintained and generally trying not to be an arsehole. It would be wrong to tell you that I have all the answers.

Plus, none of our female friendships are made any easier by the narratives we are sold in popular culture. As well as those BFF or mean-girls tropes (the ones where we fall out and then make up, start out as enemies and end up friends, or are part of an unbreakable girl squad), a new breed of female friendship has emerged: the 'real and unvarnished' type. To me, these still aren't all that relatable. Films like *Animals*, *Lady Bird*, *Girls Trip* and *Booksmart* were hailed as watershed moments in recent years and, like many of you, I was relieved to see something approaching the truth emerging about the love (and moments of hate) that can exist between female friends. But I can't help worrying that the focus is still on the intensity of having a BFF. Isn't the scene where the two characters in *Animals* pee in front of one another and peer into the bowl ('You need to drink more water') just another rarely attainable ideal of female friendship: the raw, hilariously honest kind?

I know that our everyday experiences of female friendship might not make the best movies. I'm not sure a film about two very tired women trying to arrange a date to meet for brunch over a series of increasingly terse WhatsApp messages is going to break box-office records. But aren't you just a bit tired of seeing and reading the same old female-friendship cliches over and over?

It's been going on for far too long. In her 1940 book *Testament of Friendship,* Vera Brittain wrote: 'From the days of Homer, the friendships of men have enjoyed glory and acclamation, but the friendships of women . . . have usually been not merely unsung but mocked, belittled and falsely interpreted.' I'd add to that: taken for granted.

Because, in our real-life relationship rankings, families, partners and children tend to take priority. Friendships are the first to go when life gets too hectic. It's easy to neglect them. You wouldn't dream of going for months without investing time and effort in your love interest, but you might do that with a platonic friend.

Friends are easy to fob off when things seem stressful. While I was writing this book, my pal Alexa asked to come and meet me for a coffee/accountability check, and my instinct was to say no. Too busy, sorry. What was I thinking? I'm writing a book about female friendship and I haven't got twenty minutes to give her? Those little check-ins are just as vital for reinforcing your bond as any girls' road trip or shared wee. So why are they always the first to go?

Friendships linger near the bottom of the pile when it comes to academic research, too. Where studies have been done, they tend to focus on the statistics: how many friends we have at school, college, university – and how that number fluctuates throughout our lives. But the emotional aspect? The importance of friends' support? How much value we place on them? The love? You're far more likely to stumble across one of the many studies into male–female romantic relationships that asks, 'What makes women most attractive to men?' (Answer: wear high heels[3] and make-up,[4] naturally.)

And yet, where research *has* been done, friendship has been shown to be at the heart of what keeps us healthy. As we'll soon discover, female friends can even help us live longer. That's something we should be seriously happy about. Because, at the heart of it, female kinship and connection breed happiness – so much of it. This is absolutely not a story about women being horrible to one another.

Female friendships can help you frame the world and grow into the person you are. They vibrate on a different level, inspiring you and showing you what might be possible. They're a lot like our romantic relationships. And, just as we know how to manage our love lives, so too there are things we can do to improve and deepen our female friendships.

Looking back at my own friendships now, I wonder why no one ever told me how rocky things could be. About the friendships that would go wrong and the women I would sideline while chasing the BFF myth. You probably have your own regrets, or things you wish you'd known sooner. That's why it's time to shine a light on the complexities and realities of female friendship: what happens when you outgrow a friend, how to make and keep new friends as an adult, when to let a toxic friendship go, why it hurts so much when you're the one who's dumped, the power of unlikely friendships, the laughter.

I hope to put all these on the map and present an honest picture ... and a positive one. Because female friendship is a positive story. But, friends, it just isn't always easy to get there.

Best Friends Forever?

*Myth: Every girl or woman needs a
platonic female soulmate*

'I don't think we should be friends any more,' a voice
that sounds like Ana's is saying down the phone.

'What?' I reply.

'I don't. Want. To be your friend,' she repeats, drawing the words out in that deliberate way teenagers
do – though usually to their parents, not their bestie.
Their soulmate. Their BFF.

I burst into tears.

I am sixteen, just back from a summer in California
and desperate to tell my best friend all about it. Except
that before I've even reached the part about the Juras-
sic Park ride at Universal Studios, she's broken my
heart.

Ana and I have been best friends for three years. We
met when I moved to a new school aged twelve;
awkwardly, a year after everyone else had started and
already formed friendships. It didn't help that I was

immediately nicknamed 'Posh' – this being two months after the Spice Girls had released 'Wannabe' – on account of my straight brown bob with a fringe and my straight-outta-Wimbledon voice.

I immediately gravitate towards Ana. She has long wavy hair, and neat nails with perfect white moons. Her ears are pierced with actual diamonds. She's rude to our teachers but always gets straight As. She's every-thing I want to be. It takes a while, but what finally brings us together is a shared love of the band Hanson (told you I liked long hair). We spend hours swooning over them. We memorize their lyrics, scribbling them on our school folders and up our arms in biro. When Ana gets the internet at home – the first person in our class to have this futuristic, beeping, hissing portal to the wider world – we scour chat rooms for more information about the objects of our lust. When we get tickets to see them at Wembley, we devote days to carefully crafting a love letter. It is written in fountain pen on lined A4 paper, as all respectable love letters should be, and in Ana's handwriting, which is more grown-up than mine. We draw a border of pink hearts around it.

No copy exists, but I imagine it went something like this:

Dear Isaac, Taylor and Zac,
We are two 13-year-old girls who live in London [transla-tion: we're your age and therefore fine for you to snog and maybe even go to second base, depending on your version of the bases because they might be different in America] *and are your biggest fans eva!!!*

We think it's tres cool that you write all your own
songs and we have all your albums, including the Christ-
mas one [which we inflict on our families every
December until their ears bleed].

We bought you an inflatable Jelly Belly bean as we
read that they're your favourite food. What flavours do you
like? We love buttered popcorn and watermelon [we
secretly hate them all but Haribo Tangfastics haven't
been invented yet].

Do you ever ask fans backstage? We'd love to meet
you! [Please take our virginities.]

Mahoosive love,

Ana and Claire xxx [alphabetical
order for fairness]

What MTV award-winning pop superstar could
resist?

On the big night, we tie our letter to the large
inflatable jelly bean, on which we have spent all our
pocket money, before hurling it towards the stage. It
lands in the dark pit between bouncer and band, but
we don't care. We spend the rest of the concert arm in
arm, jumping up and down, while Ana's dad waits
outside to drive us home. I had never been happier
and thought Ana felt the same. Until she broke up
with me – an event so seismic that my teenage heart
was shattered into a million tiny pieces.

If it's ever happened to you, you'll know it, too: the
feeling that your small world, which revolves around
school, has collapsed. The fear of having to go into
class the next day without the security of your BFF
beside you. The worry that everyone else will be

looking at you and thinking: 'Ugh, she must be a really bad friend. What did she do wrong? It must be her fault she was dumped.'

For years, I didn't think of it that way, though. We don't naturally use that language for the end of a friendship: *split, break up, separate*. But we should, because the heartbreaks that have, without question, hurt the most in my life have been from female best friends. Mine occurred at school and university, a time when having a best friend is as vital in Maslow's hierarchy of needs as air, water and food. But friendship fractures can just as easily happen in adulthood, causing as much agony as any romantic split – probably more.

I blame the BFF – best friends forever – myth. It's something little girls are spoon-fed from the moment we start school and our parents ask, 'So who's your best friend?' It's in the books you read and on the TV you watch: that you should have one special person to whom you are joined at the hip and with whom you never fall out. It's even in our playground rhymes: *'Make friends, make friends, never ever break friends'*.

This is when the 'girl code' first raises its head – the unwritten dos and don'ts by which every female friendship must operate: 'You've got my back, I've got yours.' It doesn't suddenly stop the minute we leave school either. I've heard grown women accused of 'breaking the girl code', having started dating the ex of some distant acquaintance, or not taking their friend's side in an argument. And it holds us back from having the freedom to find true and meaningful friendships – ones that don't demand loyalty based on gender alone.

It might sound supportive and nurturing, but it's actually pretty proprietorial when you think about it. How many of us have ignored friendship red flags because of such unquestioning devotion? From a young age, the BFF myth encourages us not to question why we are friends with someone and how that friendship might be sustained and improved, but simply tells us that we are friends because 'that's what girls do'. Having a best friend in this way can be reassuring and make you feel as though you belong, but it can also bring with it a pressure to perform and not to put a foot wrong. It can make us feel insecure: will she be my BFF? What if she likes another girl more than me? Does she want to steal my best friend? How can I win?

And the myth is quite specific to girls and women. 'The term "best friend" is not something that you hear men say very often,' says evolutionary anthropologist Dr Anna Machin. As part of her initial research into friendship, she sent out a questionnaire in which 85 per cent of the women who responded said they had a female BFF. That seems extraordinarily high to me, but Anna suggests that it could be linked to both the BFF myth and our biology.

'It is very high and there might have been some pressure to say "Of course I've got a best friend, I'm not a sad, lonely person,"' she explains. But, she adds, women do place importance on close friendships in a way that men simply don't. 'What women tend to need from their friendships is real emotional intimacy,' she says. 'They are getting something from that which is absolutely vital to being a woman. Men don't look for emotional intimacy with friends and so it's not the case that they need that very close dyadic relationship. They tend to attract bigger groups.'

As women, we place so much pressure on ourselves to find the perfect partner, the perfect job, the perfect house, the perfect family, and we are expected to juggle it all perfectly. I'd add to that list the pressure to have a perfect friendship; the sort of female soulmate with whom you can have a conversation by merely raising an eyebrow, and who knows all your secrets. It's an intoxicating idea; but the reality? Usually less than perfect. It's just as poisonous as the notion of Prince (or Princess) Charming swooping in on a white horse. Why on earth are we letting little girls imagine that their perfect BFF will turn up on a My Little Pony and that, magically, life will be complete? It's not a myth that every single girl and woman buys into, of course, but so many of us do. You might not even realize that you have.

'In childhood, when you're just discovering that someone outside the family can be very important to you, there's the myth that a friend is someone who's "just like me",' says psychologist and University of Cambridge professor Terri Apter. 'It's a myth that some girls buy into . . . *she's a sister, she's my real twin.* And then what happens is that as girls develop and change, they face a dilemma: *does that mean she's no longer my best friend? Should I change? What do I do?*'

That idea of things changing in friendship is something we all worry about. When you're young and devoted to the idea of a BFF, it can be all-consuming – the fear that your friend might be moving in another direction is intimately tied up with your fledgling sense of identity. Do you allow yourself to potentially lose your 'soulmate'? Do you also change to try to keep up? *Does* it mean you're no longer best friends?

Simply, it can be hard to find the space to change when external forces suggest that to 'grow out of' a friendship or to drift apart is somehow to have failed at being a BFF. And it doesn't necessarily get easier to negotiate as we get older – not only allowing our friends the space to embrace new challenges, but rejecting the impulse to keep old friends in a box; expecting them to remain just how they were when we first met them. Say that you and a friend are both single and sharing that life, with all the same ups and downs, and flickers of doubt about the future. Then your friend meets someone and you're left wondering where your friendship sits in her list of priorities and whether you still have anything in common. It can, as Terri Apter says, 'lead to a sense of "I've been betrayed, because she's changed".'

Of all the women I have interviewed, Lauren probably knows more about change within friendship than most, and how it can work for the better. She began to transition while living with her (cis) female friend 'M' and tells me how it helped to deepen their bond.

'We were housemates during the time when I was starting to question my gender,' she says. 'You often come out to your housemates before friends and family, because you want to try out dressing differently and it's nice to not have to be confined to your room. M and I remember vividly one night we spent lying in the garden, looking up at the stars, talking about gender and the dizzying, terrifying sense of vertigo that had enveloped my life.

'We moved apart and kept in touch. At the same time my identity was moving away from "I don't know what I am", through "I know I'm not a man" to "I know I'm a woman" and I found – whether through shifting psychology, hormonal changes or changes in social code – that the vulnerability felt more and more natural. I found it easier and less scary to say to people outside of any romantic interest: "I love you. I miss you. I'm so glad I know you." All these things that had been harder once, even when I knew I felt them. I don't want to generalize, but I always had the feeling that men are not supposed to say these things to each other.

'As I became firmer in my own identification, all these worries and barriers about showing affection and vulnerability dropped away. My friendship with M was one of the first that benefited from this process. I found I could say to her in a true spirit of platonic female friendship the kinds of things I was so scared of saying, and she could say them, too.'

*

Of course, I'm not saying there is no such thing as a best friend – they do exist for a lucky few. You only have to hear stories like Lauren's to understand that. Fashion designer Justine Tabak also has one of those precious bonds, having known her BFF for over fifty years, since their mothers met at antenatal classes.

'We often make a point of saying that we've known each other since birth, and people can't believe it,' Justine says. 'We're very different, but we share very similar values and that's why I think our friendship has endured. We say what we think and give hard-hitting advice. We've guided each other through marriages, separation, children, work dilemmas, bereavement – every phase of life. I feel so lucky to have a friendship like ours. The older I get, [the more] I realize how special and unusual it is. She is my "sister" through and through.'

That language of being 'like sisters' remains powerful for the handful of adult women who tell me they have a best friend. One is activist Nimco Ali, who has been besties with Carrie Symonds, the wife of Boris Johnson, since before she was in the public eye.

'I think the fact that it hasn't changed her and it hasn't changed our friendship has been something that's incredibly important to me,' says Nimco, thirty-eight. 'I don't think of her any differently to my other best friends, even though she's like more of a sister to me than anything else. I probably just don't feel the level of protection [for my other friends] that I feel for her. I think love is a strong thing to say, [but] the same way that I would feel for my sister, I feel for her.'

A few women were embarrassed to tell me that they had a BFF. 'I find the term quite cringey, in a Pony Club sort of way,' said one, before going on to describe the woman she can't imagine life without. It's the best-friend double bind: we can feel shame if we have a BFF, and shame if we don't. Perhaps we should accept that we're all searching for something that doesn't exist as a one-size-fits-all standard. And that re-creating the sort of intense friendships we see on screen and read about in books is incredibly difficult.

'Growing up, I always craved a best friend,' one woman in her thirties told me. 'A lot of it was to do with characters on TV always having a lifelong BFF. But the reason it works on TV is the reason it doesn't really work in real life – people are more complicated. We evolve, and have different things to offer at different times. So while I believe that best friends are possible, they're not always forever. That's the unrealistic bit.'

Forget BFF, I'm starting to think we should be saying BFFN (best friends for now). As the author of *What Did I Do Wrong?* and friendship expert Liz Pryor says: 'It's not the best of terms because it puts a lot of pressure on people who don't have one. And I don't think it's as common as our culture claims. As my mum used to say, it's a gift and not everybody gets it.'

To me, the concept of the best friend is flawed because it assumes a single hierarchy. What does 'best' actually mean? I'm best at being me and you're best at being you – but that doesn't mean we're always going to bring out the best in each other. Plus, to put all your eggs in one platonic basket is a lot of pressure, under which most relationships would crack. It's too much. No one best friend can meet all your friendship needs, just as no one romantic partner can be your 'everything'. It's a fantasy to expect that a single person can fulfil you emotionally. That myth sets us up for failure and disappointment – and it's how the 'girl code' can end up being quite controlling and possessive. But no one ever says this. So onwards we plough, trying to force a flawed model of friendship to work. No wonder it so often ends both badly and sadly.

Doesn't that sound pretty familiar in terms of adult relationships, too? The foundation for the idea that one romantic soulmate can complete you is fostered all the way back in the concept of the BFF. Eventually, most of us work out that there's no such thing as 'The One' in terms of love, so why are we still deluding ourselves that 'The One' exists in female friendship?

As well as by best friends, I have had my heart broken by men in several ways, each as uniquely painful as the last. I sometimes think mine must look like a Franken-heart, repeatedly fractured and then put back together with great ugly stitches that criss-cross it like train tracks. But when your heart is shattered by a lover, you can at least distract yourself by finding a new one, however bad an idea that might turn out to be. Friends can't be so easily replaced. You can't down a couple of wines and go out to pull a new friend in a sweaty club. Or call up an old friend at midnight and see if they want to come over . . .

What's more, after every single one of my romantic break-ups, people rallied round and asked if I was OK. After my friend break-ups? Nothing. Which says everything we need to know about how we rank our friendships compared to our relationships.

*

It's all too easy to write this stuff off as petty playground grievances, but it sticks with us for far longer than we admit. Being ditched by a best friend is one of the most scarring things that can happen when you're trying to form those first meaningful relationships outside your immediate family, using the only under-developed emotions you have: love, hate and neediness.

It might sound dramatic to say that life would never be the same again, but my first BFF-dumping started a chain reaction that gave me a mistrust of female friendship which would take me decades to recover from.

Quinn and I were in the same class at our all-girls school and had desks side by side, which, when you're five, pretty much means you're destined to become best friends. I loved going to her house. She had a bigger bedroom than me, in which we spent hours making up dance routines and playing with her Cabbage Patch dolls. Even better, our mums were friends, so entire days could pass while they talked about grown-up stuff. I was sure that Quinn would be my best friend forever. So the day she torpedoed our friendship still prickles in my chest more than twenty-five years later.

It was 1993 and a new girl joined our school. She had what I didn't: mystery. Her parents were divorced and we didn't know anyone else whose parents were divorced. I didn't stand a chance.

Quinn's parents were having one of their house parties. I've got to hand it to them, looking back: they were pretty great at it – the booze flowed, there were adults dancing to Bowie and smoking everywhere, while we hid behind sofas, watching wide-eyed. As

Quinn's best friend, I expected to be front and centre. So I will always remember the moment that she turned to the new girl in the playground.

'My parents are having a party. Do you want to come?'

Then the kicker.

'Claire will be there, but only because our mums are friends.'

My eyes burned with tears and my face fell. I didn't understand what had just happened, only that it hurt like nothing before – maybe apart from getting a splinter in my bum. I wanted Quinn to be my BFF again, but how? It was the first time in my small life that I felt as though I was not enough.

And it's happened to so many of us.

'When I was eleven at boarding school, there was a group of four of us and one girl decided that there wasn't room for me any more. So she put a note under my door saying that,' says writer and podcaster Pandora Sykes, thirty-five. 'It's heartbreaking because it feels like you've lost everything. Those experiences are so formative and, like anything that happens in your childhood, they can be traumatic.'

It's strangely reassuring to hear that other women still carry around these specks of childhood hurt, lodged deep in their bodies like pieces of shrapnel. Vivid memories about which we can recall every agonizing detail just like that, when we can't even remember what we had for breakfast yesterday.

'When I was thirteen, I came into class one day, and my best friend had moved to a different desk,' recalls Jane Lunnon. 'I felt so ashamed, as if I had done something wrong, or failed. I didn't tell my parents or anything. It was just awful.'

In 2020, Jane was named 'Best head of a public school' by *Tatler*. At the time, she just so happened to be at the helm of Wimbledon High, the school I attended between the ages of five and twelve and where I had some of my formative best-friend experiences. She thinks that the idea of the BFF has been 'cultified' and wants girls to start telling themselves a different story. 'Everything about the way girls are brought up encourages the idea that you should have close friendships,' says Jane. She blames the 'gendered childhood observations around nurturing: that girls play with dolls, and the focus on femininity being so closely aligned with effective relationships. That "this is what we're good at".'

'There's also been a commercialization around the "very best friend" notion,' she adds. 'It's been exacerbated by social media. In recent years there's been this kind of cult of the best friend.'

'My daughters were sold aggressively, from the age of about four, this idea of the BFF. I think it's really destructive,' says Emilie McMeekan of *The Midult* website and podcast. 'Endless T-shirts and charm bracelets: it's so toxic. I've got one daughter who has a best friend, but one who has found it harder and so she feels there's something wrong with her. The idea that we're all locked into a BFF is extremely difficult.'

That utter belief in BFFs and the power they wield over one another is clear from my conversation with nine-year-old Rose about her school friend Elsie.

'She's my best friend but she's sometimes nice and

sometimes not nice. She will sometimes say, "You can't play this game", but other times she will let me play,' says Rose.

She tells me that her family is about to move and she's going to a new school, in a new town. I ask if she'll keep in touch with Elsie or if she'd prefer to have a wider group of friends at her new school.

'I'd like to have a best friend because if I had lots of friends there would be lots of people wanting to play with me. And if there were lots of people wanting to play with me, then I couldn't play with all of them. And then some people who wanted to play with me might get sad because they can't,' Rose says. Which is as good a summary of my guilt about my adult social life as I've ever heard.

Do you think that you and Elsie are going to be best friends forever, I ask.

'Probably not.'

Oof. One formative BFF heartbreak coming right up.

*

The cult of the best friend has been building for decades. At school in the nineties, we would talk about who our best friends were constantly. We admiringly copied one another's school bags and butterfly hair clips. We bought necklaces that broke into two parts on separate chains, so both BFFs could wear a segment in a public display of unity and adoration. Two halves of a whole heart, sun, moon or Forever Friends teddy bear.

It might all seem sweet and innocent, but these necklaces are loaded with meaning – and not always the good kind. While they might feel precious to the pair involved, those excluded will probably feel horribly left out and hurt. It's a performative show of best friends forever that screams exclusivity and deliberately shuts out others, turning female friendship into something to flaunt like a shallow status symbol.

And the novelty can wear off even for the holders: if you begin to drift apart, despite your matching jewellery, you can feel like even more of a failure, having previously shouted about your special bond. They put pressure on girls to be chained to one another like soulmates. They can also be quite passive-aggressive if bought as a gift, the recipient having been declared the giver's BFF when, in reality, they might not feel that way. They can also lead to heartbreak. One pal admitted to me that when she found a new best friend at school, she handed her half of a yin-yang necklace back to her former BFF. Brutal.

I had my own version: a silver heart, broken in two, with a dolphin embossed on each side. My friend Izzy and I bought them together, at a time when our friendship had been rocked by our being put into separate classes at school and we were craving reassurance. It worked in that moment but, as we got older, it also came to represent a childish closeness that had been tested by time. Eventually, I put it in a little box – where it remains today – a sign of the sort of confining best-friendship ideal I believed wholeheartedly back then.

Rereading my childhood diaries from this time

was not only mortifying but eye-opening as to just how much emphasis we put on having a BFF (and sometimes a second or third best friend, just as back-up).

Friday February 10th, 1995

Dear Diary,

I rang Izzy to tell her that I had her jumper and painting but she didn't want to talk as her neighbour Sally was over again. I'm supposed to be her best friend.

Love Claire

Saturday May 6th, 1995

Dear Diary,

Madeleine says I'm her second-best friend. I get the impression that Izzy feels a bit left out. I love Keanu Reeves!

Love Claire

Thursday September 28th, 1995

Dear Diary,

I have started senior school. Izzy isn't in my class and I am frightened of losing our friendship. We are best friends. Gymnastics tomorrow.

Love Claire

Riveting stuff, I know. Move over, Samuel Pepys. Nice try, Virginia Woolf. I'm expecting a call from the British Library's important manuscripts department any minute now with a request to save my journals, *c*.1993–8, for the nation. Tantalizingly, the two front pages of the 1996 volume are glued together with a substance that has refused to perish in the last quarter of a century – I can only assume Copydex – but through which, if I hold it up to the light, I can make out the words 'A list of my best friends' ... and what looks like the names Rhiannon and Lauren, neither of whom I have any recollection of knowing.

Perhaps they were code names for real friends (I was always paranoid that my sisters were reading my diary). They could have been fantasy BFFs, conjured up from my childish imagination. Or maybe they were now long-forgotten characters on TV – because that's where the best-friend cult really did its work before social media. Blossom had Six. Moesha had Kim. Buffy had Willow. Daria had Jane Lane. Cher had Dionne. Tia and Tamera in *Sister, Sister* were twins – like my own younger siblings – but also best friends. I mean, give me a break. We fetishized real-life best friendships, too: Courteney Cox and Jennifer Aniston, Drew Barrymore and Cameron Diaz, Gwyneth Paltrow and Winona Ryder.

What really gets on my nerves is that at the same time as we're having these 'perfect' examples of female friendship drummed into us, we're also being told that we could mess it up. Right from our first schooldays, girls are painted as being 'petty', having 'catfights' and going off in 'huffs'. We tend not to stop to consider the action that might have led to a little girl feeling upset over a friendship; instead we focus on her reaction – often dismissed by parents and teachers as 'silly' behaviour. We even have terminology such as 'frenemy' – a portmanteau of 'friend' and 'enemy' – which is overwhelmingly applied to women to describe the sort of female friend who might hug you from the front while stabbing you in the back. 'Two-faced' is another one. Bet you've never heard those terms used about boys or men.

'I often hear people say, "Little girls can be such bitches",' says Pandora Sykes, who has a young daughter. 'And I know what they mean, because as you get older, if you want to be cruel to someone it tends to come buried in other layers, whereas when you're young that cruelty is just there [on the surface].' She thinks it's because little girls, while not 'bitches', are pushing boundaries; trying out exciting and grown-up ways of treating one another, and finding out how it feels to be in control.

When I spoke about this with my husband, he recalled being told by a teacher when he was six years old that girls 'fall out all the time' and 'hold grudges'. Whereas boys? Well, they are annoyed for five minutes and then 'get on with it'. The assumption throughout our lives is that if women aren't bosom buddies (even that phrase is so gendered) we must be at one another's throats. Men and boys, though? Easy-going. All they need is sport or a drink and they're bonded.

Annoyingly, there is actually some truth to that last bit. It's a generalization – something the academics I spoke to were quick to point out – but, by and large, they agreed that women want their friendships to revolve around sharing emotional intimacies. And men? Well, as Professor Robin Dunbar, the University of Oxford evolutionary anthropologist, puts it: 'So long as the other person is capable of holding a pint glass to their lips that's good enough.'

'Boys live in this kind of rather anonymous clubby group world where the identity of the members of the group – the identity of your friends – isn't really that important just as long as there's somebody there,' he adds. 'They don't think about relationships in that kind of depth. It's just kicking a football backwards and forwards across the street. I think that probably protects their friendships a bit more and makes them harder to fracture. But on the other hand, they sacrifice the emotional support that girls get from their friendships.

'If you think back to how life was when you were about eight or nine, girls' friendships are so specific to individuals, so one-on-one: if Frida doesn't invite you to a party, it really is the end of the earth.'

Or if, as happened with Quinn, they wish you hadn't been invited at all.

★

If my first BFF heartbreak had made me feel inadequate, the second would transform me into a 'beta friend' – passive, subservient, eager to please. It was 1995. I had just started secondary school and was suddenly in a different form to my friend Izzy. It meant I needed a new BFF in my new class.

Madeleine owned an amazing selection of coloured pens and we both fancied Prince William – we had to be soulmates. The only problem was that two other girls also thought that Maddy was their best friend. Outwardly, we probably looked like a happy gang of four. But in truth, three of us were engaged in a bitter power struggle, in constant competition to sit next to Maddy and share her stationery. It was exhausting and, looking back, I have no idea why I thought these girls were my friends in the first place. Maddy didn't so much play us off against one another as simply enjoy the attention – who wouldn't?

One day, though, she made the call: I was definitely not her best friend. I had crossed some invisible line. The three of them stopped speaking to me and refused to sit with me, freezing me out. I put a brave face on it during the day and burst into tears the second I got into my mum's car every afternoon, sobbing fat tears onto my exercise books in the certain and crushing knowledge that I was not good enough.

So I set about trying to change. To be the most endearing version of myself that I could be. Someone who laughed at other people's jokes and agreed with whatever they said. Who complimented their Groovy Chick pencil case. Your classic wing-woman, satisfied with second place at the expense of her own emotional needs. It's what I'd read about in books such as Judy Blume's *Are You There, God? It's Me, Margaret*, in which Margaret tries to be someone she's not, just to fit in – and even though it hadn't worked for her, maybe it would for me?

This diminishment of myself coincided with one of the most terrible things that can happen when you grow up in a happy family in suburban Zone 4: moving to a new school, partly because of my isolation and partly to help my younger sisters get in. But despite my friendship misery, I didn't want to leave the only school I'd ever known. *Things will get better,* I told my parents (because I will be better). *Please?*

But the decision had already been made. I cried myself to sleep every night for a year, probably longer. The strain of trying to fit in at my new school was awful and I always seemed to stand out when I didn't want to. My voice was just that bit more clipped, as the result of years of drama classes. My body wasn't as developed. I had always been skinny, but I hadn't realized it was a problem until my new classmates started to tell me.

Where are your boobs?

Do you even wear a bra?

You'd look all right if you wore a bit of make-up.

You look anorexic.

Girls would stride up to me by our lockers and poke my hips. On 'own-clothes day', one so-called new friend was so outraged by how my legs looked in a pair of H&M flesh-coloured flares (fetching, I know) that she slapped me hard across the cheek. 'I'm only *joking*,' she said, as a bright-red handprint appeared on my face.

If I'd thought for one second that making a new BFF in my new school as the new girl would be easy, this was a rude awakening.

You can see, then, why my friendship with Ana, when it finally happened after more than a year of making myself as likeable as possible and trying desperately to win her over, meant so much – and why it hurt so deeply when she cut me off. As far as I was concerned, we were BFFs. Life was good, at last.

California had been our first family foreign holiday, after a lifetime of rainy Cornish seaside trips. I returned, golden and full of stories. Lying on my back on the sofa with our cream Bakelite phone balanced on my chest and the cord twirled around my fingers, I remember dialling Ana's number and hearing her voice for the first time in weeks. But something was different. Solemnly, she explained that she had been hanging out with another group of girls. They had been listening to different music and 'doing things you wouldn't approve of'. I sobbed until she hung up. At school, I put the gift I had bought her from America – a notebook made from recycled paper clips – in her locker. She never said thank you.

The thing that stuck with me, the detail I would ruminate over lying in my single bed at night, was that 'things you wouldn't approve of' comment. I didn't know what she meant. It made me feel that not only was I not good enough to be her best friend, but that there was something inherently childish about me. That I was immature in a way I couldn't quite put my finger on and therefore couldn't change.

When I asked my friends now about the BFF myth, many said that they wished they'd been encouraged to think about how unrealistic it was sooner, and that it was still causing problems in their lives today. Sameeha Shaikh, twenty-seven, tells me she was obsessed with having a best friend at school and university, and kept the 'mindset going for a very long time. That was my Achilles heel, because I had great people in my life, but the expectations I had of those people were a lot,' she says. Kayra feels hemmed in by it even at the age of thirty-nine. 'I have a friend who tells me I'm her BFF, and will write it in messages and cards, but it doesn't sit totally comfortably with me because she is not my best friend,' she says. 'I don't want to have only one. Frankly I think by the time we're adults we shouldn't be using that term.'

If I could tell my nine-year-old self all this, would it have helped? Or is it better to learn the hard way? Of one thing I'm sure: if I hadn't believed that best friends should be forever, I wouldn't have tolerated some of the behaviour I did. And I might not have been so heartbroken when those friendships ended. Maybe they wouldn't have ended at all if girls were brought up to see beyond the myth. Ana could have had her new crowd, and stayed friends with me, too. It's why I think we should be encouraging children not to put all their energy into one person, but to have many friends from different social groups – hopefully preparing them better for adult life.

Friendship coach and author Shasta Nelson thinks we can all start to look at the BFF myth another way. 'I would argue that the label "best friend" isn't something we [should] bestow on somebody. It's an acknowledgement of a relationship that's already been developed,' she says. 'We walk around like, "Am I somebody's best friend? Who's my best friend?" instead of saying, "I can have several best friends" and seeing "best" as a quality, as opposed to a quantity. We can have more than one. It just means that a relationship has reached a meaningful standard. I think we've done a lot of damage, thinking that we're supposed to find this one friend, and be chosen. It's kind of crazy.'

I love Shasta's way of viewing best friendship as a quality and not a quantity. It's just something that can, in time, be applied to any significant friendship if that's what both friends want. When you put it like that, it takes a lot of the pressure off. And here's another thing: Robin Dunbar tells me that he's noticed a pattern in when – not just if – women tend to say they have a best friend. We're more likely to claim it when we're young and then again as we approach old age. 'I'm struck by the fact that there is a dip in middle life, but then it comes back with a vengeance – that's my casual observation in older women,' he explains. 'I think that has a lot to do with the fact that your capacity to *do* stuff with anybody is simply short-changed by reproduction hitting.'

That's one way to look at it. Another might be that, as we approach midlife, the BFF myth slowly begins to lose its grip. Sure, we're tired because of the impact of our careers, family, travel, doing tax returns and perusing Rightmove – but we've also been jaded by friendships turning out to be less than perfect, in ways we weren't prepared for. Then, when you're much older and your friends begin to depart this world, you find yourself wanting to restart the search, armed with a lifetime of wisdom, as 91-year-old Helge Rubinstein – whom you'll meet later – told me. Perhaps those are the two times in our lives when we need the BFF myth the most: when we're taking our first tentative steps into the social world

as children and near the end, when we find ourselves
alone again.

*

In the end, I was better off without Ana. Now that I
was free to eat lunch with different people and sit
with other girls in the park behind school (we always
went in groups to make sure we outnumbered the
flashers), other friendships slowly started to grow.

One was with Marie. For years, we had been in
maths lessons together – the only two girls in our class
to be put in the bottom set. But I grew to realize there
was so much more to her than the things that had
slightly intimidated me: her high heels, bomber jacket,
her short, layered haircut like a dark Gwyneth Paltrow
in *Sliding Doors*. She was funny, kind and liked indie
music. I began to see her as a friend, not just someone
to moan about equations with.

When we moved into the sixth form a year later,
everything changed again. New girls joined and suddenly our old friendship ties loosened. It felt like a
fresh start, with classmates who had never seen us cry
in PE and didn't know the burning shame of those
past friendship break-ups.

Marie and I formed a threesome with one of the
new girls. Suddenly, the landscape of my social life
(I had a social life!) had altered. We met a group of
boys from a sixth form in Fulham and started going to
the pub on Friday nights. We always got in, because
what respectable branch of the Slug and Lettuce
would turn away three teenage girls dressed up to the

nines? (Which in 2001 meant tweed trousers, heeled sandals and a strappy top from Bay Trading.) We would spend our history lessons passing notes dissecting every detail of the previous Friday and not learning anything about the economic history of Germany between 1889 and 1989. We went to gigs together, stumbling into school the next day smelling of Marlboro Lights.

I had other new friends: girls I chatted to in the common room, girls I bunked off General Studies with, girls I went for lunch with at our local cafe. To me, they were everything and nothing. I liked them but I didn't know where I stood. I worried they would get bored, or that I would do something wrong. What I didn't realize, and wouldn't for years yet, was that I was getting a taste of what friendship could be like if you weren't beholden to one person whom you idolized above all others – if you broke up with the BFF myth.

Because, when you think about it, finding your female soulmate or being 'chosen' or living by the girl code ... it all smells suspiciously like just another unrealistic set of rules that women are meant to live by, and which mean we put even more pressure on ourselves.

Isn't it better simply to be honest? Very few of us will have a true best friend forever, and that's OK. Instead, we'll hopefully make different friends throughout our lives, who unlock certain parts of our personalities and fulfil some of our emotional needs. The reality is that most of us will eventually learn that this is what we want: a portfolio of friends, rather than a claustrophobic little cult of two. Wouldn't it be so much more powerful (and waste less of our time) if we all knew this earlier?

It can take years to shrug off. Even if we start to see through the BFF myth, it can remain in the back of our minds like a nagging little voice telling us that we're letting our friends down. It's why we feel terrible when – instead of instantly knowing the answer deep in our hearts because we're soulmates – we find ourselves panic-scrolling through WhatsApp trying to find a friend's address to post a last-minute birthday card, or a message from when their baby was born because we've forgotten the date. It's part of what makes us feel guilty for all sorts of minor friendship blips: the weight of expectation and perfection we're sold from the start. And it's just not the truth. As one wise schoolmate put it to me, a few months after the break-up with Ana: 'I like you much better now; you're less of a sidekick.'

It was, in hindsight, a lesson I wish I'd learned there and then.

The Friendship Formula

*Myth: Your female friends will never 'get'
you like a romantic partner can*

Steaming vaginas. Jade eggs. Bone broth. Cauliflower
pellets. There seems no end to the list of extreme and
often pseudo-scientific wellness trends that are supposed to help us to be healthier and happier. To live
our best lives. You might even have tried some of
them: whether doing a digital detox or making your
home more *hygge* (a Scandinavian word for basically
shoving a load of candles and fur blankets around the
place), we're obsessed with living longer and better.
But there's one area of our lives that we can bolster to
help us achieve both and it's already staring us in the
face: friendship.

Studies show that having friends is good for our
mental and physical health. Friendships can help to
lower our blood pressure, stop us gaining weight,[5]
boost our immune systems,[6] protect us against heart
disease[7] and can prevent us from catching colds.[8] They

reduce our stress levels,[9] improve our mood and make us laugh,[10] releasing those feel-good endorphins we all crave and which help us cope with physical pain.[11] 'Friends are better than morphine', as a headline in a 2016 edition of *Time* magazine put it.

And not having friends can be actively bad for us. Professor Julianne Holt-Lunstad, who teaches Psychology and Neuroscience at Brigham Young University in the USA, found that being socially disconnected can increase your risk of death by 26 per cent, can be as harmful as smoking fifteen cigarettes a day, is a better predictor of early death than the effects of air pollution or being physically inactive, and is worse for your health than being obese. So you can be a non-smoker who lives in the countryside, runs marathons and boasts the world's best BMI – but if you don't have any mates? You might as well eat a Big Mac for breakfast every day. It doesn't matter whether you have a BFF or not, friends are the stuff of life. And while some of the above health benefits apply to all of us, others are exclusive to women.

Get this: before the year 2000, there hadn't been any research done into whether the 'fight or flight' survival instinct, which is supposedly the primary driving force of every human being, was actually the case for women. The analysis which had led to that conclusion in the 1930s had been carried out exclusively on men.

Professor Shelley Taylor at the University of California wondered whether, just maybe, the research might be biased, and women might react differently to stress. Guess what? We do. She concluded that the hormone oxytocin, when released at anxious moments, mixes with all our lovely oestrogen and means that most women display a different behavioural pattern in times of crisis, which she called 'tend and befriend' – an instinct to protect our offspring (if we have them) and form close attachments with other women.[12] It's what makes us pick up the phone to a friend, or to our mothers, when everything seems awful, rather than withdraw. It is the elixir of female relationships; to put it another way, we actively look for female friends in our most vulnerable back-against-the-wall moments as a way to deal with stress or danger.

'The fact that men may be somewhat more likely to cope with stress via fight or flight and women to cope with stress via tend and befriend may help to explain the worldwide gender gap in mortality,' the study concluded. Isn't that incredible when you really think about it?

Fundamentally, female friendship is written into our genetic code. Our evolutionary past suggests that women who formed strong social support structures were more likely to survive. Across continents and throughout human cultures, we have come together to raise young and support one another. We sat round the fire, telling stories and creating our own communities, while the men were out catching the tiger who came to be tea.

The evidence is still there in some societies. The Japanese island of Okinawa has the oldest average life expectancy in the world for women, at ninety. One of its secrets is thought to be the *moai* that residents form from a young age – a social bubble of five friends, who offer each other a lifetime of support.

We've all seen how powerful that female solidarity can be with the #MeToo movement. The demonstrations against restrictive abortion laws in Poland, America, Argentina, Mexico. The mass protests and outpouring of anger in response to the rape and murder of women in Spain, India, Algeria, Austria, South America, Kyrgyzstan, France, Sierra Leone, Kosovo, South Africa, Clapham Common.

Being a woman can be dangerous and female friendship can be a comfort. The women I've spoken to have supported one another through the worst of life: domestic abuse, murder, divorce, addiction, depression, dementia, infertility, cancer, loneliness, grief. They've held one another and left food on doorsteps. They have been honest and vulnerable.

Their stories, which you'll read throughout this book, shared so much in common that it made me wonder: is there some sort of unspoken formula for female friendship? A set of techniques or a blueprint that we all unwittingly follow, or try to?

Dr Anna Machin, author of *Why We Love*, has studied female friendship for years and knows more than most about what it means to us. She tells me she was 'surprised' by what she found when she first started to explore the subject: that heterosexual women get more emotional intimacy, can more easily be themselves and have more in common with their female friends than anyone else in their lives, including their male romantic partners.

When you consider how strongly we believe romance to be the answer to everything, it is surprising to stop and reflect that women are getting this vital connection and support from female friendship. We take it for granted that our partner will 'complete' us – 'you're my best friend', we tell them – but, according to science, they cannot fulfil us emotionally nor understand us to the same degree that the women in our lives can. That is huge to me: that the 'truth' we are told about how romance is the route to eternal happiness has a formidable rival in female friendship.

'When we look at brain scanning studies, women experience emotionally intimate moments with their friends in a very positive light,' Anna says. 'We see a lot of activation in the reward centres of the brain and a decrease in amygdala activation [the part of the brain that governs our emotional responses], which means that they are not fearful or stressed about being intimate. If you put men in that situation, they actually get quite a negative response. Their amygdala fires off and that's a sign of fear: "I don't actually want to be having this intimate conversation with my male friend."'

It's why, she explains, in general women would much rather be sitting across from a female friend in a bar over a glass of wine – enjoying eye contact and deep discussion – while men might choose to go on, say, a group bike ride. Yet, despite how fantastic female friendships can be for our physical and emotional health, how highly do we actually rate them in the hierarchy of love?

'We have a real issue,' admits Anna when I ask her why we find it so hard to articulate how we feel about our female friends. 'I would interview people and say to them, "Do you love your dog?" And they'd say, "Of course." [Then I'd say] "Do you love your friends?" . . . "Umm, I don't know." There's a real reluctance to say "love" when it comes to friendships. And I find that quite funny. When you speak to people from the Mediterranean countries they say, "I love my friends passionately." So it's a real cultural thing that we have to question whether to apply the word love to friends, whereas we're perfectly happy to attach it to our dogs.'

I find this staggering. We are so fixated on romantic relationships being the defining element of our lives that we're missing what's right in front of us (and putting our pets firmly before our pals).

Women are taught to make our lives revolve around men and we do it from the start of our first crushes, spending hours unpicking the meaning of a throwaway comment or moment of eye contact. We learn to exist for some imaginary male audience that lives in our heads: shaving and waxing our body hair even though our only weekend plans involve tracksuit bottoms and the TV remote; sitting in a cafe with a book and thinking only about whether we look sexily mysterious enough; closing our eyes and tilting our heads back in the shower as though we're in some soft-porn shampoo advert. In her novel *The Robber Bride*, Margaret Atwood writes: 'You are a woman with a man inside watching a woman' – and that inner eye, that internalized male gaze, is what means heterosexual women aren't placing enough value on their relationships with each other.

As we know, women are raised on fairy tales, which

means we think falling in love and getting married is still going to make our dreams come true. Having done both those things, I can tell you that while it was wonderful, it certainly isn't the pinnacle of my achievements. Yet we talk in those terms all the time – 'my other half' – and I say that as someone whose friends and family were made to sing 'Two Become One' at her wedding.

'It's ludicrous because you block out this massive spectrum of love,' says Anna Machin. 'As humans, we are so lucky that we have these big brains that enable us to fall in love in so many different ways and with so many different people. But we denigrate all that and think romantic love is the main force. And it just isn't. That makes me quite cross because I think we as a society focus entirely on romantic love. It's weird.'

We need to start having a proper conversation about love within our female friendships. To reframe where they sit in our lives. To get more comfortable with telling our friends that we love them. Can you imagine how much more relaxed and secure our friendships might feel if we were able to do that? If there was a formula for our friendships that included saying 'I love you' and there wasn't anything strange about it? At the very least, we'd all know where we stood.

'We are indoctrinated into believing that we say it to our romantic partner and we say it to our children – that's the acceptable face of "I love you". Beyond that it's all a little bit uncomfortable,' says Anna. 'But with your friends, every day, you're saying, "Do I want to be here?" in a way that means that if you're with them, that love is a chosen love, and that's arguably more powerful.'

Friend love is entirely conditional. Every time you speak to a friend, meet up with her, share something personal with her, you are making a conscious decision to invest in that relationship. As the author Hanya Yanagihara put it: 'Friendship is the most underrated relationship in our lives . . . It remains the one relation not bound by law, blood, or money – but an unspoken agreement of love.'

Yet we have no proper love language for talking about it. Of course, we all give and receive love in different ways: for some people acts of kindness are the most important thing; for others it's quality time, or physical closeness. But a universal way of speaking about the importance of our female friendships would be a significant step in elevating their status.

At the moment, so many of the terms and phrases we use around female friendship are either twee or ultimately a bit meaningless: sisterhood, sisters before misters, tribe, girl squad, hoes before bros, hovaries before brovaries, life force, power posse, BFF.

Perhaps it would actually be more impactful to use the language of romance to describe our female friendships; then, everyone would know what we meant. We've put down social markers when it comes to talking about 'dumping' or 'heartbreak'. We know, on the emotional spectrum, how love and grief make us feel. If we described a 'frisson' with a potential new platonic friend over tea and cake, it would capture just how the conversation fizzed – little jokes and new intimacies flying backwards and forwards to create that sparkling New Friend Energy. We could admit to having 'butterflies' about meeting a new pal, or reconnecting with an old one. We just need to get over the idea that every time we talk about intimacy with someone that we mean sex – more often than not the intensity of our feelings is emotional, rather than physical.

Yet we still get the two mixed up. It's why Simone de Beauvoir's 1954 novel *The Inseparables* – about an intense female friendship, and based on her own life – was deemed 'too intimate' to be published at the time and only came out in 2021. It captures perfectly the platonic love that can exist between girls, without midnight feasts, social media posts or broken-heart necklaces, and is entirely based on emotional intimacy – which is, as we have learned, the cornerstone of female friendship.

Before my first date with my husband, Tim, I was sweating so profusely on the train that I considered getting off and turning around. Or at least popping into Boots for a travel-sized deodorant that I could surreptitiously spray up my top on the Central Line. I can remember just how my stomach churned – nervous excitement and dread all at once. Yet I've felt exactly the same with friends: making sure I wear something nice and applying my make-up just that bit more carefully; imagining what we might chat about, feeling clammy.

'I treat each friendship like its own romance – so while I love group dinners, I actually tend to see my best friends one-on-one. And not on, like, a Monday where we have an early dinner with no alcohol. But a Friday night, where we dress up to the nines and go out somewhere,' says Pandora Sykes. 'Dolly [Alderton] and I always make an "event" out of our dinners and I get butterflies in my stomach in the same way I would going on a date with my husband, probably more so. When you've cohabited with someone for a while, the excitement in your belly comes from your friendships. That never has to get old, unless you give up on the romance of friendship, or believe that friendships are not worthy of romance in the first place.'

I for one believe that they are – to my mind, just as the best romances are based on friendship, so the best friendships are based on a bit of romance.

My husband always jokes that I only shave my legs, get a bikini wax and buy new underwear before going away on mini-breaks with girlfriends. He's not wrong. It's like having a dirty weekend away, with all the cosiness, in-jokes, red wine and open fires that the heart desires – just minus the sex – and I want to feel my best for that. To be around female friends is often more nourishing than any 48-hour shag-fest during which you have to pretend that the feather-covered thong they've bought you from Agent Provocateur is the most comfortable thing you've ever worn and definitely not a one-way ticket to thrush.

But as well as not telling our friends that we love them, we're also totally dysfunctional when it comes to anything remotely difficult, such as conflict. So many women I spoke to in the course of writing this book told me that female friendship should be straightforward and that they would end one if it got 'too hard'. It was a sign that something was fundamentally wrong, they said.

I mean, yes, occasionally that might be true. But we do cling to this myth that female friendship should be sugar and spice and all things nice. It's so easy to idealize it, just as we do romance, from the unrealistic narratives we've been given. But every intimate relationship in our lives is a mixture of emotions: the highs and lows, the disagreements, the potential to cause one another pain; the excitement, anticipation and joy. The ability to hold a special place in one another's hearts, for better or worse.

We know and accept this when it comes to marriage – it's right there in the vows you make and the tips you receive from well-wishers. Here is a snippet of the advice my husband and I received before our wedding:

> *Both admit you're wrong sometimes.*
> *Always be kind.*
> *Respect each other, support each other and laugh often.*
> *Push each other hard to love your lives.*
> *Always make time to go for a pint together.*
> *Sort out every disagreement with a game of paper, rock, scissors.*
> *Go bra-less (the only suggestion I've truly taken to heart).*

I found it reassuring that, amid all the congratulations, there's also the acknowledgement that marriage isn't easy. That it takes work. It gives you encouragement that it doesn't have to be perfect all the time, and confidence that you can get through the wobbles. It takes a bit of the pressure off the fairy tale. By contrast, then, isn't it patronizing to tell girls and women that our friendships – often the most intimate and important relationships in our lives – should be easy and conflict-free? Why aren't we giving ourselves permission to experience the full range of human emotion with our friends?

Before I'd ridden my own friendship roller coaster, I didn't think of it this way. My world was divided into people I thought had been 'good friends' and those who were 'toxic'. But it's ridiculous to think that your good friends are going to be aligned with you all the time. Of course they're not. How exhausting would that be? How fake. Every single friendship, even with the most wonderful women in your world, will have ups and downs. You can't reach the top of Everest if you haven't been at the bottom.

It all boils down to the fact that, when it comes to female friendship, there is no set formula. No rule book. We have any number of rituals in place when it comes to our romances, to symbolize renewed commitment to one another, but with our close pals? Nada.

Plus, friendship security is pretty easy to unpick. What hard proof do we actually have that anyone is our friend? That they really do like us? Texts, sure. Birthday cards, yup. But do these things count? Or are they just markers of duty and obligation?

As humans we crave milestones to reassure us and

to measure a relationship's significance. 'It's normal to label a romantic relationship and let people know that's your person, but we're more reluctant to label a friendship and say someone is your friend, maybe out of fear that you're not theirs,' Rebecca, thirty-five, tells me over email. 'Shades of grey which are common in friendships would be unacceptable to many people in dating. I think a best friendship takes commitment to evaluating and understanding what that relationship is and how you both define it if it's going to last.'

We only tend to get that show of commitment at life's most intense points. At weddings and baby showers, fine, but also when tragedy and illness bring into sharp focus the passion we feel for our female friends and the almost animal desire to show it. It happened for me when a friend's father died unexpectedly, shockingly and so young. I wrote her a letter; I went to his funeral. Years on, I still think of him often and of the burden of grief she has to carry with her. I felt it again when a friend went through the agony of losing her baby. Even writing those brief words now, I can sense some of what I did then – the clenching of my internal organs and the helplessness. The love I desperately wanted to show.

'When I was diagnosed with breast cancer, I was overwhelmed by the way in which my friendships deepened and strengthened, at exactly the point when I needed them most,' says journalist Rosamund Dean, forty-one. 'Friends sent me headscarves and silk pyjamas and cashmere socks – and their eagerness to make me feel better during a bleak time made me so grateful that I could cry (and often did). On long walks, we talked about death and fears and ambitions in a way that we never had before. And it wasn't just my closest friends who stepped up. Old university mates messaged for the first time in years, just to let me know they were thinking of me. Women with whom I had barely exchanged a word at the school gate were suddenly leaving casseroles on my doorstep and offering to look after the kids so that I could rest. They helped me feel calmer, and cared for, while I was facing the brutal triumvirate of chemo, surgery and radiotherapy. Having cancer does not have many silver linings, but a new appreciation of the women in my life is certainly one of them.'

The love is there. We just need to learn to vocalize it on the mundane days, as well as the most painful or joyful.

One of the symbolic markers we do have to celebrate our friendships is Galentine's Day. Yes, that's a thing – coined by character Leslie Knope in a fictional comedy series, *Parks and Recreation*, in 2010. The idea is that you get together with your closest gal pals on 13 February to have dinner, drink fizz, get a manicure, paint mugs or whatever floats your boat. In the last few years, shops have sold greetings cards to mark the occasion (*'You are my best bitch, always and forever'* should give you a flavour). There are gift lists in women's magazines, encouraging us to show our love for our friends by buying them T-shirts embroidered with nipples. Or as *Cosmopolitan* put it: 'OMG! Don't be stressed. First off, just like Valentine's Day, you are free to skip Galentine's Day. But considering it's all about showering your friends with affection, why would you want to?'

No pressure though, right?

I don't think we need an enforced 'day' on which to celebrate our female friends and buy one another presents; especially as Anna Machin found[13] that gifts don't actually improve female friendships and can make them less emotionally intimate, so save your pennies. For me, to mark it in such a way is too commercial and contrived. Wouldn't it be nicer if we created our own individual milestones, just as we do in relationships?

Linguist and friendship expert Deborah Tannen, author of *You Just Don't Understand*, thinks this is trickier because our friendships don't tend to have a watershed moment such as a first date or kiss. 'There's no "We were friends but then we became lovers",' she says. 'With "We were acquaintances and then we became friends and then we became better friends", there isn't as much of a specific starting point.'

Relationship anniversaries tend to be burned into your brain: the day you first met / snogged / moved in / got engaged / married / got a cat. But does that lack of a specific starting point mean we can't celebrate our friendship milestones? Yes, it's more admin. Yes, another date for our diaries. But what those milestones or markers look like is up to you – whether a cuppa, a phone call, a card or a simple text. The point is not to give ourselves more emotional labour or put ourselves under any more pressure. It's to find a way that works for you, and your friend, to acknowledge what you have built, *despite* life's pressures and endless responsibilities. That's surely worth celebrating just as much as any snog or set of house keys.

A huge part of the problem today is time – the conflicting pressures on our daily lives mean that we often feel there isn't enough of it. It's a wonder we manage to maintain friendships or even make friends at all, given how long it takes. Brace yourself: you might need chemistry to spark a successful female friendship but there's maths involved, too. A 2018 study by Jeffrey Hall at the University of Kansas[14] concluded that you need to spend fifty hours with someone to go from acquaintance to casual friend, ninety hours to go from casual friend to meaningful friend, and more than two hundred hours to become close friends. It's about putting the effort in. 'You can't snap your fingers and make a friend,' said Hall. 'Maintaining close relationships is the most important work we do in our lives.'

Still, I don't know about you, but two hundred hours seems overwhelming. A hundred two-hour drinks at the pub. Or two hundred coffee dates. Maybe sixty-five or seventy meals out. That's a lot of booze, caffeine and cheese plates for the sake of one new mate.

It's not what any of us want to hear, is it? If you're anything like me, you already feel pulled in a million different directions and walk around like a great big churning ball of guilt about not seeing, calling or texting your friends often enough. You worry about being seen as a 'bad friend' when you have nothing but good intentions; you imagine that they're feeling neglected, when you're simply bogged down with life – but then you also feel overlooked when they struggle to find time to contact you.

The key to alleviating all this is learning to prioritize, which is where Dunbar's Number comes in. It's the brainchild of evolutionary anthropologist Professor Robin Dunbar of the University of Oxford, whom you've already met. He began his career studying primates and became convinced there was a link between brain size and social group size. He and his colleagues decided to apply the theory to humans, extrapolating primate ratios to estimate that the 'magic number' of social contacts for people is around 150. This, they discovered, is part of a pattern to do with the number 150 throughout human history: as an ideal maximum group size, it applies to early hunter-gatherer communities, units of Roman armies, villages in the Domesday Book, modern Christmas-card lists and phone records of the number of people we tend to call over the course of a year. Any more than this, and the network tends to drift or collapse.

According to Dunbar's theory, our individual 150 is divided into circles. The closest consists of just five people, our loved ones, whom we interact with daily. Then come our 'best friends'; the ten people we value deeply and probably contact weekly. Next are 'good friends' (around thirty-five people) and finally our 'just friends' or acquaintances (approximately one hundred). People can move in and out of these circles and any new friend will likely usurp one of the existing members of our group if it's full. There are nuances in personality, too: while introverts focus more tightly on their inner circle of five, extroverts will spread themselves more thinly. Women, in general, have more close friends than men.

Even if you don't agree with Robin Dunbar's conclusions, his theory makes the point that we all have a limit to the number of contacts with whom we can realistically maintain a relationship. Each of us will decide, consciously or unconsciously, who slots into which layer of our friendship circle and how much time we apportion them.

My hen do was the perfect example. I looked around the country pub at the random assortment of women wearing waterproofs and wellies . . . one from school, a trio of university friends, my sisters, a few friends from past jobs, another I'd met through an old boyfriend. Not many of them knew each other; I was their glue. They were bound together only by my friendship circle. Because after years of trying, failing, and trying again, that is now my personal friendship formula. I don't have a BFF. No platonic life partner or soulmate for me.

Instead, I have a portfolio of female friends: a loose group of women from different parts of my life. Some are subdivided into smaller groups of three or four; many I meet one-to-one. That's my method. Yours might be different. But however they look, our friendship circles take their energy from a mixture of past, present and future. You might have old friends who go way back, or you might have learned valuable lessons from past friendships that are crucial as you make new ones. The point is, your friendship grouping probably doesn't follow some set formula at all – only the one you want it to.

What we need to realize – and what I'll unpick in the coming chapters – is that there are many ways to experience female friendship. You just have to find what works best and feels healthiest to you. Vaginal steaming, cauliflower pellets and *hygge* optional.

Toxic Friends

*Myth: Toxic friendships
are always one-sided*

I need a drink. But I can't go to the bar, because three of my friends are staring at me. They are willing me to agree to a plan which, in hindsight, should have sent me running – but which I am about to go along with.

It's my first year of university and, having lived cheek-by-jowl in student halls for little more than a few weeks – with over six hundred of us in an asbestos-filled building that will be razed to the ground the year after I leave – we are suddenly being asked to subdivide into clusters of future housemates. I am convinced that I will be rejected. At best, the pity pick. *Someone has to live with her . . . you do it . . . No, you.*

What this feeling means is that I am desperate to make friends with anyone who will have me. Quality control has gone out of the window. So instead of taking my time and seeing who I might connect with, or joining societies . . . I latch on to the nearest set of girls. And when those girls, with whom I share a corridor, but not much else, suggested that we cohabit in our second year? I'd have lopped off a limb to make it happen.

The four of us are sitting on my lumpy single bed, with its spotty blue-and-white Debenhams bedspread (the same one they had in the *Big Brother* house the previous summer), when it happens.

'Claire, do you want to live with us next year?' says Naomi, in a sing-song voice.

My heart almost bursts out of my chest.

'It'll be so fun,' cries Leonie. 'We can go out all the time and *everything*.'

What 'everything' means, I'm not sure, but I want to find out. Maybe this is my entry to the secret club of BFFs at last.

I glance over at the photo collage on my bedroom wall, with the cut-out faces of my family, Izzy and Marie smiling down at me. They'll be pleased I'm making new friends, I think. And maybe these girls are actually more 'me'? I start to imagine that maybe I am *growing up* and finding *my people*.

The reality, of course, turns out to be far more complicated than that. It's no secret that many women struggle with friendship at university – living away from home for the first time, with all the expectation of forming close bonds for life and few responsibilities other than making that happen. It's a high-pressure environment that is bound to boil over for some.

I've buried a lot of what went on during my second year. Dredging it up for this book has actually been pretty upsetting. At times, I've had to confront my own less-than-ideal behaviour, and I've been forced to understand that my former friends may not even recognize themselves in this chapter at all. They will no doubt have their own perspectives on everything I'm about to tell you. But by sharing mine, I hope that anyone experiencing a similar situation might begin to recognize toxic traits in a friendship and be able to step away, saving themselves heartbreak down the line.

If I'd been able to, I might never have taken part in the great bedroom swindle of 2003.

The plan is this: we are picking numbers to decide who will sleep where in our new house.

There are to be five of us. Naomi is the self-appointed leader. She's pretty, quick-witted and self-deprecating – but not without taking you down with her: 'I've got such pointy feet ... but look how long your toes are.' She subtly negs me from day one: 'You've got such lovely eyebrows, even though they meet in the middle.'

Leonie and Poppy are her numbers two and three. Crucially, all three already know each other and have mutual friends. Looking back now, that should have been a red flag: university is not where you go to meet a girl clique and try to insert yourself into it. But at the time, it seemed to me like the pinnacle of female friendship.

Another girl from our halls, Malia, has also been recruited as this particular house is deemed too good to pass up. After all, it's slap bang in the middle of Birmingham studentsville. There is a master bedroom with a king-sized bed, two comfy medium-sized rooms, along with one much smaller rabbit hutch that can barely hold a single bed, and one bedroom downstairs, with a window that faces the street, at which the clientele of the nearby chippy enjoy hurling their empty cartons.

The three girls now staring at me in the pub want to make sure none of them is lumped with the hutch. What they are suggesting is that we pre-pick the numbers one to four at random, choose which bedrooms we want (one being the first to select), then when Malia arrives at the pub we go again – pretending that we haven't already done so. This time *all* the pieces of paper in the draw will have the number five written on them to guarantee that she is the resident rabbit. '*I've got number one!*' the victor will exclaim, having already swiped the king-sized room and swiftly hiding her slip with the number five on it.

Sitting at a high table, with the sort of precarious bar stools that make you feel as though you're at the world's worst job interview, I weigh up my options: 1) Go along with this devious plan, say nothing and find my BFFs; 2) Tell them that I want no part of it and be forced to live by myself in the new-build student flats unaffectionately known as the 'loser block'; or 3) Drop out.

'Who's going first?' I ask, forcing a smile.

I burn with shame to recall this now. Such is my longing to be accepted that, instead of standing up against what I know to be wrong, I rummage in my handbag to find a receipt on which we can write the numbers with my Collection 2000 eyeliner.

I've long asked myself two things about that day. First: what had our fifth housemate done to deserve it? Answer: I think the other three had simply identified her as someone who wouldn't kick up a fuss at paying for a bedroom so tiny that the chances of her ever being able to invite someone back were non-existent. Equal rent for unequal sex.

Second: did they swindle me, too? I pick number four from that sticky pint glass – which has, until moments earlier, contained a snakebite – lumbering me with the freezing downstairs bedroom next to the front door, which would slam all night as students came and went, and saw me stuff my ears with Blutack in an attempt to sleep.

I have every reason to be suspicious. Naomi picks number one, Poppy and Leonie numbers two and three. In the moment, I don't care – I have been included and am euphoric. So this is what it feels like to be part of a girl squad. This is what it feels like to be in control.

That's the thing about false friends: they don't immediately reveal themselves to be fool's gold. They dazzle you with their generosity ('*You must borrow my new boots*') and attention ('*Claire, can I sit next to you at the cinema?*') to make you feel somehow indebted to them. Then they subtly put you down, in ways so small you hardly notice. Worse, they might not even know they're doing it.

University is a vulnerable moment for this. It's

when you're supposed to meet 'your tribe', who aren't mere friends of circumstance thanks to growing up in the same postcode. It's not only a formative experience for your academic future, it is where your friend-family is born. But many of the women I know would agree that they struggled to make friends when first living away from home – and that they made bad choices. I certainly did, right there in The Gunbarrels pub at 4 p.m. on a wet Friday afternoon.

Learning to cope with these experiences earlier on, says Jane Lunnon, can give us the tools to deal with them throughout our lives. Which is why, when she was head of Wimbledon High in 2016, she introduced lessons on toxic friendship to teach girls that disappointment is a part of friendship and not to berate themselves if something goes wrong. 'It seems really crucially important we are teaching children about the realities of relationships and that they won't always be rainbow-coloured and sparkling,' she explained at the time.

'I don't think it's far-fetched to say that a really toxic friendship can have a similar impact to more traditional forms of abuse,' Jane adds, when we speak on the phone. She has come up with a list of questions we can ask ourselves to assess if a friendship has potentially turned toxic.

1. Do you feel anxious when you meet up? You might occasionally feel nervous to see a friend – say, if you haven't for a while – but if it's a recurring theme then you should interrogate it.

2. Is there an imbalance of power? Are you always meeting in the place that your friend wants to meet, or doing what they want to do?

3. How do they react? Does your friend ignore it if you try to suggest something you'd like? Do they react in an extreme way, abusing or dismissing you?

4. The fourth is trickier to pin down, because the truth is that these sort of friendships are often really fun. 'The friend with the power can often be very charming,' says Jane. 'What will happen is this sort of awful seesawing of emotions ... you're having a great time, and then something happens that impacts it, so you think you've done something wrong.'

That's exactly the point – a 'toxic friendship' isn't toxic all the time. It's appealing enough to keep you constantly coming back, and to make excuses for the bad moments. It's why terms like 'frenemy' exist. The painful parts hurt all the more because five minutes ago you seemed like BFFs.

And here's another painful truth: your toxic friend might not be seen as toxic by everyone. Often, as friendship coach Shasta Nelson explains, it can be the dynamic that's poisonous – rather than the people themselves.

'I had a friendship that I would have been tempted to use that word about a couple of years ago, but other people loved her and had a great relationship with her,' she says. 'So I don't think that person is toxic, I think that the pattern that she and I developed had become toxic. But that's not to say that person, or every single friendship that person has, is toxic.'

Could that be the case with my former housemates?

After the great bedroom swindle, Naomi and I become close during that first year in halls. We watch *Sex and the City* in her room, help one another with essays, swap clothes, and date boys from the same friendship group. What could be more perfect? Outwardly, I am happy. Inwardly, I feel as though my head (*Do you actually have anything in common? Are you being yourself?*) and heart (*You finally have female friends, do not rock the boat now*) are constantly fighting. And when we move into our new house, it threatens to become full-on war.

It happens gradually at first. Naomi invites me on shopping trips, then claims she never asked me, or that there isn't room in the car. They all stop talking when I walk into the room. Leonie ruins my new suede Adidas trainers by dropping tuna brine on them. I scrub them for days and can't get the stench out. I keep my bedroom door locked after that.

They're the sort of small behaviours that, when I was living with these girls, quietly and slowly ate away at me, making me anxious that I might say or do something to turn them permanently against me.

I start sleeping badly for the first time in my life. I've always been the sort of person who's asleep before their head hits the pillow and, if undisturbed, can put in a solid ten hours. It's something that has infuriated the insomniacs and early risers in my life, as I happily snooze with my eye mask pulled down and – I'm told – a serene smile on my face. As a student, I was known for being able to fall asleep standing against the speakers in clubs. In my twenties, it morphed into the loo at house parties. More than once, I've had a bathroom door kicked in because the people queuing on the other side thought I must have had some sort of terrible incident. But there I would be, catching forty blissful winks. Now, however, I am a zombie. Even Malia, who often stays at friends' houses (see: The Hutch) begins to notice. 'Are you all right?' she asks, her own eyes ringed with dark circles.

Exhausted and unhappy, I start to act out around my boyfriend, Dan. By now, we've been together for a year. We've met each other's families. I know the names of his dead pets and which song he listened to while having his first wank. On paper, we don't really work: he is scientific and sporty; I'm an English student who thinks sport means throwing myself around the Walkabout dance floor. But I try – even going on a university ski trip and attempting to blend in with a crowd of people who own salopettes (mine are borrowed and too short) – and call my boyfriend 'Danny boy' and 'Dan the man'.

Slowly, I become attention-seeking, insisting that Dan walk me home from campus in the dark, even though I only live a couple of streets away. I am starved of small acts of kindness. I constantly ask him for reassurance on how I look. What is in fact my increasingly low self-esteem, he mistakes for vanity. Whenever I try to tell him about my living situation, he brushes it aside as petty girl stuff. 'Can't you all just be friends?'

he says, as if I've spent the best part of a year trying to do anything else.

On the night he breaks up with me, we sit side by side on my bed, the green light of the chip shop flickering through my window and across his face.

'I just don't think I can make you happy,' he says, as I fiddle with my fingernails. 'I'm sorry.' He kisses me on the forehead and walks out.

Naomi is furious. In her eyes, I have ruined our cosy arrangement with the boys. She starts to freeze me out for days at a time, the rest of my housemates doing the same. It feels brutal, and that I might be heartbroken over the end of my relationship doesn't even seem to register with them. I start to miss lectures, and the handful of fledgling friendships I had made with my course mates quickly drift away.

I remember feeling gripped by panic. How could I be halfway through my university experience – this supposedly magical period – and have no friends and no boyfriend to show for it?

The final nail in the coffin happened while I was in the midst of trying to cope with my stalker. Actually, let's just call him Stalker so there can be no room for doubt – because I did doubt that was what was happening to me for a long time, something not helped by the dismissive reaction of my housemates.

Stalker was in the year above – someone we'd bump into on nights out, over eight pints of vodka Red Bull and a tactical chunder. I'd never given him any thought beyond that. But a few weeks after the break-up with

Dan, during the holidays, he messaged me: 'Hey, in London and thinking about you. Want to meet?' I was busy with a newspaper internship: 'Sorry, see you in Brum' I texted back. I've often asked myself whether I should have just gone for one drink. Perhaps I shouldn't have replied at all. What would have been the least triggering option?

I understand now that this is classic victim-blaming. So let's end that poisonous myth: stalking is not your fault. And it has nothing to do with unrequited love. Someone who refuses to leave you alone because they claim to like or love you *so much* is not being 'romantic' – it's harassment.

Back at university, I started to feel nervous. Stalker's texts escalated and the 3 a.m. phone calls started, often just heavy breathing. He would message, asking me to meet him in random locations on the edge of town. I started to look over my shoulder and always checked that my bedroom window was locked before going to bed. But when I confided in my housemates, they acted as though I was making the whole thing up for attention. 'He's *such* a nice guy,' they gushed, if his name came up. 'Is that your *stalker*?' Naomi would coo, whenever my phone pinged, as if I should be flattered. 'He just likes you,' they said, exchanging glances (almost) behind my back. It made me feel as though maybe I had got it all wrong; that I didn't have to scan every face as I left my lectures just in case he was waiting for me.

It all comes to a head the night before an exam, when I am panic-revising in my bedroom while Naomi blasts out cheesy pop music directly above. By this time, I'm staying at my new boyfriend Stephen's house regularly – not convenient, as he lives in a different part of the city. But it gets me out of that house and away from the worry about Stalker appearing at my bedroom window.

Stephen and his housemates are everything my student home is not: generous, kind, fun. Even if it's the kind of middle-class laddish fun that is easy for women to play along with – games of Mario Kart until 2 a.m., cooking steak as though they're in the *MasterChef* final, calling everyone 'squire' – but is ultimately a bit unfulfilling unless you have female friends with whom you can gently poke fun at it.

My increasing absence is interpreted as a direct snub to Naomi. She stops speaking to me entirely, as do the others. When I walk into the living room after one weekend away, she stands up from the sofa and marches out, practically shoulder-barging me on the way. 'Oh, sorry, didn't realize you were actually *living* here,' she says.

Perhaps I should have tried to sit my housemates down and explain to them exactly why I was spending so much time away. But it seemed futile to try to make them understand what to me was obvious – and I felt as though they didn't want to hear me, even if I could have found the words. It's an example of all the things that go unsaid in female friendships; something University of Arizona academics Walid A. Afifi and Laura K. Guerrero called 'topic avoidance' in their 1998 study.[15] They concluded that we tend not to disclose certain things to friends largely for reasons of self-protection. Opening up and making yourself vulnerable is often tricky, even more so when the person or people concerned have a question mark over their heads. Can you trust them? Will they reject or betray you? It feels easier to stay quiet and protect yourself – and we've all worn that emotional armour at some point in our lives. Even if, as you'll discover, leaving small issues unspoken can make things harder in the long run.

On that evening before my exam, I creep up the wooden stairs to Naomi's room on all fours, like a frightened animal, and knock.

'Naomi, would you mind turning the music down?' I ask, my voice straining with the effort of sounding congenial.

No reply.

'It's just I'm trying to revise . . .'

The volume doubles.

Something snaps inside me. Hot with rage and shame, I storm back down to my bedroom and deploy the only weapon available to me: the fuse box, which just so happens to be in a small cupboard above my bed. This is my nuclear button and I am not afraid to use it. Satisfaction flows through my body as I flick the 'upstairs electricity' switch off and the music dies. I hear Naomi stomping and Leonie complaining that her essay has disappeared. But I no longer care. I pack a bag, get on a bus to my boyfriend's flat and don't go back to that house until my dad comes to collect me a few weeks later, at the end of term.

The incident feels to me like the absolute proof of what my two decades on earth have been trying to tell me: female friends aren't to be trusted. They will let you down. They will discard you like last night's dirty knickers. I tell myself that I am a guy's girl; the sort who enjoys cheap, badly cooked steak and Nintendo.

For a long time afterwards, I asked myself the same questions over and over: did they intend to humiliate me? Was it all in my head? Were they perversely creating a tighter bond between themselves by singling me out? Some of their actions were probably thoughtless mistakes, but there's surely no way they all could have been.

There was probably a bit of responsibility on my part. I went into that living situation expecting to be disappointed. I was trying to be someone else. I relinquished too much control over my own emotions, in the same way many of us might when trying to fit in, or when we go along with a situation because of peer pressure. The same thing can happen in a romantic relationship, too, when it can (falsely) seem easier to give yourself over to the other person in order to show your devotion and win their love.

My only contact with Naomi, Leonie and Poppy after that is limited to a few terse messages about bills. I'm relieved, but – what now? I am beginning my final year of university with no female friends and living with two boys, whom I know through Stephen.

Seeking a distraction, and with nothing to lose, I join the university newspaper – an eclectic group of people who spend most of their days in a small, airless room in the bowels of the student union building. I've only been writing for a few weeks when my features editors, Eleanor and Bella, announce they are quitting and are looking for a replacement. I put my name forward.

Eleanor and Bella are twins. Identical, beautiful and very posh, they float about campus in long skirts, their hair caught up in velvet scrunchies. They intimidate the hell out of me, but somehow they decide I am the woman for the job. They send me a charming email, outlining my responsibilities and offering gossip about the team. 'One thing,' they write. 'Your deputy is Agatha. She's OK but not ur sort of person. U guys seem quite different.'

Sixteen years later, Agatha and I still laugh about this. Within about a week of working together, it is blindingly obvious that she and I are going to be friends. The twins were right: we are different in superficial ways. I'm a southerner with poker-straight hair and a taste for biltong. Agatha is a curly-haired Brummie who, when I ask her what her biggest turn-on is, replies 'houmous'. She always thinks of others before herself and spends most of that third year giving blood. I occasionally manage to think of others just after I have thought of myself and (still) don't even know my blood type.

Agatha is intensely sociable and has an amazing ability to keep up with friends from all corners of the country. I pretend to be sociable but secretly like nothing better than a night in and a bath. And because the one in her student house gets so little use, Agatha lets me wallow in it. I arrive at her front door, towel and novel under arm, much to the bemusement of her housemates, and lock myself in their bathroom, burning my way through their term's supply of IKEA tealights.

What matters, though, is that we have the same sense of humour. We like the same music and the same books. We're both close to our parents. We have also both been through bruising housemate experiences – like me, Agatha lived with one girl in her second year who, for reasons unknown, decided to give her the cold shoulder. In the years after graduation, many other women tell me the same thing happened to them.

These confusing dynamics aren't always toxic in the most obvious sense. To me, toxicity is any behaviour that makes you feel small, or where the power balance is off. It could be a friend who is always judgemental when you confide in them. Or someone who reacts jealously, so much so that you start to feel like you don't want to share your good news. They might be possessive, acting hurt if you've spent time with other friends. They might thrive on gossip – a significant reason that some women told me they found it hard to trust female friends and preferred not to go on 'girls' trips'.

It could be a friend who is so wrapped up in their own dramas that they never listen to yours. Perhaps they make you feel as though you have to walk on eggshells, or they are constantly negative. Maybe it's someone who likes to buy your affection. Or a friend who pressures you: 'Oh go on, share a bottle of wine with me' – when you've already told them you're not drinking. A pal who never takes the initiative in making contact or plans, leaving you to do the heavy lifting. Someone who only ever seems to pop up when they need something: a shoulder to cry on, a work contact, someone to hang out with when they're single again.

I bet you have, or have had, a friend in your life who fits into one of those categories. And such friendships aren't confined to school or university. It can happen at any time in your life and with anyone. Sometimes, a friendship you've had for years can be the most damaging of all, any negative behaviour masked by a sense of loyalty. You might have got comfortable with feeling uncomfortable.

Radhika Sanghani, author of *Thirty Things I Love About Myself*, has a points-based system for working out whether a friendship is unhealthy. When she meets up with someone, she asks herself whether she has come away feeling buoyed up (plus two), just 'meh' (zero), or actively worse (minus two).

'For me, it's a way of figuring out if a friendship or a connection is positive or not. Because sometimes you just hang out with your friends on autopilot,' she says. 'But take a moment afterwards to ask: how do I feel? Do I feel like their conversation drains me, or fills me? And if it fills you, fantastic – that's what I want more of. And if it drains, and it keeps happening, then you have to think, "This friendship isn't giving me anything. I need to see them less."'

It might seem like quite a calculating way to consider your friendships, but it's something I think many of us do naturally anyway – you know when you come away from seeing a friend full of happiness, unable to stop smiling and buzzing with energy. And you know when you get home after meeting up with someone and just feel flat or exhausted. It's about taking a moment to really acknowledge those feelings and place them into a pattern.

We see this negative dynamic play out so often on screen that we've become almost immune to it. I'm not the first person to point out how flawed Carrie Bradshaw is in *Sex and the City*, and it pains me to do so because I strongly believe we need more imperfect women in TV and film, and fewer 'good girl' stereotypes. There is nothing wrong with showing the less likeable parts of our personalities and the things we do out of guilt, jealousy and self-preservation. It's why shows like *Fleabag* are so popular – they refuse to shy away from the pain female friends can cause one another, as well as the joy of guinea-pig cafes.

We need to talk about how flawed these characters are and not buy into the toxic fantasy that what we're watching is a model of picture-perfect female friendship. That many women have expressed relief at the character of Samantha Jones not being included in the *SATC* reboot *And Just Like That* – because it 'destroys the myth of friends for life' and means she has become 'the elusive text friend' as two headlines put it – shows just how little we talk about the crumbling of our female friendships and the suddenness with which they can reveal themselves not to be forever after all.

★

We are more aware than ever about toxic romantic relationships and how harmful they can be. Coercive control was criminalized in 2015, meaning that a pattern of psychologically abusive behaviour in an intimate or family relationship now holds a maximum prison sentence of five years. But when it comes to toxic friendships, we still find them hard to recognize.

Of course, it's tricky to compare controlling friendships with toxic romantic relationships – there are factors in play that often mean romantic relationships carry higher stakes and can be genuinely dangerous.

But there are some striking similarities, especially when it comes to the warning signs that can point to an unhealthy friendship. Natasha Devon MBE – who has volunteered in refuges and is the author of *Toxic*, a novel about a troubling female friendship – wrote the following checklist for the *Times Educational Supplement* of things to look out for, and has kindly given me permission to reproduce it here.

- The friendship will often develop at a time when you feel vulnerable – perhaps another close friendship has just come to an end, you are being bullied or you have problems at home. Your new friend will swoop in and make you feel special at a time when your confidence is low.
- Your friend will enjoy this dynamic (that of 'saviour') and will want to keep you vulnerable. They will spend a lot of time comforting you when things go wrong, but disappear, or

show a less than enthusiastic response when your life takes an upward turn.

- Your friend will have had a lot of intense friendships that have gone wrong in a dramatic way in the past. They will tell you about these in a carefully edited way, so that you are left in no doubt that it wasn't their fault.
- If your friend is annoyed with you, they'll take great delight in punishing you by withholding their company, or not texting as frequently as you are used to, leaving you wondering what you have done wrong.
- When your perceived transgression comes to light, it will often be something you couldn't have possibly known about, such as accidentally offending them by referring to an aspect of their past they hadn't yet told you about. You will start to feel like you have to walk on eggshells.
- At first, the friendship will be incredibly intense. Your friend will usually have issues (which is fine; we all do) but, crucially, they will refuse to seek help for or manage these, instead confiding in you and demanding secrecy or special treatment. They are likely to be very charming and to tell lots of stories in which they emerge looking like a hero. You'll buy into their self-publicity, believing that they are special and you are less so.
- Toxic friendships are hardly ever completely one-sided. You'll behave in ways you aren't particularly proud of, too, because you'll be

confused and upset by the other person's behaviour. Whenever you think about confronting them, or breaking away from the friendship, you'll remember that you are not blameless and worry that they will list all the reasons why you are a terrible person.

- Most importantly, your friend could read all of the above and would absolutely not recognize themselves in any of the descriptions.
- If a significant number of the above are present, it doesn't mean the 'perpetrator' is an awful person, necessarily, just that the dynamic between them and their 'victim' won't bring either party anything positive. The healthiest thing for both of them would be to keep the other at a distance.

Those last two points are so important. This is not a story of good versus evil. There's no such thing as 'good girls' and 'bad girls'. It's not as simple as me being the wronged heroine and my university housemates the vile bullies. There is every chance that they might read this chapter and, as Natasha puts it, not recognize themselves. They might never have realized how I was truly feeling. And just because I began to understand that our situation was toxic, that doesn't mean that they ever did so. After all, it's not easy to recognize negative friendship behaviours in yourself – to realize that your brutal honesty might come across as critical; that your 'great advice' is unsolicited and might feel judgemental; or that wanting to spend all your spare time with a friend might feel stifling, controlling and isolating to them.

We're all on the same spectrum of female friendship and we hit different points on that scale at different times in our lives. Think about the absolute basics of what you want in a friend: someone you can talk openly with, someone you can turn to for support, someone whose company you enjoy. But this friendship base layer is constantly buffeted by life's changes, and which element you need most from your friends can also change, with one demanding more attention than the others. It can throw your friendships off balance. The key is not to let your needs at any one moment tip over into behaviour that could negatively impact the other person.

That imbalance is the reason why I gratefully picked out a number from that sticky pint glass: because in that second, I wanted to be accepted. It's why I reached for the fuse box: because at that moment, I realized that none of my friendship needs were being met. It's why I went to a fancy-dress party at Agatha's student house dressed as a giant pair of tin-foil scissors, despite having known her for only a couple of weeks – because I knew I'd found someone whose company, and pure silliness, I could enjoy.

It might sound as though I'm letting her off the hook, but Naomi is no more the monster of this story than I am. University was a formative friendship period for her, too, with all the pressures that brings. I see that now – and even if she didn't at the time, she did come, I think, to realize it later. Almost two years after we'd graduated, I received a text message from a mutual friend.

'Hi Claire, Naomi asked me to pass this on, hope you don't mind. She feels really bad about how things ended between you and was hoping you might consider being her friend again? Up to you.'

Up to me. Now I was the one with the power, and with great power comes great responsibility – to myself. I deleted it.

That's the thing about experiencing a toxic friendship dynamic: eventually, you have to put yourself first. Maybe that means trusting your intuition that something isn't right. Perhaps that means trying to talk to them about it. But more likely, it means telling them that the friendship isn't good for you – deep breath – and walking away.

It's not easy and you'll probably feel shame, guilt, confusion, regret and loneliness. You might miss your friend – as we know, every toxic friendship has fun bits, too. But if you give it some time, you'll start to realize that you feel better without them in your life, and that they weren't the right friend or friends for you.

Then you have to forgive yourself, which sounds seriously corny but is true. You're only human and people make mistakes. It's why I spent a long time trying to reframe my 'What did I do wrong?' questions into 'OK, I did a few things wrong and tried *way* too hard, but I *was* consistently being made to feel bad about myself.' For me, that forgiveness included doing things I enjoyed purely for myself, like going to the cinema but on my own – a small action to reclaim your sense of self and start to reset – and diving head-long into a positive new social situation like the student newspaper, intimidating though it felt at first.

You can't change other people, but you can change how you treat yourself. It's not easy but it's the way forward. Because as soon as you let go of what doesn't work? You start to make space for what does.

Work Friends

*Myth: It's not a good idea to
make friends with colleagues*

It began with an email.

*'So sorry for having gone on about my boyfriend all day,
you must think I'm really insensitive. Hope you're alright.'*

It was Valentine's Day, 2006, and I had just had the
equivalent of a bucket of cold water thrown over my
head by a colleague. Someone I admired and had seen
as potential friend material, but who I now knew pit-
ied me. Great.

Let's just say it: workplace friendships can be deeply
weird. You're essentially being paid to interact with
people you would never have chosen to see more of
than your own family and friends. Just like in the
school playground, you have a finite number of potential work friends to choose from in an office setting
and it can feel tough to know where to begin (even
trickier if you're freelance or self-employed).

Many of us find it pretty confusing to know how

to make a friend who becomes personal, but still remains professional. Who is more than just somebody to walk to the coffee machine with, and whom you can mutually rely on and trust just as you would in any other friendship – but who might be going for the same promotion as you, or pitch for the same project.

However, as Shasta Nelson, author of *The Business of Friendship*, puts it: 'Not all of us are sure that we should be making friends at work. But we're all happier when we do.' Given that we spend anywhere between a quarter and a third of our adult lives at work – and the boundaries are more blurred than ever – it can be helpful to find the people you get along with and who don't send too many passive-aggressive emails at 11 p.m. ('Just kindly putting this to the top of your inbox.') Having someone who understands the unique pressures of your workplace or industry, the horrible bosses and their bad attitudes, and with whom you can rant, plot and celebrate, is helpful. Someone who can make work feel a little less like work. But there are bigger benefits to work friends than just helping us get through the days. They can actually make us less lonely, more productive and generally happier.

In his book *Vital Friends*, Tom Rath found that people who had at least three good work friends were 96 per cent more likely than those who didn't to report being 'extremely satisfied' with life. There can be a positive impact on our mental health, too, with almost half of us rating 'practical and emotional support' as the best bit of workplace friendships, according to a survey by jobs website Milkround in 2019.[16] (Though I'd rather gloss over the study that found we millennials apparently see our bosses as 'work parents'. I've had some brilliant managers but, unlike my mum and dad, not a single one of them has repeatedly phoned me asking how to copy and paste, or asked my partner to come round and fix the printer.)

The evidence points one way: we should value our work friendships just as much as any other. And if one in five of us has identified a person we would sleep with at work[17] (and, if you're anything like me, eventually marry), surely it can't be beyond us all to form a friendship?

Except it can be. A Totaljobs poll in 2018 found that 60 per cent of people felt lonely at work compared to in their personal lives.[18] Young people find it particularly tough to make work friends due to social anxiety and a lack of money with which to go out. Almost half have called in sick as a result of workplace loneliness and one in three actually quit their jobs because they felt friendless. With vast student debts, high rents and low wages, is it any surprise that there isn't much left over for making work friends? And the shift to digital communication – not to mention freelancing or starting your own business – has only made it harder: those Thursday-night drinks with co-workers or contacts just aren't the same over Zoom.

Arguably, then, there's never been a more important time to form a workplace bond. And it is possible. Shasta Nelson has a three-point method to help us do just that – a samosa of friendship, if you will. She has identified the elements she says are vital for making a connection in the first place and then helping that to become a fully-fledged friendship.

1. Positivity: the friendship makes you feel good and supported.
2. Consistency: you put in the time getting to know one another.
3. Vulnerability: you share who you really are.

These apply to all types of friendships but are even more important when it comes to the office environment, Shasta tells me.

'With almost every workplace friend, it's not that we would have chosen that person out of a line-up of other options, and it's not that we chose them because they were better than all the other people we could meet,' she says. 'We chose them because we saw them regularly. We were paid to interact and the consistency happened, and then we bonded with the people who we were seeing regularly, who we felt like we got to know and who left us feeling good.'

Remember that University of Kansas study[19] that found we need to spend fifty hours with someone to morph from acquaintances into casual friends, ninety hours to become meaningful friends, and more than two hundred hours to become close? We're putting in the time with our colleagues by default – so it's little wonder that many of us end up making lasting friendships in the workplace. Which is not something I thought would be possible in the slightest.

I was back in London after university and had

started my first job, as an intern in the PR office of an
auction house, which, in the infamous words of Dan-
iel Cleaver in *Bridget Jones*, meant that I spent my days
'fannying around with press releases'. But, between
working, I was also trawling Facebook for pictures of
my ex-boyfriend – who had dumped me over the
phone after graduation – and his new girlfriend. I was
distraught, sending countless messages to Agatha to let
her know that I had just been crying at my desk or
that I was 'so sad and puffy today'. I must have had a
face like Eeyore for at least six months, because that's
how long had passed when I received that apologetic
Valentine's Day email from my colleague which, though
meant kindly, I found seriously embarrassing.

No wonder Agatha was telling me to put my face
straight. She was right. I was twenty-two, living rent-
free (read: back at home) and had a stable job. My
only real worry was the fact that I'd managed to break
the £500 office laminating machine on my first day
by putting in the plastic the wrong way round, and
never owned up. What did I have to mope about?

But I couldn't shake the feeling that I was doing it
all wrong. This was supposed to be the great beginning: the post-degree utopia of earning your own
money and having to think about grown-up things
like upgrading your student bank account. Yet I felt
unhappily single and far away from the few female
friends I had, who were all busy getting on with
their own lives. Izzy and Marie were still studying,
while Agatha had decided to stay in her Birmingham student house, which meant I became very
familiar with Friday evenings on the Megabus. After

a week at work, I could hand myself over to the ruddy-faced cartoon conductor in the yellow cap and let him whisk me back in time to our third year of university. Back to the comfortingly familiar house with its deep bathtub. Back to the pubs where we had worn wrinkles in our favourite seats. Back to a moment when I hadn't seemed friendless.

But during the week, sleeping in my childhood bedroom, I felt lost and lonely. I would lie awake trying to make sense of how I had got back here. How I had so few female friends for two decades of trying. Whether they were even still my friends now we had different lives, in different cities.

'Once we think we're not liked or once we think that we're not safe, our brain is immediately looking around and trying to find everything else that's proof that we're not,' says Shasta Nelson. 'So you're going to see things and take them personally; assume the worst and feel left out. Whereas if you can feel like "I'm worthy, I'm chosen", your eyes and your brain are going to be looking around for that evidence.'

Being surrounded by the paraphernalia of my childhood – my grubby pale-yellow Care Bear and several Trolls with matted hair – did not help my eyes or brain seek out anything positive. It seemed to bring it all together; my mind tracing a line from those first school-friend break-ups like a vapour trail left by a plane of which I was behind the controls but didn't know how to fly. What would the black box of my friendship crashes reveal if I could play it?

The path of least disappointment, I decided, was to

revert to the guy's girl act I had started to hone at university; that tedious 'cool girl' stereotype of someone who gives the impression of loving football and dirty jokes. Who plays video games, drinks cheap beer and mainlines fast food. This was the artifice I had constructed for myself to keep my heart safe from the unpredictability of female friendship, as I saw it. I wanted to be the sort of girl that women couldn't touch because I was one of the boys and therefore protected by my laddish indifference. Freeze me out, shoulder-barge me. I. Don't. Care.

What this meant in reality is that I spent most evenings watching *Top Gear* with random male acquaintances. I knew I wasn't happy, but I didn't know what to do about it until that Valentine's Day email. It might seem relatively insignificant, but to me it served as a wake-up call. I had been so unhappy and self-involved at work that I hadn't made a single friend; instead I'd inadvertently pushed people away and given the impression that I was unapproachable.

I had to start thinking about what I wanted instead of just letting life happen, and I had to trust again. If my miserable face hadn't already ruined my chances, surely I could make more meaningful friendships, and work seemed like the best place to start. More precisely, the work canteen.

I know what you're imagining: that auction-house lunches are surely a Regency-style affair where the gentlefolk of the art world would gather to take a turn around the drawing room before enjoying a three-course feast. Probably a bird stuffed inside a bird stuffed inside a swine. In reality, it was more a grimace at each other across the room at the lingering smell of fish. The canteen was also where the main business of the day was conducted – and by that I mean the raking-over of the events of the previous night. For a 22-year-old looking to make new friends, the auction house had one big thing going for it: an enthusiastic drinking culture. Monday to Friday, there was always a group of colleagues at the bar next door to the office; come one, come all. So I did, and everything started to change, with the help of several vats of alcohol a night.

Happy hour was taken seriously: we'd leave the office in our wrap dresses like a herd of thirsty wildebeest crossing the parched desert and stampede into the bar, knocking back kir royales until the money ran out, or until someone more senior turned up and opened a new tab. We snogged, we danced like drunken Diane von Furstenberg mannequins in the 151 Club on the King's Road. We ate kebabs in Chelsea and fell asleep on night buses and trains all over London. I once woke up in Woking.

At the heart of it all were the women. Chloe and I worked in the press office, Eve in the posters department, Johanna in decorative arts, Amanda in modern art. Mostly, I don't know where they are now, whether they're settled down or if they live on the other side of the world – except for one, who asked me to be godmother to her daughter. More on that shortly. For now, we were too busy getting to know each other, sharing Marlboro Menthols while shivering outside pubs and playing 'Shag, Marry, Kill' about our male colleagues.

Or trying to. Eligible men were thin on the ground, or too thin on top. They were the sort of chaps that, if one of them managed to persuade a woman back to their Kensington flat, would ask 'Do you mind awfully if I undo your bra?' and serve tea in a Burlington pot the morning after. Everyone seemed to be part of a dynasty. If you let one of them stick their tongue down your throat, you could spend days afterwards at your desk idly fantasizing about marrying someone *landed*, even though you didn't fancy them, didn't want to be a kept woman and had spent ten minutes scrubbing your tongue with your toothbrush the moment you got home.

But every snog, flirty text or hair extension accidentally left under a boss's bed brought us closer together as female colleagues, as I learned first-hand what it was like to share secrets (and not all about men), admit fears, laugh and support one another – and then spend all day at work acting as though nineteenth-century ceramics were the only things in the world we cared about in the slightest.

*

One woman who knows what it's like to blend friendship and work is Pandora Sykes, who co-presented the popular *The High Low* podcast with Dolly Alderton. The pair's obvious affection won them a devoted army of fans who sprayed the hashtag #friendshipgoals all over social media, with one woman even admitting that she'd changed the names of her own best friends to Pandora and Dolly in her phone. Stay cool, ladies.

The two first encountered one another through work, with Pandora commissioning Dolly to write articles for the now-defunct feminist website The Debrief. 'Then we were set up on a friend date,' explains Pandora. 'And we were there for five hours just chatting. I knew immediately I'd made a really good friend.'

The key to their success as friends and business partners, Pandora thinks, was a good old-fashioned mix of chemistry and compromise. 'We're really different in some ways: I am much more responsive and efficient, and Dolly's a bit more dreamy. But we're really similar in terms of what we find funny, what we find moving, the values that we hold in the world, and in other people. So it definitely made it easier to have a business.'

Pandora tells me that they never kept score, splitting their responsibilities fifty-fifty.

'She was available one week if I was having a shit time with the baby or whatever, and I would do the bulk another week – so there was no counting in our friendship. And I do think that's rare,' she says. 'That said, we did have to make sure that we checked in with our friendship as well. So, we'd agree not to talk about The High Low at dinner. But to be honest that was never really something we had to try too hard at.'

On social media, they've referred to one another as 'my work wife' – surely a term originally thought up by a man trying to convince himself there were two women who wanted him.

'I definitely would call it a romance, in fact one of the great romances of my life,' says Pandora. 'Equally, though – and I do find this quite depressing – there were some people who were cynical about it. I remember doing an interview where the writer was like, "People ask me if you're really friends." You would really be able to tell, I think, if we weren't. I am way too honest and earnest for that; I'm not cynical enough to fake a friendship for a bloody podcast.'

How sad that our default mode when two women achieve friendship and success while working together is to call into question whether they secretly hate each other. It's straight back to those BFF or mean-girls tropes; the boxes we love to put female friends in. The reality, as Pandora explains it, is that sharing values, boundaries, a sense of humour and emotional trigger points is the stuff that helps to bind women together. Those commonalities are what, over time, can take a colleague-level bond to a friendship one – the qualities around which you'd hope to establish a connection with any new friend, and which are no different when it comes to a workplace pal. Proximity isn't enough in itself; it's when you can also identify similarities and establish a relationship based on support and reciprocity that true friendship can blossom. Work isn't another country – our real lives play out there, too: success, failure, disappointment, joy. And to find someone who makes all that seem better, both professionally and personally, is what you're aiming for.

Which is not to say that there can't be a drop of healthy rivalry involved. I loathe it when women are pitted against one another. It happened to me in my first newspaper job when, as one of two twenty-something women, the attitude was that only one of us could climb the ladder and competition was almost actively encouraged. And yet ... just because women are often put in that position by others, it doesn't mean that we don't also do it to ourselves.

This polarization was experienced by Jane Garvey, fifty-seven, who found herself pitted against her *Fortunately* podcast co-presenter, Fi Glover, for years – something that stopped their friendship progressing.

'Because we were both female broadcasters competing for the same jobs, let's be honest, I think we'd never been really close,' she says. 'We were both women of a certain age, we're both white and about the same height. We've both got dark hair. We have a similar sense of humour. And genuinely a lot of people at the BBC couldn't tell us apart. So the podcast was the first time we'd worked together, while being aware of each other, and often being in the same company. Now, we are now a lot closer. We had lunch last week. We've written a book together.'

Whisper it: competition is one of the last taboos in female friendship. Don't tell me you've never felt it – a little lurch of envy in the pit of your stomach when a friend tells you she's got a new job or had a promotion. If you've made a lot of work friends over the years, it can be even harder as you might share goals and ambitions in the same industry, and while you're pleased for your friend, it can also reflect what you haven't got back at you.

It can cause sleepless nights. But it's almost impossible to vocalize that without sounding like a monster. Without sounding like you don't want your friend to have their success at all. Of course I want my friends to do well. Someone else's success doesn't have to be at the expense of your own. It isn't either/or. But, if I'm being totally honest, it can set a little fire burning inside me. It makes me envious at the same time as I feel pleased for them. I don't think the two are mutually exclusive – and I don't think we confront it enough. (Needless to say, if you're actively happy when your friends fail, there's a word for that and it's a lot ruder than *Schadenfreude*.)

Being friends with successful people forces you to look in the mirror: something none of us likes to do. 'It can be painful seeing your female friends succeed where you feel you've failed,' one friend told me. 'You're proud of them and you don't love them any less, but there is pain there, too. Especially if you are drawn to people you admire – as many of us tend to be.'

Journalist and author of *Careering* Daisy Buchanan, thirty-seven, wrote for *Grazia* magazine about her envy over a friend's success: 'Our working worlds are similar enough for me to be in a constant state of comparing and despairing. I don't hate her, I'm not angry with her, but I have spent the last couple of years feeling nauseous with the shame of not being her,' she said. It was a refreshingly honest admission about this hidden layer of female friendship – how seeing a friend succeed at work can not only be painful but introduce something approaching heroine-worship into your friendship, as you long to be where they are and doing what they do.

'It's been really hard because it felt as though we were coming from a very similar place,' Daisy tells me. 'You're both on WhatsApp moaning about unpaid invoices – and then suddenly your friend isn't facing the same struggles.'

What can help, she says, is knowing what's going on behind the scenes. Where someone's career can outwardly seem enviable, the truth can often be messier. They have bad days, too and it's helpful for the more successful friend to pull back the curtain and expose the full picture, so your friends can commiserate when things are rubbish and celebrate with you when they go well, just as they always have.

'You have no context a lot of the time,' explains Daisy. 'All you see is everyone just being brilliant, and feeling like you are not. There are days you [as the successful one] need to tell your friends about in detail, so that any envy ... doesn't go away, but they realize it's not all glossy and perfect.'

One of the most difficult things, she adds, can be if a friend doesn't pat you on the back when you've previously made an effort to cheer them on. 'I've felt quite wounded when I feel like I've done something [successful] they've not really responded to, or acknowledged. And I've been like, "Oh fuck you then",' she admits. 'But maybe that was hard for them in the way that it's hard for me sometimes.'

But while a little gentle envy doesn't have to mean a big green-eyed monster trampling all over your friendship, what if it runs deeper? That Totaljobs survey also found that six in ten of us have a 'work enemy'. Madeleine Albright might have said 'There's a special place in hell for women who don't help other women' – but she might not have accounted for the fact that some women would happily go to hell rather than give their nemesis a hand-up.

I don't want to give oxygen to the false narrative that professional women are all at one another's throats, talons out. It's reductive to paint a picture of us as backstabbing bitches, clambering over one another to get to the top – a stereotype that long suited a largely male-dominated workforce keen to keep us down. I'm not saying it never happens, of course, but we've come a long way since women were often made to feel they had to be rivals. By and large, these days I think we're all much happier to cooperate, not compete.

But I do believe that many of us encounter a work nemesis at some stage, even if we don't vocalize it: someone we compare ourselves to, and whose success we ruminate over when we should be concentrating on our own. It can be a big waste of energy. There's nothing you're likely to regret as much as spending time imagining your life should look like someone else's, when in reality you know nothing about the choices they've made or whether those choices would even be right for you.

That said, anyone who triggers such a strong emotion in you is worth paying attention to. Stop looking at them and look at yourself. Ask what your feelings towards them say about your own choices and ambitions. Ask whether you could even help one another.

Holly, twenty-nine, became friends with her work 'nemesis'.

'A few years ago, I got down to the final two for a job but was told the other candidate was more experienced,' she says. 'A few months later I got a call saying that an identical position had become available. I was nervous about working alongside the person who had been deemed "better" than me and very aware of the direct comparison between us. I remember thinking she was incredibly grown-up and seemed to have this massive network of people. I still felt like a child who was testing out being an adult.'

Unexpectedly, Holly's colleague invited her to meet outside of work one weekend.

'We ended up in Spitalfields Market and I saw a dress that I liked. There was no changing room so I just hid behind her and tried it on. She was slightly shocked, then said, "I guess we're friends now." That actually became a bit of a theme. A year or so later I got badly burned from topless sunbathing. We were the only two people left in the office one evening, so I undid my bra and showed her. On her advice I saw a doctor; it turned out to be a second-degree burn. So it seemed fitting that when I got married years later, she was the bridesmaid who helped me into my dress.'

The idea that you should befriend every accomplished, smart, kind woman you meet, instead of seeing her as a rival, is something that would benefit us all. *Woman's Hour* presenter Emma Barnett is the absolute queen of this approach.

'One of the things I love doing is trying to help connect people,' she says. 'In fact, I see it as kind of your duty if you've had a bit of luck, or you've found a way into something, to then help others – because I didn't have any connections in this industry when I began. Through that, I've met some really nice women, and kept in touch with them.'

Emma also met a woman she calls her 'IVF fairy' at a corporate work event and formed a unique bond. 'She was the only person I could bear to tell about my IVF at the time, because she didn't know me,' she explains. 'She's in my phone as "IVF fairy" because I don't even know her real name. But she used to send me texts to encourage me during the process.'

I love that you can make a connection at a random work event, with a woman whose name you don't even know, and have it play such an important role in part of your life – a friendship that lasts for a moment in time, but which is no less meaningful for that.

Others can last much longer. Emilie McMeekan tells me that she's 'absolutely a work-wife person'. She and Annabel Rivkin set up *The Midult* website in 2016 to, as they put it, 'pop the perfection bubble' when it comes to women's lives. They met in an office almost twenty years ago, became work friends, started a business together, write books and columns together, record a podcast together and, when I speak to Emilie, have just returned from holiday together.

'Annabel and I absolutely fell in love with each other at work, at a point where both our lives were extremely complicated, with dead dads, addictions, and a difficult work environment,' says Emilie. 'I think one of the reasons that we have such a successful relationship is because we have forged it on honesty. There was a really crucial point in our relationship when I was drinking very heavily and I'd had a fight with someone and I said to Annabel, "Oh my god I don't know what to do, I'm in such a mess." And she looked at me and said, "I cannot help you, unless you help yourself."

'It was one of those moments where it shot through my heart because I knew what she was saying and she knew what she was saying. She threw me a lifeline, but it was a hard lesson. So the fact that we can be brutally honest about how we feel means that there can't be any awkwardness between us, because it's all out there.'

This level of brutal honesty can be easier said than done at work, though I have noticed work friends and women I've met professionally being more open about having therapy, or struggling with anxiety, particularly in the wake of the pandemic. It's something Emilie has also experienced, after suffering an episode of mental illness in 2013 that left her having a breakdown in the work loo.

'I didn't tell anyone for a long time that I was struggling, until it got really bad and I was hearing voices and having chronic panic attacks,' she says. 'So I told my best work friend, who was also my boss, and she was immediately like, "Do what you have to do to get better." I got thrown so many lifelines. But it doesn't happen until you start sharing and talking about it. That's the thing we forget. When people finally talk about their vulnerability there's just the most astonishing reaching out. But you have to get to that point. It's all about laying your vulnerabilities down and then women supporting each other.'

If you get to that stage with a work friend, creating a strong support system that allows you to rely on one another and offer total honesty, it can be jarring to lose it. If a close colleague moves to another job, you can feel as though you've lost a limb somehow – like a vital piece of you is simply no longer present. Even if you know your friendship will survive in the real world, the hole left by not seeing them most days can feel vast.

And should your bond be severed in more tragic circumstances, the impact can be devastating.

Jess Phillips had that supportive relationship with her former colleague and fellow Labour MP Jo Cox, who was murdered outside her constituency surgery in Birstall, near Leeds, on 16 June 2016.

'She was a woman from a similar background to me, elected on the same day as me, she had small children like I did, she thought she was doing a shit job of being a mum, she thought she was doing a shit job of being an MP,' says Jess. 'I didn't need the context with Jo because I knew that she got it. She understood that we felt spread too thinly, and not being able to find our way into the system, and constantly messing up at work and not understanding what we were meant to be doing. And it was that sort of universal experience that meant my friendship with her grew very, very quickly.'

Jess tells me that she was at Jo's house the day before she died, having dropped in on the way to the airport for a girls' holiday. It meant that she was in a villa in Spain when she heard the news that her friend had been killed.

'I just fell silent. My girlfriends would just come in and put dinner in the room. I couldn't speak,' says Jess.

'I was in denial, if I'm honest, because there was the whole day – even though I knew she'd died – waiting for the reporting. So I just convinced myself that somebody had got it wrong. I thought to myself, "I can't see a person fourteen hours ago, tell her I love her and give her a cuddle. And then she's dead." I couldn't make it make sense in my head.

'I sent her loads of WhatsApp messages to say, *I love you. I know you're going to be all right, like don't worry about it. We'll laugh about this one day. Don't worry about responding to me, focus on yourself.* Even though she was dead. You can't come down from being a close friend of somebody to nothing overnight.'

Jess tells me that she has found ways for their friendship to live on, particularly by befriending Jo's family. She has become close friends with Kim Leadbeater, Jo's sister – who won her sibling's former seat, Batley and Spen, in a July 2021 by-election, also making the two women work friends. When Jess heard the news of Kim's victory, she texted her, simply saying: 'I love you.'

'You have to find a way of extending that friendship that you felt towards them,' she says. 'And so my friendship with Jo's family: I made it replace that. We take the piss out of Jo all the time – especially when somebody is publicly beatified, you lose that element of being like, she was sometimes annoying.

'I remember at her funeral, we just sat around and traded stories about what a nightmare she could be, and continued to laugh … because you can't just switch off a friendship like that. It doesn't go somewhere, it doesn't dissipate – you have to sort of try and continue it. But dealing with it publicly was, in some ways, really helpful. It's really nice to see people caring about the thing that you care about. I don't stop missing her.'

What really struck me when speaking to Jess about her friendship with Jo was that sense of having met a kindred spirit through work – the idea that you didn't need to colour in the context; she just got it and that allowed their connection to flourish – and, of course, that meant it left a terrible void when her friend's life was suddenly taken.

Just because you 'get' one another's working situation, however, that doesn't mean you're on the fast track to friendship. Sometimes, it has to be more deliberate than that, with the slow sharing of small confidences.

'But we should never be doing a vulnerability dump,' warns Shasta Nelson. 'We should not be sharing everything, and we should be doing it in a way where nobody feels vomited on. We should be sharing in a way that leaves us and them feeling good – and it's even more important in work that we show curiosity about the other person's life and make sure that there's time for them to talk. We want to be mindful that we're not using people just to feel better ourselves.'

You definitely don't want to scare off a potential work friend on day one by telling them how you once got an upset tummy in Trump Tower in New York and almost shat yourself on the golden escalator. But sharing flesh or feelings with someone you'd like to know better at work can have an almost magical effect. Take the colleague who, one day, told me that she had a strange rash on her thigh.

Now, I know rashes. My family is rashes. One of our favourite stories is the time my mum texted my rashy sister saying *'In Boots, got your ointment'* and sent it to her entire phone book by accident. My dad maintains that he gets a rash every time he eats Quavers.

It's probably a bit of an eyebrow-raiser to see two female colleagues going into a loo cubicle together in the middle of the day, but that's where we ended up as my work friend held up her skirt, lowered her black tights to half mast and revealed the rash – about the size of a 50-pence piece and blotchy.

'I don't want to be alarmist,' I said, leaning down towards her inner thigh in the manner of Sherlock Holmes peering through a magnifying glass, 'but to me that looks like it could be shingles.'

A few hours later I received an email: *'It is shingles. Well done Doctor Cohen,'* my colleague said, having taken herself and the rash to see a GP. She still calls me that now – it was a moment of trust that broke any last remaining ice between myself and someone I had actually been a bit intimidated by. Maybe she suspected that when she took me into her confidence. Either way, it was the shingle best thing that could have happened to us.

*

I wish that my work friend Kate and I had shared a skin condition or two before we decided to go from colleagues to flatmates. I'd had enough of my child-hood bedroom and she'd just broken up with her boyfriend and needed to move out, sharpish.

Looking back, it was a hasty decision. We didn't really know one another. I just saw someone who worked in the same place I did, went drinking the same places I did and was a bit older than me: a proper grown-up, I thought. What could go wrong? Plus, she'd regaled me with tales of her former flatmate – horror stories about maggots. If grubs were her red line, that was fine by me.

Our budget didn't stretch far in West London. We saw one flat in Hammersmith that had no central heating and another near Fulham that I should really have reported to environmental health. In the end, we found a slightly shabby first-floor apartment that was over-priced, had fag-burned carpets and the sort of kitchen that at first glance seems to have a subtle swirly pattern on the lino but, on closer inspection, turns out to be decades of ingrained filth. Otherwise, it was perfect.

We cooked together and chatted on the sofa most evenings. We grew to have mutual friends. We com-muted home together.

It was all going so well, until it wasn't. Our differ-ences started to outnumber our similarities, which suddenly seemed superficial. Turns out you can't just move in with a casual work friend and become instant BFFs.

Kate might have drawn the line at maggots, but she didn't care about leaving half-eaten cheeseboards on the floor when we were in the midst of a ferocious mouse infestation. She didn't care about borrowing my clothes and getting fag burns on them. She didn't care about keeping her bike in the living room, so that the floors were always muddy and you had to navigate handlebars to get to the TV.

Like any mature person, I texted my grievances while I was out, which she mostly ignored (and fair enough).

'Hi chick, would really appreciate it if you could keep your bike downstairs. It's a touch in the way. Thanks SO much!'

Then, she started seeing a truly unpleasant man, who liked to tell her she looked fat (she did not) despite the fact he had more hair on his knuckles than his head. He was rude and unkind, which made me feel protective of Kate. I started ignoring the bike and cleared away their cheese silently. But then I made a fatal mistake. They broke up after a particularly nasty argument, and as I comforted her in her bedroom the next day, Kate asked me what I had really thought of him.

'Honestly?'

'Yes please,' she sniffed.

I took a deep breath. 'I thought . . . that he belittled you. I thought he never seemed very affectionate. I think you can do a lot better. And,' I said, warming to my theme, 'I absolutely don't think you're in any way fat.'

Kate nodded. 'He was a bit horrible, wasn't he?' she said miserably.

Then they got back together – of course they did – and our friendship never recovered. I got a job at a national newspaper and so we no longer worked together. When our flat contract came up for renewal a couple of months later, we decided to go our separate ways.

Her final message to me was on the Friday that she left. 'I've done all the cleaning in the kitchen, so there shouldn't be much for you to sort before you go,' she wrote. I got home from work to find the lino even swirlier than when I'd left that morning and all my cutlery missing. We never spoke again.

Many people have horrible housemate histories, especially in their twenties. I have a friend who returned home to her flat one day after work and put her key in the front door, only for her lodger to start screaming, 'No, no, don't come in!' Turns out, she was poaching salmon in the kitchen, starkers and covered neck to ankle in hair removal cream. Another friend lived with a girl who used up an entire loo roll every single day – three-ply, quilted – with no explanation ever given. Just an empty cardboard tube in the wastepaper basket next to the sink every twenty-four hours.

But I was crushed. This was supposed to have been my fresh start when it came to living with female friends: mature, relaxed, respectful. The happy home that would erase those upsetting university memories. Looking back now, I can see that I was repeating the same pattern – clinging to the first female-friendship life raft that came along, and not questioning whether it was good for either of us. Assuming that because someone is right in front of you, that mere convenience and consistency are enough.

Mainly, it didn't work with Kate because I still

hadn't understood what it would really take to form a close connection, and what good female friendship looked like. Without that, we never had a chance to go from co-workers to confidantes. But I did slowly begin to understand after we moved out. In some ways I'm thankful, because the end of that work friendship led to the deepening of another.

Eve was an auction-house girl, and had also become a friend of Kate's. She had always been someone I could email with a problem that might have seemed trivial to anyone else (she was the only person who knew about the laminator), with whom I could roll my eyes at life's maddest moments and who seemed genuinely interested in me, despite my Eeyore period. After I'd left that job, we'd stayed in touch and I still enthusiastically joined her for the happy hour stampede.

When I told her that Kate and I had fallen out, she simply said: 'Oh well, that's the end of her and me, too, then.' I really hadn't anticipated that. She unquestioningly had my back. It wasn't the 'girl code' – it was something more meaningful; a conscious choice. And that loyalty changed me – even if I didn't know it at the time. From then on I went to every gig her band played, even though I knew no one else there. When she had her heart broken, I did my best to distract her. When I called her hammered from the back of a taxi, crying about what a mess I was making of being a grown-up because I'd lost my favourite pink wallet with a rabbit on the front, she listened but gently told me to get a grip.

When she found out she was pregnant with the

baby that would become her wonderful eldest daughter, my god-daughter, I was the first friend she told as we stood ashen-faced outside a theatre in Leicester Square the evening after she'd taken the test. Inexplicably, we went through with seeing the play. I *think* it was *Who's Afraid of Virginia Woolf?* but I can't be certain. Neither of us took in a word, as we silently went through her options in our heads, me occasionally squeezing her arm.

When I told her I was writing this book, she told me I could say whatever I liked about her, because 'you're the most loyal friend'. It was Eve who had shown me what a work friendship could become. That if you didn't hide your feelings, if you were trusting, if you refused to be anything other than yourself, then not only could you be friendly with a colleague but you could become lifelong friends, too.

How Women Became My Job
(Because of a penis, naturally)

'How many women actually know ... the size of ... their man's penis?' I type out, slowly.

It is early 2014 and I am writing an article about penis size. Max Clifford's penis size, to be exact. Democracies might have been falling, Rome burning and monarchies crumbling, but for me the hot topic of the day is the late celebrity agent's manhood. It has been mentioned in court during his trial for indecent assault (he was eventually jailed for eight years), with one woman calling it a 'micropenis'.

There is one reason, and one reason only, that I have agreed to write this masterpiece: a job. A new deputy women's editor is needed at the newspaper I am already working at, and I am determined it will be me. So when the women's editor asks me to pen the penis article? I stand to attention.

It works: after a round of interviews (but we all know

it was the penis piece really), I get the job. Suddenly, I find myself in unfamiliar territory – working on an all-female team for the first time in my career. More than that, I am thinking about, writing about, interviewing and meeting women all the time. Menstrual leave, bum implants, how we're apparently too bossy, abrasive and ambitious at work. There is so much to cover when it comes to this half of the population – 51 per cent to be precise – of which, at that time, I still secretly feel wary. Despite literally being a paid-up member of the Sisterhood, inside there's still a part of me that isn't sure I can fully trust women and my new job is making me confront that truth, day in and day out.

I now recall the first few months with a full body cringe. I was so earnest. I didn't want to be seen as difficult or unlikeable. I was desperate to get along with my two female colleagues. I wanted to please. My old friendship patterns were playing out in my professional life. Whenever I conducted one of those 'How she does it'-type interviews – the sort in which the person claims to rise at 5 a.m., be in the gym by 5.15 and drinking a green shake, having caught up on their email and brokered world peace by 6 a.m. – they would tell me that the key to their success was their trusted 'support network' of women they could turn to as sounding boards and truth-tellers. To admit to myself that I didn't really understand what such a thing was made me feel like a massive fraud.

About a month into the job, I launched a shiny new online 'Work' channel, encouraging women to share their professional dilemmas, ask for advice and not be afraid. At the same time, I was terrified and felt out of my depth because I realized I still couldn't do those things for myself. It felt a bit like living a double life. It's not that I didn't believe what I was writing, or feel passionately that women shouldn't be second-class citizens. I threw all my weight behind campaigning for reproductive choice, a stalkers' register, help for victims of domestic abuse, a level playing field for women in business – all these things and more are my oxygen. They're the reason I've got out of bed every morning with a clenched fist and jaw, determined to make a small difference.

But, in those early days, there was a nagging feeling that I still wasn't paying as much attention to the women in my personal life as the ones I was writing about. That I was having intense, probing conversations with strangers and still keeping my female friends slightly at arm's length.

What helped me to start uniting these two parts of my life was Taylor Swift. It's not very sisterly, but Taylor really started to get on my wick. I'm not someone who obsesses over celebrities, but at that time it honestly felt as though I couldn't escape from Taylor and her so-called 'girl squad'.

It seemed as though she had gathered every superhuman specimen of womanhood she could find, made them her best buddies and photographed them all baking cookies in their pyjamas. Every girls' night was carefully documented via group selfies on Instagram. The hashtag #squadgoals took off, as if having anything less than a glossy pack of perfect BFFs was, quite simply, tragic.

Maybe I shouldn't have cared. Probably I was too

old to care. But there was something about this gratuitous performance of female friendship that I couldn't stand. It was like those BFF necklaces made human. And it was everywhere – it's hard to explain now just how much the press pushed Taylor's squad and the volume of noise around it. It felt relentless to me, as someone feeling so uncertain about her own female friendships and desperately trying to understand what made them tick. The 2015 MTV Video Music Awards was the squad's peak performance. Swift arrived at the event accompanied by nine other women as her dates. It was elite. It was mostly white. It was mainly Victoria's Secret models. The singer paraded her friendship with these superwomen at every opportunity, including her video for 'Bad Blood' and on stage during her '1989' tour. It was so obviously being commoditized. We were being sold a picture of perfect female friendship.

The whole thing hit a nerve after a lifetime of being told that such cliques are the be-all and end-all. Where was my squad? Why wasn't I having weekly sleepovers when my schedule was, let's face it, decidedly less busy than Taylor's? And if I felt like this about a woman I'd never paid a huge amount of attention to before, how were her devoted young fans taking it? The message it sent was that it only matters what female friendship looks like, not what it feels like – the cause of so many of my own heartbreaks.

I wasn't the only one feeling queasy. *BuzzFeed* called it 'strategic girlfriend collecting'. There was speculation that Taylor's squad had been manufactured to rehabilitate her reputation as someone who 'feuded' with other famous women. I didn't care about any of that, but I did object to the ramming-down-our throats of this unhealthy and one-dimensional portrayal. I actually wrote an article about it, with the headline 'Female friendship has become big business. Cheers Taylor Swift', in which I chastised the singer for turning gal pals into an acquisition model. But in hindsight, I think poor old Taylor was just as lost as I had been.

Not discounting that it could be PR spin, she later wrote an article for *Elle* called '30 Things I Learned Before Turning 30' in which she addressed the backlash around her 'squad', which by that point was conspicuous by its absence.

'Never being popular as a kid was always an insecurity for me,' Taylor wrote. 'Even as an adult, I still have recurring flashbacks of sitting at lunch tables alone or hiding in a bathroom stall, or trying to make a new friend and being laughed at. In my twenties I found myself surrounded by girls who wanted to be my friend. So I shouted it from the rooftops, posted pictures, and celebrated my newfound acceptance into a sisterhood, without realizing that other people might still feel the way I did when I felt so alone. It's important to address our long-standing issues before we turn into the living embodiment of them.'

That's it, right there. The honesty about female friendships we so desperately need to hear and which – had I read it when I was the same age as most of Swift's fans – would have made me feel less like the odd one out.

For me, it was thinking about Taylor's squad that

helped me to understand how much of female friendship in popular culture is performative and how what
we don't see is actually far more important. Because
behind all the support networks, perfect-looking
social-media posts, girls' getaways, films that pitch
women as soulmates or soul-destroyers – somewhere –
lies the truth.

That truth might not be sexy enough for #squadgoals,
but it's what we need to hear to understand that we
are all doing female friendship right, in our own way.
That there is no one model for how yours should look;
whether you should have one good friend or an
entire catwalk's worth. That actually, as Taylor herself
came to see, being vulnerable is a hell of a lot more
relatable.

Erin Brokovich told me something similar, when I
interviewed her that same year: 'It's OK to be vulnerable, it's OK to talk about our fears – often we don't
and I think it's that suppression of our voice that can
lead us down a path where we feel angst,' she said.

It was what I needed, to understand that I didn't
have to live a double life, torn between championing
women professionally and being wary of them personally. Because if perfect female friendship was an illu-
sion, then so was the idea it was permanently broken
in my own life. And if I could open myself up to talking
to women I'd only just met through work, then perhaps I could do the same with those I called my friends.

New Friends

*Myth: Making new friends isn't
worth the effort*

Saturday, 4 January 2014 was my thirtieth-birthday
bash. The whole evening was a bit surreal. Not because
I was having a party in a bar kitted out like a sweet
shop, which you accessed through wardrobe doors as
though entering a hedonistic Narnia. Not because I
got to name cocktails after myself ('Cohen Down a
Treat'). Not even because after too many of said cocktails, I fell down the stairs and gave myself carpet-burn
blisters up my right arm.

No, the bizarre thing was that, looking round the
room, many of those stuffing flying saucers into their
mouths were people I wouldn't have invited to any of
my previous birthdays. They were new friends; women
I'd only known for a short while, but whom I already
couldn't imagine celebrating without.

Two years earlier, my birthday had been very different. That afternoon, my boyfriend had taken me to

the cinema. I can't remember what film we saw, only that I left the auditorium in a foul mood – made even worse when my phone started beeping with messages from friends flaking on my pub drinks that evening. They were only meant to be low-key. No big deal, I'd said. Which in hindsight was possibly why people felt it was no big deal. Someone had decided to stay at their parents' house post-Christmas. Someone else wasn't feeling well, with an indeterminate illness that I immediately put down to can't be arsed-itis. One friend backed out because her dog had diarrhoea.

I chucked my phone at Tim in a strop and declared that I was calling the whole thing off. 'Just forget it,' I spat.

By that evening, I'd managed to pull myself together. But it did make me think about who my friends were and who was prepared to put a dog with the runs before me. It often happens that in our late twenties we start to find certain friends flaky, where once they'd been fun, spontaneous or popular. As we begin to value intimate nights in as much as going out, and life becomes more complex, it matters who is prepared to show up for you – and who isn't.

I'm going to say this now, for the record: you are not too old to make new friends. I learned for myself that it's never too late. I asked several women, across the generations, including two in their nineties, when they had last made a new friend and the answers they gave me were more reassuring than a furry hot-water bottle on a cold day. Every single one had made a new friend in recent memory.

Yet they all claimed *not* to make new friends easily.

That's the thing about forming new friendships as an adult: we don't expect it. We're often not even looking to grow our networks. Plus, meeting new people can seem almost impossible. When you're at school or university, there are options on a plate, even if they don't always work out. And you have time. There were hours in the day not accounted for with doing laundry, worming the cat and talking to the Amazon delivery person. What did we do with it all?

A 2016 Finnish study[20] found that we reach our peak number of friends at twenty-five, the age at which we're most 'socially promiscuous' – meaning that we make more social contacts and are more open to putting ourselves in situations where that's possible. After that, the numbers begin decreasing, particularly for women. It does make you wonder whether making new friends later in life is even worth it. Why bother?

Well, firstly, there are any number of reasons you might *need* to make new friends: moving to a new town, a break-up, getting a new job, everyone else deciding they're over daytime drinking sessions as 'the hangover isn't worth it'. Often it's a simple matter of priorities: as your existing friends couple-up, settle down, have children, or move away, your friendship balance changes. Your life stages can start to feel off-kilter. It doesn't mean you're no longer friends, just that you might need some new people to hang out with – but more of that later.

The key, friendship coach Shasta Nelson says, is 'starting with saying friendships matter to me and I can build them'. That statement sounds so deliberate, but you do have to be intentional about it sometimes. By making a new friend – which, remember, takes fifty hours to go from an acquaintance to even a casual friend – you are actively selecting someone to be in your life. Which means you need to choose carefully and not just jump on the first person, or first group of people, who come along, like I have done. It can be helpful to imagine what your other friends, or your family, might think of the person you're investing in. Do they share attributes with those you would consider closest to you, or with anyone you've left behind in the past?

Just as experience teaches you what you want, or definitely do not want, in a relationship, so your heart learns friendship lessons along the way. It makes sense that you wouldn't open the door to just anyone. But when you do? I lost count of the number of women who described the blossoming of their newest friendship in the same terms as you might the start of a relationship, with butterflies and a rush of intensity. A honeymoon period, during which you make an effort, get past the awkward small-talk stage, share confidences, wear perfume. Woo one another, basically. It's exciting and daunting, like a teenage crush: the idea that this is someone who could potentially be in your life forever, if you manage to peel back enough layers and like what you find in each other.

'A few years ago, a woman I could hear chatting to someone else behind me at a work event caught my ear – she sounded so incredibly fun – and when the host introduced us, I have never felt an immediate connection like it; we were grinning at each other

from ear to ear,' admits one of my friends. 'Quite seriously, it felt like the early stages of a relationship; like
a teenage crush in my thirties. We met up for a walk a
few days later and I came away wanting to talk about
her to everyone – other friends actually started making jokes about being jealous.'

Possibly, I was one of them. It can be disconcerting
when your adult friend makes a new friend, stirring
up insecurity. It harks back to the BFF myth; the idea
that the pinnacle of female friendship is a soulmate,
sister or twin. And even if you've seen through that by
now, the message we've internalized about the girl
code – always having one another's backs, no matter
what – can mean it stings when your friend looks
elsewhere. It can be hard not to compare yourself, or
wonder what they're getting from a new friend that
you couldn't give them. It can diminish your sense of
importance in their life. Harder is to see it as an opportunity: for your friend to be even happier and even for
you to meet this fantastic new person, too.

'It feels lovely to make a new friend; it's a sense of
acceptance, of feeling liked and valued,' says Cathy,
thirty-six. 'A new friend is making the active choice
to invest in you. It's nice to be able to try out a new
dynamic and be a different version of myself. It's
exciting to learn another person's stories and get a different perspective on yours.'

That idea of trying out a different version of yourself
doesn't mean faking it, or pretending to be a person
you're not. It's just acknowledging that one of the
gifts a new friendship can bring is the ability to see

yourself through a different lens; to expand and grow into a new space, with a person who ideally has zero expectations and is just getting to know you. Where older friends might have a set idea of who you are, with newer friends the additional layers you've gathered through life's constant churn can become the core of who you are in that friendship, rather than ways in which you have 'changed', as your old pals might see it. And it's always a thrill to find someone who doesn't know that you fell down the stairs at your own birthday party.

My mum, Jane, told me how she made a new friend in her sixties during a lecture at Tate Britain.

'We sat next to each other and began talking, and we have scarcely stopped since,' she says. 'Our lives seem to run on parallel lines: we both have daughters, and we are the same age with similar backgrounds. We can say absolutely anything to each other and are able to roar with laughter at the absurdity of our lives. In difficult and tragic times we are able to support each other, and I feel that I have rarely come across a more caring female friend – we are always saying how blessed we are to have found each other. She doesn't live close by but we speak on the telephone two or three times a week and meet up regularly. I love her to bits. Ours is the most important friendship of my life.'

No, you've got something in your eye.

Lauren, whom we met in an earlier chapter, tells me that 'butterflies' feeling is something she's experienced in her female friendships since transitioning. She likens them to friendships in your formative years, when you're showing each other new experiences – alcohol, how to use your sex appeal, the joy of travel – but instead you're being shown a potential new self.

'Honeymoon period is absolutely the term for it,' she says. 'They feel a lot like how people talk about teenage female friendships, where there is some element of mentoring and support, and some giddiness. And maybe it actually doesn't last, because you're not that well suited to each other and grow apart, but while it lasts it's very urgent and intense, because you're both at a point in your life where you need it.

'I met a girl on Reddit who was a couple of years ahead of me in transition terms, despite being slightly younger. We weren't that similar in our personalities and interests, but we *were* alike in our specific experiences of transness. I had been unsure whether various feelings that I had were "really" what a trans person would feel, and she had the experience to be able to tell me: "Yes, actually, they are, because I am trans and I felt that and look where I am now." That was an extremely powerful feeling, and I wanted more of it.'

Lauren and her new friend spoke constantly, having phone calls that stretched late into the night. 'She'd talk about her experience and I'd be like "*What?*" because I thought it was just me. I was at a very low ebb with my mental health and it really broke a dam for me, forcing me to stop suppressing things and vocalize them. As I wrote in my diary, in those moments, I felt giddy, bottomless, suspended in the air, like flying in a dream. It all felt like falling in love for the first time: amazing and unstoppable.'

In the end, Lauren tells me, she and her new friend didn't actually have that much in common – theirs was a new friendship that blossomed at a pivotal time in both their lives and, though it wasn't destined to last, was no less important for that.

'Our conversations about other stuff didn't click in the same way and we eventually fell out of touch,' says Lauren. 'We met at exactly the right time and what I got from her was something I needed tremendously. Even if we never talk again, I hope she knows how much she changed for me. I hope she knows she saved my life.'

*

There are, according to Professor Robin Dunbar, seven pillars of friendship – the boxes we tick as we make friends and which demonstrate how much we have in common. The more we tick, the closer we become; but we won't tick more than a couple with some people, and that's OK.

1. Having the same language or dialect
2. Growing up in the same place
3. Having the same educational/career experiences
4. Having the same hobbies/interests
5. Having the same world view in terms of morals/religion/politics
6. Having the same sense of humour
7. Having the same musical tastes *(see: Hanson)*

When you read that list, it doesn't seem so daunting. And some of the seven pillars probably apply to a few people you already know but wouldn't necessarily count as friends, whether you work with them, go to a boxing class with them, or live next door.

I'd actually add another point to the list: having the ability to be honest. By which I mean the sort of naked truth-telling that doesn't come easily to me.

A study by the University of Kansas in 2018[21] found that small talk is friendship kryptonite. If you never get past chatting about the weather and what you're doing at the weekend, there's a limit to how deep your bond is ever going to be. Making yourself vulnerable and revealing details about your life will strengthen a friendship bond in a way that just having a superficial catch-up won't. To become firm friends with someone, you need to focus on 'self-disclosure' — or being honest, as the rest of us call it.

I have never been one to pour my heart out, even to people I would consider close friends, looking on in awe when women describe phoning their pals while crying in the middle of the night. I'd always much rather have sobbed into my pillow until it was damp and covered in mascara stains. If I unburdened myself to anyone in the small hours, it would be Becky, my long-suffering soft rabbit and one of the world's greatest listeners.

I really feel like an alien when I hear women say they sunbathe topless together, or had a party where they all ended up getting their boobs out. I've always preferred a pie-crust collar and a buttoned-up emotional life. The moment that a very new friend pulled her top up and asked me 'Are my nipples like dinner plates?' will go down, for me, as one of the most surprising in friendship history.

It all goes back to something Ana had said when she broke up with me aged sixteen: 'We never *tell* each other anything.' At the time, I had no idea what she meant. She knew that pizza was my favourite lunch. She knew about my favourite shop in which to buy yin-yang earrings. What more was there to tell? Honestly, I still felt that way in my twenties, even though I did have quite a bit of stuff worth sharing by then. I just wasn't sure I could voice it after two decades of self-preservation or without the help of a five-hour solid drinking session.

'It is sometimes really hard to tell your friends the things that you feel inside, because if you articulate them, then maybe they're real,' says Midult Emilie McMeekan. 'It's hard to say, "You know what? I'm not OK and this perfect life that I've put forward is not perfect." But perfection is a chilly mistress. If you can't share vulnerability, or disaster, or fragility, it's very hard to reach people. I think it's really important to let go and step over the dirty knickers of the past. It's OK to be imperfect and to share those imperfect experiences.'

Perhaps the most famous experiment designed to show the power of emotional intimacy is the thirty-six questions. You might remember it from a *New York Times* 'Modern Love' column a few years ago, in which writer Mandy Len Catron tried it and fell in love.

The experiment, created by Arthur and Elaine Aron in 1997, originally involved fifty-two sets of heterosexual male and female strangers. Two of the participants entered a lab, before sitting opposite one another and answering a series of increasingly intimate questions ('What would constitute your "perfect" day?'; 'What do you value most in a friendship?'; 'What is your most terrible memory?'). At the end, they stared into each other's eyes for four long minutes. Six months later, one pair married.

But the experiment was never designed to help people fall in love; it was to test emotional intimacy between strangers – a study in how self-disclosure can accelerate closeness. And it did so, with many of the participants saying they felt unusually attached to one another after just forty-five minutes, and exchanging contact details. As well as the male–female pairings, nineteen sets of heterosexual female strangers also took part.

'The clear finding – and as far as I know this has been consistent with other studies since – is that women–women pairs got just as close as cross-sex pairs,' Arthur Aron emails me.

Basically, if you make yourself increasingly vulnerable with a potential new female friend, and they reciprocate? Bingo. To 28-year-old me this would have sounded like the most nerve-racking thing imaginable. When you've been betrayed or had secrets used against you by supposed friends in the past, it can be tricky to navigate how much to open up in the future.

'I've noticed that a lot of women are over-sharers;

I would say they are too vulnerable too fast, and it often comes from a place of having felt lonely, and they just need to be witnessed,' agrees Shasta Nelson. 'Or they have felt rejected in the past so they come burdened with a fear that they will eventually be rejected again. But then many women make the mistake of under-sharing and feeling more closed. And that happens a lot, because women have felt hurt, or they don't trust easily.'

That really resonated with me – the notion of exposing yourself, only to have it thrown back in your face. I wanted to dig more into why that might be the case.

'Somebody I interviewed put it this way: "When I reveal personal information to a friend, it's like saying *here's a piece of me. That means I like you*",' says linguist Deborah Tannen. 'And then my comment back was "Yeah, but what can she do with that piece of yours?" So if the trust is well placed, it brings you closer and you have not lost anything, but it's possible for people to misuse that information – maybe not realizing they shouldn't have repeated it, maybe repeating it by accident, or maybe intentionally repeating it either to hurt you or to show off that they know it.'

It's a risk. You have to trust the other person not to misinterpret, judge, or repeat whatever you choose to share with them. You have to lower your defences and learn to show the parts of yourself you might have hidden away when friendships went wrong. It can be hard to relinquish control over your personal information. The self-preservation instinct is strong. But it can be worthwhile.

For writer Radhika Sanghani, the key to making new friends is putting yourself out there. After breaking up with her boyfriend and quitting her job to go freelance, Radhika realized she was lonely. Most of her friends lived abroad, while her London pals were increasingly at different life stages. So she decided to consciously go on a mission to make new friends.

'I began working in a new office, and there were people there who looked cool, so I just started asking them out for drinks,' she says. 'And some freaked out and were like, "Why is this girl so intense?" But the good ones said yes. And they just started to morph into real friendships.

'I got on well with one of them but we'd only ever have chats by the watercooler. And then one day, I just called her in the evening. She answered and said, "What is it?" and I replied, "I just called to say hi." And she was like "But ... why?" We laugh about it now and she says, "Thank god you did that." Because she, and another woman from that office, are now my best friends in the whole world and I met them three years ago. It's never too late – you can find good friends at any point.'

Radhika also discovered the power of being vulnerable when she found herself at a wedding and sat at a table with a group of women she knew from school – the perfect opportunity to fall into old, comfortable habits. 'But there was this one girl who was the girlfriend of the groom's colleague, so the most distant relationship to me,' she says. 'I started talking to her and it turned out that we were both freelancers, and we both felt lonely. Suddenly, we just moved seats and sat next to each other. And a month later, I went to stay with her. We became really good friends. That's now my big thing when you're meeting new people and trying to make friends: if you want it to be an actual friendship, you have to be vulnerable in some way. That's why I shared that I was struggling and she was like, "Oh my god, me too." Then it was a real connection because it was about something big.'

What I really like is that Radhika also created different layers of new friendship – acquaintanceships as well as close friends – by speaking to her neighbours or hanging back to chat to people after a yoga class. 'And suddenly I found myself quite busy,' she says. 'Not all of them stuck and some just became the occasional coffee. But it felt nice that I'd widened my community.'

Probably the easiest way to make new friends as an adult is to pinch your friends' friends. After all, someone you like has already done the hard work by vetting them. I met Iona through a work friend and our paths began to cross professionally, mostly over email. Memorably, I once sent her to interview a man who had discovered a way to put his pet rabbits into a trance (nickname: 'the Hopnotist').

Even though my friendship with the workmate who had introduced us didn't last, my one with Iona did. The moment I knew we were going to be proper pals came when I left my first newspaper job. For some unknown reason, I decided that I was going to have two leaving parties. For entirely logical reasons, my colleagues all came to the first one but cried off the second; in fact, the only person who showed up was Iona. I was mortified, but she didn't seem bothered in the slightest. It made me wonder whom I was trying to impress. We ordered multiple bottles of wine and settled in for the night, suddenly realizing that the great bonus of no one else being there was that we could put all the booze on expenses and talk about them all.

I thought back to my university housemates; to my school BFFs. They would have made me feel like a right prat for throwing myself a leaving 'party' for two. But Iona didn't care, so I didn't care. It helped me to be vulnerable – and let's face it, the most embarrassing thing that night had already happened. It wasn't about the quantity of guests, suddenly it was about quality. I didn't make Iona feel as though her company wasn't enough, because it was.

Just as it was a decade later, when we found ourselves at an impromptu dinner party attended by several famous types, including a Radio 4 presenter who had once called me a 'silly girl', having not noticed that the important email I'd sent them was, in fact, in their junk mail.

To my slight relief, there wasn't space at the long kitchen table for us all, so instead of awkwardly trying to nudge people along, Iona and I sat on a sofa, plates of beef-shin pappardelle on our knees, and gorged ourselves on pasta, red wine and laughter. One woman sidled up to me afterwards and said, 'You two looked like you were having the best evening out of all of us.' She was probably right.

At around the same time, I met Rachel. I say

'met' – we had worked in the same office for almost five years, but had never really spoken. I'd occasionally see her wafting past looking stylish, and wonder whether she was as nice as she seemed. Word clearly having got around about how popular I had been made to look at my second leaving do, Rachel walked over to my desk one day and suggested we have a drink before I departed. I was clearing my desk anyway, so figured if it was painfully awkward, I never had to see her again. I realize now that I was experiencing friendship imposter syndrome – the feeling that you don't measure up, or are a total fraud. It's most commonly used when talking about work and is a subject I became interested in after having a major case of it myself.

It happened a few years ago, when I was invited to take part in a panel to mark International Women's Day. Sitting on stage, alongside some highly successful women, I began to feel as though there was a sign flashing above my head: WHO THE HELL DO YOU THINK YOU ARE? I felt sure I was about to be exposed as someone who didn't deserve to be there. I remember cringing; dreading being asked a question that would reveal that I didn't know what I was talking about. Oh, and the topic of that discussion? Imposter syndrome. Now, having interviewed some amazing women on the subject for my *Imposters* podcast – actress Priyanka Chopra Jonas, Trinny Woodall, Samantha Cameron, June Sarpong – I've come to understand that it has impacted areas of my personal life, as well as my professional one. I think that's true for so many of us.

When it comes to new friendships, the symptoms are all there. We put it down to fluke that this person seems to like us and convince ourselves that we'll be 'found out' any minute, that we're not good enough – or likeable enough. It's why I genuinely couldn't see what a friendly, popular person like Rachel would want with me.

How glad I am that she asked me for that drink, and that I didn't let my own self-doubt get in the way of nervously accepting. We got on really well. I was in the middle of a massive upheaval – ending my relationship, planning to move back in with my parents and changing jobs – and I gave myself permission to talk about all three. I didn't pour my heart out; I started small, with honest answers to her questions; the sorts of things you might tell an existing friend. If you treat someone like a friend, maybe they'll become one.

Rachel introduced me to two other women from our office, Cecilia and Louise. The three of them were close, but never acted like a clique. Quite the opposite, in fact; they opened the door for me to join them. I really couldn't understand why at the time . . . actually, I'm not sure I get it now. Only that they enjoyed making new friends – that was a revelation to me. Maybe I could learn to enjoy it, too. Perhaps if I tried my best to throw out everything I thought I knew, and every bad experience that had left me feeling suspicious of female friendship, I would start to see things differently. So I tried. I encouraged myself to share secrets and disappointments in a way I'd felt too defensive to do before. I talked about them, rather than bottling things up in case they were seen as a weakness.

The result? It felt good and it worked. I bloody love sharing now. I am a vulnerability queen. Rejection? I *laugh* in the *face* of rejection. Bad day at work? *Read all about it.* Cervix-twisting cystitis? *Here's every detail and do you want my GP's number for the urine-test results?* I am last night's dirty knickers in human form. OK, maybe not. But over time, those three women became some of my dearest friends. I lived with Rachel. I am godmother to Cecilia's beautiful daughter. Louise flew back from her home in Spain for my wedding.

Our WhatsApp group – called 'Ladies!', because it's not as if all four of us work in the creative industries and could have come up with a better name – is a user's guide on topics from the merits of *Question Time* to whether or not to wear knickers (in life, at all) and the guy who, at the end of a first date, put down a towel on the bed before sex. We've often talked about moving into a commune when we're old, sending one another links to suitable minor stately homes.

My new-found ability to talk more openly didn't mean that I was suddenly spilling my guts to strangers every five seconds, but it slowly and solidly helped me forge new friendships, as well as strengthening the ones I already had. I found that I was able to go deeper with Izzy, Marie, Agatha and Eve. And it had another surprising side-effect, bringing me closer to some women I'd always considered other people's friends, not mine – such as Agatha's university housemates. Now, I realized how much shared history of our own we had and what I needed to do to help those friendships solidify.

It was as if I'd set off a chain reaction in my own life.

Little fires of female friendship began to spark everywhere. Kiko, a stylish and smart woman I'd always admired from afar – the sort who can wear clashing patterns, hi-top trainers, huge earrings and look incredible rather than, as I would, like someone the 1980s threw up on – started to become more than the friend of a friend as we spent more time together. We talked about life, about other people's lives, about whether it was better to make the penis-shaped pinata for our mutual friend's stag do from cardboard or papier mache.

I knew we were truly pals when she and her husband invited us for dinner and then asked us to adopt Maybe, the sweetest, smallest cat, with thick black fur and tiny white socks, whom they had recently rescued and we had been swooning over for weeks. Turns out Kiko's husband is steroid injections-level allergic to cat fur. If a friendship can survive someone near-pinching your pet, I think you're set.

'I honestly can't believe you weren't at our wedding,' Kiko said, a year or so after she'd got married and a few months after our friendship had solidified. It's something she and her husband mention self-consciously from time to time, but actually it makes me feel strangely reassured. Yes, I'd have loved to be there – not least because there was a bottle of whisky on every table – but I like being reminded that I've made a dear new friend when I didn't expect it. Two, actually.

Doing things two by two is an attractive prospect for couples. It can help you see your partner in a different light; interacting, sharing intimacies, laughing and generally being fanciable in a way they probably aren't at home, in their tracksuit bottoms and vacuuming cat hair off the sofa.

A 2014 study by the University of Massachusetts[22] found that couple friendships can even reignite a passionate spark in your own relationship. And couples are happier when they have close friendships with other couples, which is obviously why I encourage Tim to go out cycling with Rachel's husband while she and I have long lunches and get our nails done. See? Good for everyone. With new friends, creating a foursome can be even nicer, as you get to know them and their relationship almost in tandem. It can take some of the intensity out of being vulnerable and help you to share things, with your own partner by your side for back-up – and, of course, to lovingly kick you under the table if you're oversharing.

*

Looking around my thirtieth birthday party, I couldn't believe what a difference two years could make. I felt like someone who had the beginnings of that friendship portfolio: Izzy and Marie, who were loyally still in my life; Agatha and Eve, who had shown me that I didn't have to be a 'guy's girl' hollow cliche of a person; Rachel, Cecilia, Louise, Kiko – new female friends with whom I felt, if not totally sure of myself yet, then getting there.

I started to understand what it was that I hadn't been giving in friendships: myself. I had presented a version of Claire that I thought would be desirable as a friend. A person who was always 'OK, thanks' and struggled to be vulnerable. A people-pleaser, who made herself small so others could feel big. Who, in doing so, set a pattern that contributed to the uneven balance of power in her friendships. Who, in putting up a barrier, was never properly seen, heard or understood.

Until that point, I had always felt as though the few female friends I did have were pals with me because they knew my flaws and inexplicably liked me anyway. I still think that's true for most female friendships. But what I hadn't understood was that they weren't focusing on what was wrong with me, or judging me in the way my inner critic constantly judged myself. They wanted *more* of me, not less. So that's what I slowly found the confidence to give them.

It might not seem revelatory to you that being more open and honest is actually pretty key to making new friends, and bringing old ones closer, but it was to me. And even if you're armed with that knowledge, which I think I had been deep down for years without appreciating it, it's not always easy to put into practice. But friends, believe me, it's worth it.

The Friendship Gap

Myth: Once a friendship fractures,
it's impossible to repair

Have you ever felt as though you're looking at a friend from the opposite side of a vast chasm? You can see them – almost reach out and touch them – but there suddenly seems to be a huge distance between you.

Welcome to the friendship gap: the space that opens up between even the closest of female friends, when the tectonic plates of your lives move apart and leave you staring into a gaping void. Where once you were aligned, moving to the same rhythm, now you've never felt further away. Imagine the earthquake in *The Land Before Time* and you'll have some idea of what I'm talking about.

The friendship gap isn't usually anyone's fault. No hurt is intended. The reason for this big, scary abyss can be any number of perfectly pedestrian life stages: falling in love, buying a house, being promoted, getting married, having a baby, moving away, the

menopause, divorce. (Though it can also be a difference of opinion over something fundamental, or a
lack of understanding around a friend's lived experience, more of which later.)

These are the rituals of adulthood that help us to
keep travelling forward, whatever your personal milestones might be. There's a good reason that marriage
and babies have been codified in our society for
centuries – they keep the supermarket conveyor belt
of humanity chugging along. Milk, butter, bread, Mar-
mite, marriage, pasta, jacket potatoes, terraced house,
extra-mature Cheddar, baked beans, babies.

The friendship gap is perhaps the most painful the
first time that a friend tells you they have *big news*. It's
an unenviable position to be the one who chooses to
step back and do some adulting. And it can throw an
unwelcome spotlight on your own choices. They're
engaged. (Why are you still going on awful dates?)
They're buying a flat. (Why are you sleeping on your
sister's futon?) They are pregnant. (You still feel like
a baby and aren't even close to being ready to have
one.)

It's not just that you won't all be travelling at the
same pace, at the same time, or want the same things,
but those choices can impact your friendships in
unforeseen ways. Gaps will inevitably open up; it's
how you bridge them that counts.

Our major life stages are now happening later and
later, which can make the contrast between friends
especially stark. The average age for a heterosexual
woman to get married in the UK is thirty-five, while
the average age for becoming a first-time mother is

twenty-nine and rising. So when a friend tells you that they're getting married at twenty-four or having a baby at twenty-six, it's a *thing*. An active choice that sets them apart and often creates a friendship gap in the process.

The first time this happens for most of us is when a friend falls in love – or maybe we do. Falling in love, says Robin Dunbar, means that you lose two friends. Because your new partner is now firmly in your inner circle that means something – someone – has to give and a couple of people get bumped down your priority list. It's because, he adds, 'time is the basis of friendship' and by investing that in your new relationship you have less of it to go around.

It's something Greta Gerwig captures in her 2013 film *Frances Ha*: the feeling of being replaced that can occur between female friends when one of them gets a boyfriend and the shifting of our friendships as we enter the next stage of our lives. As the character of Frances tells her closest friend, Sophie, who has fallen in love: 'If something funny happens on the way to the deli, you'll only tell one person about it and that'll be Patch and I'll never hear about it.'

'I had quite loving relationships with my friends in my twenties. I used to joke that I would put on perfume and lipstick to meet my female friends, but I would wear tracksuit bottoms and not shave my armpits with my boyfriend,' says *The Panic Years* author Nell Frizzell. 'We would go on holidays and drink sparkling wine on balconies, which I didn't do with my partner. And then to have all that intimacy put on someone else . . . and I know love isn't a finite resource.

But time is a finite resource. There was a period where I had no one higher in my priority list than my friends, but they all had either a partner or a child, and that was trumping me. Ultimately, there is a decision of time and priority, and you are down their list. I found that really sad.'

Undoubtedly, children are one of the most dramatic things that can happen to a friendship. Suddenly, a breach has appeared that's bigger than almost anything – and I'm not just talking about the dilation. After all, women are never really the 'right' age to have kids. Get pregnant 'too young' and you're chucking away your education, career and youth. Wait 'too long' and you're a selfish, tired geriatric with withered eggs. No wonder we feel so mixed up when our friends take the plunge.

'The first time someone tells you they're pregnant, you think, "Oh my god, are people getting pregnant now? Am I ready to be pregnant?"' says Nell. 'What has been abstract suddenly becomes an urgent question settling in your life. And it can happen with anything: a promotion, getting a dog. We all do it.'

That's how I felt when one of my friends married and got pregnant when we were twenty-six. I couldn't get my head around it. Everything we'd done up to this point had been in the pursuit of fun. Having a husband and a baby seemed like the undoing of that. Would we ever have a night out again?

A huge part of what I think causes the friendship gap, particularly when it comes to those early outliers, is that they're not only pulling the pin out of a grenade in their own lives, but they've also exploded how you'd imagined yours. All the adventures you'd hoped to share with them suddenly seem out of reach. Or, as Nell puts it, 'It's as if they've taken away your debit card without telling you.' If only NatWest had a fraud hotline for that.

I remember going to visit my friend shortly after she'd broken the news, excited to hear all about it – and I wanted to know *all* about it. This was the mate with whom I'd shared every detail of my teenage fumblings, so the nitty gritty of how she'd got pregnant was the next natural step. But when I arrived? I couldn't get her alone. Her husband just didn't understand that I needed us to talk in private. About him. About which of their shags had made a baby. I suggested that we go for a stroll, hoping he'd get the hint. He didn't and so the three of us ended up at the local pub. Finally, at the bar, I had two minutes of alone time with my friend, but the pressure was too much. I couldn't just blurt out 'So how many times did you have to *do it*?' in a genteel market-town watering hole.

My status had slipped and, rather than doubling down and trying to prevent the gap from growing wider, as with the benefit of hindsight I wish I had, I let our friendship drift. She was preoccupied and I felt pushed out. I didn't know then what I know now, about the friendship gap and how it doesn't have to stay billowing forever. Instead, I lost a close friend to nothing more than a happy change in her circumstances.

As time goes on, these friendship gaps start opening up everywhere. It feels a bit like a game of

Whac-A-Mole – as weddings, housewarming parties and pregnant bellies pop up all over the place. Eventually there are so many molehills that anyone who hasn't started down a similar track starts to seem as though they're making a mountain out of things. You feel like a novelty: the last woman standing who can entertain your pals with 'hilarious' dating stories. You sense it at weddings, christenings, birthday parties in your friend's gorgeous family home after which you return to the single bed in your rental flat. The material aspects of your lives can appear insurmountable, even if the fundamentals of your friendship remain the same.

Where the gap really opens up is if you think a friend is judging you; that their priorities are somehow a pronouncement on your choices. That by not taking whatever 'next step' your friend has, your life has somehow fallen under a shadow and is the negative to their positive. I recall one pal, after having her baby, making nudge-nudge-wink-wink references to how I'd soon be in the same boat. I think she wanted to reassure herself that our friendship might not be 'uneven' for long, but it made me feel as though I was letting her down by not being ready to follow her lead.

Chances are your friend won't be judging or trying to upset you. Just as the gap gets into your head, it can get into hers. She might even be longing for what you have. But it can be easier said than done to confront. Admitting to a friend that you're feeling left out when they've just given birth, for example, probably isn't going to go down well. Being jealous of a newborn is not a good look. Actually, for me, one of the hardest gaps has been those new 'parent friends'. I sometimes feel a bit left out when my friends talk about NCT pals, or school-gate mums. I like to rationalize it by telling myself that I'm not a terrible person, and they just need someone they can WhatsApp at 1 a.m. to moan about having to clean up another human's faeces.

But Christine Armstrong, author of *The Mother of All Jobs*, doesn't think we should dismiss so-called 'mum friends' as merely friends of convenience. 'Motherhood is the basis of so many female friendships. And those mum friendships aren't superficial,' she says. 'Lifelong bonds are born in the fire of 3 a.m. feeds, children with diarrhoea, identifying special needs, or when someone falls out of a tree. Some women I've interviewed have said that their college or school friends had been replaced in importance. This was now the friendship group that defined who they are, rather than a younger version of themselves.'

Ouch. I'd like to think that wasn't the case for most of my friends with children. Yes, there's a certain empathy gap: it's harder to genuinely understand the demands of night feeds when you're not dealing with it first-hand. But that doesn't mean I don't care. And, in my experience, if both of you can adapt then no one has to be replaced by anyone. It's a matter of accepting that things are different. It basically involves shelving your ego – recognizing that your birthday dinner won't be the most important date on your mate's calendar for a bit, even though their child's birthday is on yours.

'When I had a baby, I couldn't be the friend that I'd been before. Trying to be that person was exhausting, and made me resentful,' says Nell Frizzell. 'What I could have done is just leaned into it and said, "I'm not ashamed. I'm not going to be able to come to your party. But I'm still going to phone you when they're having a nap. And if you come round, I can still make you dinner. But it's going to be different to how it was. And in a few years' time, it will be different again."'

That's another thing that it's important to accept – it is likely that they won't be gone forever. Just as you might wait for a friend in love to come up for air from her new relationship (or for a friend writing a book to finish it and re-emerge from her cave), so a friend in the parenting trenches could use the same patience.

They might even be struggling with their own gap, as Nell did when she found herself part of an NCT group of parents-to-be who were all wealthier than her. 'We would all go to each other's houses and I put off having people round to our flat for as long as I could, because I was embarrassed,' she says. 'When they finally did [come], they were all perfectly nice. I got flustered and I put out weird snacks, but it was basically fine. And I remember thinking "What's going on here? I don't particularly care about money, but I am worried that these people are going to pity me, or be revolted by me, or talk about me behind my back." The financial inequality between us made me feel inferior, judged, edgy and uncomfortable. And that was my problem, really . . . I don't know what the solution is other than get therapy so you don't feel monumental self-criticism every time someone has a different life to you.'

Pandora Sykes tells me it took her a while to work out how her two 'identities' could sit together: being a friend and a parent. 'With a friend who hasn't had babies there does have to be a necessary renegotiation of your friendship,' she says. 'You're not going to get invited to everything and sometimes that's going to hurt. Sometimes you might have actually really been up for going out on a Friday night but your friend assumed, trying to be sensitive, that it wouldn't suit you and so they never asked. Those kinds of miscommunications are common; it's how you react to them and deal with them.'

At a certain age, the subject of fertility is like an unexploded bomb in our lives. There's always someone trying to get pregnant and someone else excitedly telling you what fruit their foetus is currently equivalent to (Mango! Avocado!). Several women shared with me how they had avoided putting pregnancy announcements on social media, as they knew friends were struggling. I've seen pals who were trying to have children quietly withdraw from friendships where the other person had young kids, as it felt like a constant reminder of what they so desperately wanted.

Nor is it always helpful to know that another friend is going through the same difficult thing as you. As Emma Barnett told me: 'When you're having fertility issues, older women and younger women are your favourite people. You basically want to ignore everyone who's thirty or forty and could still potentially use their womb, because at any moment they could say, "I'm pregnant!" Or the opposite – "I'm really struggling, too" – and maybe I don't feel like hearing that either.'

It's so personal and a really delicate thing to handle well, with the potential to cause hurt on both sides. Labour MP Jess Phillips says that she 'lost a lot of friends' when she had her children young. 'I found that there were very few people left in my life when I was twenty-two and had a baby. And actually my new group of women friends came along because they had children as well,' she explains.

Now, she is the one navigating a fertility gap with one of her best friends, who is trying to have a baby on her own. 'I really feel for her because all of us – at every point in my friendships, whether we decided not to have children, had kids, had miscarriages or abortions – have always had some experience to share; some knowledge, some understanding,' says Jess. 'But having a baby through IVF on her own, we've got nothing at all. I've found it really hard that we can't offer that help to her. So much of the fundamentals of our friendship has been because we've all had shit boyfriends, we've all struggled with money – we have a universal experience. It can feel quite lonely when your female friends don't immediately know the right thing to say.

'We just had a massive blow-up row about it – and the deficit is mine, not hers, without question. I just don't know how to handle this particular situation,' she admits.

'What I've often found with women – and it is difficult and dangerous – is you cannot explain what does and doesn't matter to somebody who hasn't experienced it. So I say, "It's not the be-all and end-all of being a woman, being able to carry a child." But it's OK if you *can* carry one; it's easy to say that, isn't it? Yet it's not OK to say that to somebody who feels that they're failing, or that they can't have something they really want. I know that afterwards, when she's successful in doing this, she will end up with the same universal experience that we all have, where we say, "Oh, you know, being pregnant is a bag of shit."'

Psychotherapist Jody Day, fifty-seven, knows exactly what it's like to feel outside of your friends' shared experience. She runs Gateway Women, a network for those childless through infertility or circumstance. The friendship gap she experienced through not being able to have children has defined her adult life.

'I was one of the first in my circle to get married,' Jody tells me. 'But we didn't start trying for a few years, and during that time, everyone else had children. There was never any reason for me not being able to get pregnant, so I stayed in denial, even when my marriage broke down under the strain. It wasn't until I was forty-four that I woke up to the fact it was game over.

'That's when my friendships started to change. They had been quite difficult to keep up with but I had done it, as I imagined that one day their children would be my children's playmates. I shouldered that emotional labour because it was part of my dream of being a mum.'

When she accepted that she wouldn't be having children herself, Jody says, her friends didn't want to acknowledge that fact or talk to her about it, instead offering solutions and advice that plainly weren't feasible. 'I started to realize that I was the one keeping the friendships going, and I couldn't do it any more. I was in too much pain. So as a sort of semi-conscious experiment, I withdrew a lot of my emotional labour. And it was like I'd dropped off the face of the earth,' she says. 'I lost my entire social group to parenthood. I call it the #FriendshipApocalypse – and I now know it's extremely common, but at the time I just thought I must be a bad friend. I felt utterly abandoned.'

Her friends, she adds, had a 'fantasy' view of her life. 'Because I hadn't had kids, they compared my life in my forties, single and childless, to life in our twenties, single and childless. They thought I was having a great time. It probably never occurred to them that I might be lonely. There's so much unspoken stuff and that's what derails the friendship; not the difficult conversations. But perhaps because we've been brought up with this idea that female friendships can survive anything, when it gets sticky we don't have the skills to talk about it,' she says. 'If we had, I might have been able to save a couple of my friendships.'

It's important to accept that having such difficult conversations with friends won't be easy – if it were, there might be no friendship gaps at all. The key is listening: for me, problems arise when you presume you know what a friend will feel or think about a certain situation. Jody's pals assumed she would want advice on how she might still have a child, but really she only wanted their acknowledgement of her grief. Comments like 'Here, have one of mine' or 'You're so lucky you get to sleep in' widened the gap because she wasn't given the space to express her emotions openly with her friends, who in trying to empathize actually ended up making her feel as though she couldn't say how she really felt. And when she has plucked up the courage to ask her friends why they've not invited her to certain social gatherings, they have told her they were trying to spare her from all the 'boring parent chat', or from pain. But is that worse than being excluded and not told why?

The skill in having these tough talks is to be curious; to ask questions of your friend rather than directing them down a particular conversational path. To listen and not rush to interject before you know how they really feel. As Jody puts it: 'Whatever you're thinking of saying, park it. Maybe just ask an open question instead.'

*

Marriage and parenthood might be some of the most significant gap-makers, but they can open up at any age.

'As a child, my two closest friends were from middle-class families,' one woman in her thirties tells me. 'They always had so many things I coveted, from toys to holidays and birthday parties. These friendships were affected by the barrier of my family being traditional working class and short on cash and the impact this had on being able to do the things my closest friends wanted to. Going to school in the "posh" area of my town and being surrounded by the children of aspirational middle-class parents could be isolating.'

Ninety-two-year-old Audrey Lamontagne-Defriez explains that fading health has opened up a gap with one female friend whom she's known since 1955.

'We've been through thick and thin. We had a break when I was travelling around and I lost touch a bit, but every time that I surfaced, we met up,' says Audrey. 'Now, she phones me up, gosh, nearly every other day. Sometimes I dread picking up the phone. She's deaf, so we have rather inconsequential telephone calls about her neighbour's mother-in-law, whom I don't know and never shall. It's a monologue really and she doesn't listen to a word I say – I think possibly because she can't.'

Perhaps the biggest gap to hit female friendships after that initial settling-down period, however, is divorce. It's one of the most heart-rending things anyone can go through and a time when you'd hope to rely on your friends more than ever. Yet what is surprising is that many women report losing female friends when they divorce – between 10 per cent and 40 per cent, depending on whom you ask. The reasons are obvious to psychologists: you may be seen as a threat, one single woman in a sea of couples; they might be your partner's friend as well as yours and think they have to 'choose'; or it could be plain old fear. After all, if it can happen to you, it can happen to them. And they're not wrong – the 'divorce cluster' theory has been proven by academics, with one US study[23] concluding that you're 75 per cent more likely to divorce if someone close to you has done so.

'Divorce is brutal. It rocks your world like you can't believe,' says friendship expert Liz Pryor. 'Your husband will have brought certain people into your life and you could have become extremely close. And regardless of the divorce circumstances, there is an unspoken loyalty to your husband: he gets them and you don't. There are so many people that I felt pretty close to over the years who, to this day, I feel slightly uncomfortable seeing.'

'I was the first person to get divorced [in my friendship group] and that was really difficult,' agrees Jane Garvey. 'I found out very quickly who was there for the long haul and who'd always been my friend. And who perhaps was not that fascinated by me as an individual, but was along for a different sort of ride.'

Navigating the issue of mutual friends during a break-up or divorce is rarely straightforward, with some feeling as though they have to take sides and others just quietly drifting away in an attempt to avoid conflict, or because they were never really invested in your happiness in the first place. But what really took me aback was the number of women who told me their oldest friendships – ones that long pre-dated their marriage – had been shattered by a split.

One woman, who asked not to be named, was blindsided by a gap that opened up with her oldest friend.

'Over breakfast my husband told me something he

had been hiding for a long time and ended our twenty-two-year relationship,' she says. 'I hadn't seen it coming and until that point I'd been one of those annoyingly blissful married people. Our relationship was the envy of many of my friends. In those first weeks, I struggled to tell them what had happened and confided in a support group. It was easier to talk to strangers who weren't thinking it had served me right to have been so smug.

'Then I found the courage to tell one of my oldest friends. She was amazing. We both come from the same town and right from the beginning I explained that I didn't want anyone "back home" to know yet. I wanted to be at a certain point in my own grief before my story was available for human consumption. But one evening she called me in a panic saying that she'd been chatting to a friend from our town and it had slipped out. I felt deeply betrayed and it brought to mind all the red flags that I had explained away over the years. I also had another friend who got very upset that I hadn't reached out to her and took it as a lack of trust, saying as much. It blew my mind that in my darkest hour one of my dearest friends could make it all about her.'

She has now deliberately drifted from those old friends, despite feeling 'guilty' about it. Even more surprisingly, she adds, 'It was actually the people I least expected who rallied; offering to have my children, inviting me for walks or sending messages of kindness.'

Liz Pryor also found that divorce can help you form new friendships, even as gaps open up elsewhere.

'The beauty of divorce is that it's a little bit of a club,' she says. 'It's a huge bonder between women: "You know what I've gone through."'

That is such a powerful sentiment within female friendship and something so many of us have felt with another woman, whether to do with loss, illness, addiction, unequal pay, sexual harassment or any number of things where a 'me too' means so much. Grief should be one such bonding experience, and yet when Lauren Libbert's mum died, her best friend of more than twenty years ghosted her.

'She was on holiday when it happened. So I was expecting that, obviously, when she got back she would immediately get in touch,' says Lauren. 'But she just didn't. It was really bizarre. I was also separating from my husband at that time, so I was going through all these things and she was completely absent. I can understand when people don't get death or feel awkward – but she'd actually lost her father a few years previously, so that was even more shocking.

'I bumped into her shopping a few weeks after she'd got back and I remember how good she looked; she had a great tan and all this gold jewellery on. She was just like, "Hello!" It was very weird.'

After that chance meeting, Lauren's friend did try to get in touch and persuade her to meet – which they eventually did, in a cafe around six months later.

'I was so nervous. It felt like seeing an ex or something,' says Lauren. 'She apologized and we probably could have worked through it all but I wouldn't allow her. I'd moved on. I just feel like she's not the person or the friend that I thought she was and I can't close that gap with her. I suppose it's almost like a partner cheated on you – I mean, how do you get the trust back?'

Lauren's experience comes down to how much we expect from our friends. We overlook the odd missed birthday or last-minute lunch cancellation, because life is busy and overwhelming. But when it comes to those big milestones, whether joyful or painful, we expect them to come through. To drop everything and be there. So when they don't? It can shake our friendship belief system; the one built on mutual support which means we feel able to reach out and tell a friend that we need to bitch about our boss or talk through a relationship problem. It has us questioning what we thought we knew about the friendship and can easily feel like neglect, betrayal, or a form of grief in itself.

There is also the kind of grief which fuses with the promise of new motherhood. My friend Marie lost her baby boy, Lenny, almost halfway through her first pregnancy. She'd messaged me a couple of weeks earlier, as Tim and I were on our way back from our honeymoon, to say that she was expecting – the happiest news. 'That's so exciting, yay yay!' I replied. 'Want to hear all about it asap'.

She was living abroad, and we played phone ping-pong for a few days. Then she went strangely quiet. When she next messaged, it took my breath away. 'Sadly, at our scan on Friday we got some difficult news about the baby. We're going to go off the radar for a little bit and spend time with each other and our families,' she wrote. 'Love you lots.'

It was midday on a beautiful spring Saturday. I'd just had coffee with a friend in Crystal Palace and popped into the garden centre to buy some bulbs. Everything had seemed fresh and full of promise: one of those days that feels too wholesome to be true; as though you're walking through Hugh Grant's changing-of-the-seasons scene in *Notting Hill* and emerging into the sunlight, taking your jacket off and slinging it over your shoulder ready for summer.

I stopped in the middle of the pavement and sat down hard on a broken bench outside Sainsbury's, as the weekend shoppers swarmed around me. I felt winded and couldn't swallow. She was suffering; my wonderful friend was in unimaginable pain, and I couldn't reach her. I felt a gap opening up there and then, between my need to help and comfort and her very understandable desire to retreat.

I felt useless. Utterly useless. So I just messaged – saying that I didn't expect a reply but that I was going to send kisses, photos of my cat and 'thinking about you' texts anyway. She could get in touch when she was ready, no pressure. I had no idea whether it was the right thing to do, but the thought of staying silent filled me with horror.

One sunny April afternoon a few days later, my friend and her husband said goodbye to their dear little boy.

'We feel so lucky to be his parents,' Marie messaged.

'He will always be remembered,' I promised her.

'I can't tell you how much that means,' she replied.

I sent her some books – something to make her laugh and something to transport her to another, far-away land. I called. A few weeks later, I flew out to visit for the weekend and told her that I loved her – perhaps the first time in our twenty-year friendship. I meant every word.

'Losing Lenny affected my friendships in different ways,' said Marie, when I asked her about those terrible weeks and months. 'The first time I saw some friends afterwards in the pub, they didn't say anything to my face even though they had messaged me their support at the time.

'That really threw me, especially with those of them who had previously lost someone close. I thought they might have pulled me aside to say something. I left feeling quite disappointed in those friends, and since then there is a bigger gap between us. Not consciously; it's just grown.

'But others have become closer through this; the friends that really recognize and talk about Lenny. For me, they are an extra little link I have to him and because of that they are even more important than they were. I've made new friends, too, and have become close to some of my mum's friends because of Lenny.'

Recently, after an afternoon spent planting flowers underneath his memorial tree in her new home town and chatting to locals about its special meaning, Marie returned the next day to find that someone had added another plant overnight. The next time she went to water them, somebody had already done it.

There are, we agreed, friends everywhere if you're open to seeing them.

*

There's one thing that's caused a friendship gap for me and that I haven't yet addressed. I'm half-Jewish, through my dad's side of the family. Growing up, we celebrated Passover and Easter, Chanukah and Christmas, with all the food and all the gifts. As an adult, well, I couldn't tell you the last time I set foot in a synagogue and I mainline bacon. But I'm also acutely aware that my grandfather's parents and siblings were killed in the war. Oh and I have one of the most obvious Jewish surnames out there, which means that people wrongly assume they know all about my beliefs.

One morning at university, I walked into the library for my ritual of sitting at a desk pretending to work on my dissertation while silently panicking. I made my way along the bookshelves in the English department and found a spare seat, next to a friend from the student newspaper. Barely glancing up, she said: 'Oh, Claire, I thought that was you. I could see your big Jew nose coming round the corner.'

I sat down. What was I supposed to say? I felt powerless and bloody shocked. This woman was someone I'd considered a friend, so I didn't know how to confront it. The hurtful prejudice and stereotype was the cause of an unbridgeable gap. It had felt just like being back in my A-level history lesson when my teacher had turned to the class and said, 'Claire, you're a Jew. Tell us about the Holocaust.' I stayed silent then, too.

This isn't going to be a catalogue of my experiences of anti-Semitism. But in thinking about them for this book, I did start to question how much I'd asked my friends about their own brushes with discrimination. I'm not directly comparing 'isms' – there isn't a hierarchy of hate – it's simply that thinking back to that so-called student pal made me realize that I too had friends with painful stories to tell. And we're often really bad at telling them. If you think friendship in general is a woefully under-analysed subject among academics and poorly represented in film and on TV, then try friendships between lesbians and straight women. Or interracial friendships.

My friend Joan, whose mum is Black and dad is white, told me that she has reassessed some of her own friendships in light of the Black Lives Matter movement.

'There have been a handful of times when I've attempted to explain something that is different for me than it is for white friends and, until BLM, people were mostly quite dismissive,' she says. 'I was once telling a friend how you rarely see Black women in positions of power with natural hair. Afro hair is often seen as unprofessional and so I would feel at a disadvantage if I turned up to a job interview with my hair completely natural. My friend dismissed this as an issue, saying that it's the same for her because she wouldn't turn up to a job interview without washing and brushing her hair. She didn't get the difference between the two and I didn't feel comfortable elaborating. With most differences of opinion with friends, I've always been fairly confident in making my point, but race has definitely been the one that I've never felt comfortable tackling, probably because it's the one that has a direct impact on my friendships.'

That is so depressing to me, that we lack the vocabulary and awareness to have these conversations. Joan admits that it can be lonely to feel like you can't be fully open within friendships.

'I've had issues with race in romantic relationships, which meant that when things weren't going well, I wasn't actually able to give my friends the full picture of what was wrong. It's a conversation I've had with a few close friends recently and they were really surprised that I'd kept so much in. They had just assumed that I needed less support than other friends and they now feel sad that they weren't able to be there fully when I needed it.

'After BLM, lots of people were curious about my thoughts,' she adds. 'If friends want to learn then I'm happy to help, but it has been a bit overwhelming. Some people don't understand that as a white person you can look at some of the awful footage and be horrified by it, but it's not personal to you. It doesn't stay with you in the same way as it does me. It's definitely difficult to balance how I manage talking to friends about it. I don't want them to stop asking, but it can be quite tiring and there are definitely people who could be more respectful of that. I've not fallen out with anyone, I just chose to avoid them until BLM stopped being headline news.'

Joan's words shine a light on the emotional labour

that can run through friendships, where one person is either dismissive of another's experience or regularly expects their friend to educate them, with little regard for the toll that might take.

Ann Friedman and Aminatou Sow describe it in their book *Big Friendship*: 'When it comes to inter-racial friendships that involve a white person, it's likely that the non-white friend is going to feel more nega-tively stretched, while the white friend gets to have a "learning experience",' they write.

Abbie Naish, thirty-three, has also felt this 'learning gap' with her straight friends. She is often asked what she and her girlfriend do in bed. At one hen do, she recalls, the whole group fell silent while everyone took turns to interrogate her about the mechanics of lesbian sex.

'There are some things that people don't really get,' she says. 'I'm in the early stages of seeing someone, and all of my straight friends are like, "If she really likes you, she'll do the chasing, don't act too keen." And the impact of that can be to slightly erode my confidence, actually – I don't think they realize that, but it's quite a defeatist point of view. The problem is that they are giving me advice they'd give to their straight friends. Whereas it's kind of expected that I do a bit of the chasing. I adore my friends and I'd be nowhere without them, but they're just a bit out of step.'

Dating and relationship advice runs through the core of female friendships, but many women told me how it had led to a gap; from the woman who thinks her best friend's husband is a bully, to the one who lost touch with her lesbian friends after they disapproved of her girlfriend not being out. If you feel protective of a friend and her relationship seems as though you're watching a car crash in slow motion, it can be hard to button it – even if you know it could create a gap between you, or put her in a risky situation.

'I once told a friend's partner what I thought about him,' says my friend Sal. 'He insisted they kept their relationship secret, supposedly as his parents are religious. But it felt disrespectful and I know it upset her. It was only when she got pregnant that he introduced her to his family. Then he arranged a surprise baby shower and I found out he hadn't included one of our good friends. I asked if he could fit her in and he said no, the subtext being that he didn't approve of her lifestyle. And so I sent one of those emails that you should always sleep on, basically accusing him of being controlling. It wasn't horrible but it was confronting. The baby shower went ahead and I thought it wasn't an issue. But when I made plans to visit her after the baby had been born, he refused to let me go. My friend was caught in the middle at a vulnerable time, so I backed down. We're still friends but it's totally changed our relationship.'

Judi, seventy-seven, whom I speak to over the phone on a grey day, tells me that her school friend – whom she'd known from a very young age and spent many holidays with – did call out the bad behaviour of her husband, something that created a huge gap between them.

'We had both married and I went to stay [with her] with my husband and young child,' Judi says. 'My husband was extremely controlling and reluctant to make this visit, and it was a disaster as he was mostly uncommunicative and rude. My friend and her husband attempted to talk to him about his attitude, which just made things worse. Tearfully, she asked me why I was with this man. I felt hurt and embarrassed, as this felt like the end of my friendship with someone to whom I had been very close. We left early, and despite my sending a note of apology, our friendship was fractured and we had no further contact for many years, which upset me terribly. But I do understand that she found it impossible to continue: I was with someone who was destructive and it was easier to end all contact with me.'

I find that so sad: that having arguably done her duty as a good friend, Judi's childhood pal then felt she had to back away, probably when it became clear that her friend intended to remain in the marriage. It stems, I think, from a feeling of helplessness, worry and rejection of your advice – something that can ultimately lead to resentment.

That's how Esther, thirty-seven, felt about a close friend she'd lived with throughout her twenties, who got together with a colleague. 'After a year, he moved in with her and from that day he suddenly became a horror,' she says. 'He didn't like her spending time with other people. She started dressing dowdily as he didn't want her wearing fitted clothes. They were about to break up when he proposed. They planned a wedding, then he called it off as she was "a slob" and he couldn't "train her out of it". Then they got back together, married quickly and had two children – moving far away from family and friends. When I went to see her, I couldn't stay in their house, and he didn't want her to visit me.

'I tried to get her to open up, but she just leapt to his defence. Our friendship became superficial and I got pissed off as she withdrew. A breakthrough came last summer. She called me and acknowledged that her husband was abusive. She said she wanted a divorce. Being able to speak openly again was amazing – my old friend was back. Sadly, she didn't leave. But I know now what a hard position she's in, and I have to just be there for her on whatever terms she needs.'

The idea that a friendship gap can begin to narrow and that women can come back together is a really powerful one. It needn't be a situation as fraught as the one Esther describes – sometimes a simple realignment can do it. There's no doubt that when the shape of your lives has more in common, it can close a friendship gap. It might be your financial circumstances or the children starting school. The important thing is simply to recognize that friendship gaps can lessen as your worlds turn again, and that friends can turn to face each other, reaching out across that gap and meeting in the middle.

Sometimes a candid conversation is enough. Remember Judi, whose childhood friendship ended after that disastrous visit with her controlling husband? Here's how her story continues: 'About fourteen years later, I had been through a divorce and decided to track my friend down. She had moved, but I found her address and telephone number and out of the blue I called her. She was so delighted and we spoke for over an hour. It was easy to pick up our friendship and we have stayed in touch. We were a big part of each other's formative years and such shared history is an unforgettable and meaningful part of our lives.'

I find that reassuring: that it's OK to drift or press pause. Sometimes you'll come back together, even if it's not in the same way. It's about patience, understanding and being realistic. It's either waiting for your lives to realign or ultimately accepting they won't and looking for a way around it.

'I'm incredibly grateful to my child-free and single friends, who I can talk to about the stuff that is uncomfortable and the regrets I do have,' says Nell Frizzell. 'I feel it's really nice to be able to speak to people who don't have all those same kinds of conventional markers, and to say, "Oh, god, what am I doing?" And then they will look at me and say, "Oh my god, what am *I* doing?"

'I also have friends who I've not felt particularly close to for a while, but who are now pregnant or having babies, and we have found a new language with each other. I don't want to say you can only be friends with people who are exactly like you – that makes you a bit of a psychopath – but I do think if you are worrying that things are falling apart, or people are drifting, it might be temporary.'

It's really hard to look at a friendship and acknowledge out loud – sometimes even just to yourself – that it's not the same as it was. But by facing up to something that is a universal experience we can also accept another: that it doesn't have to be forever. Even if a gap opens up for years, it can turn out to be a stretch, rather than a clean break.

And if it doesn't close? Our mess-ups can make us better friends in the future, whether you failed to grasp the true demands of new parenthood among the first of your pals to have children, or didn't handle your friend's grief well. Next time, you might not fall through the gap at all.

Unlikely Friends

Myth: Your closest friends
will be just like you

'They started out as enemies but ended up best friends.'

How many film or TV show taglines could that phrase describe? In 2020, *BuzzFeed* compiled a list of twenty-two unlikely female friendships on screen and that was what most of them boiled down to. 'They began the series as rivals and grew into true friends.' (*Gilmore Girls*.) 'They didn't even like each other ... but they ended up being each other's maid of honour and godmother to each other's children.' (*One Tree Hill*.)

It captures perfectly what twists my ovaries about female friendships in popular culture: they are so contrived. There is a certain set of predictable rules and tropes, plotted by Hollywood scriptwriters, that every character must follow – and which don't leave any space for the nuances that make up every single one of our real-life female friendships. And if that friendship could be perceived as being 'unlikely'? You can add another layer of unbelievability to the whole thing.

Where unlikely friendships blossom in our actual lives, it's so much more subtle than 'Mean Girl turns BFF'. And they have nothing to do with the photo spreads so beloved of newspapers, showing a piglet that's bonded with a lion, though I do love those. I saw one on Instagram recently of a woman and a wingless bumble bee (her Bee-FF?) that reduced me to tears, the only sane explanation for which is where I was in my cycle.

What I'm talking about are friendships between women who have a significant age gap, who are on opposite sides of political lines, or from different social classes. In this context, the word 'unlikely' isn't something negative, but rather – for all the women I interviewed on this subject – a source of positivity, inspiration and happiness. Frequently, they told me that these friendships were unique in their lives; the woman they had unexpectedly befriended was unlike anyone else they knew or could talk to. Isn't that great? Doesn't *that* deserve the Hollywood treatment?

It's how I feel about Liz. We met at my weekly pottery class – the perfect place for a millennial like me to pick up an unsuspecting baby boomer. Pottery is my happy place: a room where I don't have to think about taking the bins out or the state of the world, but can just focus on clay. In the six years I've been going, I never set out to make a friend. Often I didn't want to talk at all. I felt as though any chat would lead to questions about work – the very thing I had started pottery to unwind from.

That's probably why Liz and I didn't really speak for a while, despite sitting at the same table, hands working away, kneading, rolling and manipulating clay. Perhaps she thought I was another flighty youngster, who would soon lose interest. Perhaps I thought she was far too grown-up to want to chat to me, as I stole lustful glances at her amazing creations compared to my own lumpen pots.

As pottery is a gradual process – wedge, mould, dry, fire, glaze, fire again, moan about how it's not turned out as you imagined – so our friendship has also built slowly. And I confess, the boring truth is that we initially bonded after we discovered how close to one another we live and Liz started driving me home, saving me an awkward train journey. (Yes, even more awkward than sitting in the car for half an hour beside someone I didn't know and who is thirty years older than me.)

Strangely though, I can't remember it feeling strained. As I recall, we just launched into random bits and bobs of minutiae about our lives; the sort of relaxed patter it usually takes time to achieve. Like a novel where you land in the middle of a character's life, knowing that their tale was being told before you opened the first page and will continue after you donate the book to a charity shop. For me, our age gap is a bonus. Liz is every bit as switched-on and sweary as my peers (the first time she said 'fuck' I felt internal fireworks go off). She's taught me that it's perfectly possible to live the life you want, whatever is handed to you. To stay upbeat and busy. To be creative. That you can make new friends at any age. That after using underglaze you absolutely have to put your pot in the right kiln or it will crack.

During the Covid lockdowns, I missed our car journeys. I missed hearing about Liz's life, and her genuinely rock 'n' roll stories. I'd love to tell you that I was regaling her with anecdotes of wild nights out in return, but in truth I love nothing more than listening to *The Archers* in the bath with a Harvey's Bristol Cream. If she thought she was making a younger, cooler friend, she'll have been disappointed.

I'm far from the only one to seek out this sort of friendship. So much is made, now, of the divide between generations, in particular millennials and boomers. It's all 'avocado toast and woke politics' versus 'mortgage-free second homes and a passion for Brexit'. Wild generalization never got in the way of a good intergenerational-spat headline, but it can sometimes feel as though the gap between us is insurmountable. My generation is, after all, the first in history to be worse off than our parents, so when you do manage to make a friend who's significantly older, or younger, it feels somehow even more triumphant. Like you're doing something positive to smash a stereotype.

And what really surprised me when I asked the younger women in my life about their 'unlikely friends' was the sheer number who had an age-gap friendship but had never mentioned it before. They felt the same way I do: that a) they had almost forgotten the age difference and b) the friendship was separate from any other, and held a special place in their lives for that reason.

Livia, thirty-four, tells me of her most unlikely pal – a colleague who, aged fifty, left a career in the charity sector to become a dominatrix. 'I've got some incredible perspectives on life from her; things I would never have heard from my usual friend demographic,' she says. 'And I've loved seeing her change – she has now stopped drinking, become vegan, quit sex and re-evaluated her career again. She is entirely unconnected to the rest of my life and makes no judgement about anything – there are things I shared with her that I've told no one else.'

My friend Alexa recalls the time she went to a health retreat in Austria and gained a new friend. 'I hung out with her over herbal tea and colonic chat. She lives near me so I see her regularly and we've also been on unhealthy holidays together. She's twenty-three years older than me and so has a different perspective on a lot of things, although I hardly notice the age gap. It's strange when I think that she's only a few years younger than my mother.'

I don't have a godmother but have always loved the idea of having an older woman I could turn to for independent advice. As a godmother myself now, I've started to think more about what it might mean when my god-daughters are older and actually need my input into their lives. How we might be able to have a meaningful relationship that goes both ways.

It's something Emma Barnett – a woman who has a front-row seat on women's lives – has experienced.

In 2021, she lost her beloved godmother, Jean, who had been her grandmother's best friend and lived into her nineties.

'She was really my kind of woman. She had a very glamorous hair salon in Manchester; always had a cheeky wine on the go,' says Emma. 'She was a lot of fun and very independent, but also really loved her husband. She always just knew when to take you out and when to do nice things. She once sent me a card when I had done badly on a test, with a boat on it, and she was like 'whenever you want to sail over I'm here' – just effortlessly cool and thoughtful. Our relationship grew at her kitchen table and once I could drive, after going to the chippy she was the first place I wanted to drive on my own and sit there with. I rang her every week of my adult life, if not more than once a week. My godmother and I would have been friends, even if we hadn't been introduced through family.'

Emma also formed a dear friendship with her former drama teacher, Mrs K, who sadly died during the pandemic. Because she was unconnected to anyone else in Emma's life, when she couldn't reach her friend on the phone, she was forced to contact her old school to find out the sad news.

'For me, she was this wondrous woman who knew so much,' she recalls. 'I wanted to be in her world, a bit like you do with your favourite teacher.' When Emma was leaving school, after her A levels, Mrs K offered to take her for lunch when she was next back in Manchester. 'And that's where it all began. I was like oh my god, we're taking it to the next level,' she says.

'Our relationship was on the phone for a large part of it in the end. But I felt like we always spoke at key points in my life – probably less key points for her because it wasn't like she was getting her first job or getting married or having a baby. All those things were happening to me but she had done them. And that's part of what you get from the friendship; that you can talk about your life and they respond to the things that they've done.

'I think she was very touched that I wanted to have a relationship, so there was a warmth that she was getting out of it. And I think, as her world got smaller I kept her world quite big in our conversations, and in a weird sense I feel like she had enlarged my world when it just consisted of going to school. So we sort of swapped roles.'

Although Emma never stopped calling her former teacher 'Mrs K', even though she asked her to. 'I do think when you've got an older friend some barriers remain,' she says. 'I found myself not asking as many questions about her personal life as I would with a friend who I'd known on equal terms from the beginning. I think with older women it's almost their choice what they tell you a bit more. You don't know where the emotional landmines are. But she was good to just tell stuff to. I find that generation could give really good advice succinctly. They weren't afraid to admit something was awful, and then tell you to just keep going.'

That dynamic is familiar to Audrey Lamontagne-Defriez and her friend Charlotte Massard. Audrey, ninety-two, and Charlotte, in her early forties, 'met' during the first Covid lockdown through an Age UK telephone befriending service. Neither had any expectations: Audrey tells me that she 'hadn't even asked for a friend' and Charlotte merely wanted to do something for her community. Turns out they had masses to talk about, and their one-hour-a-week chats soon became three or four.

Audrey puts their connection down to Charlotte being French, something that has transported her back to her life spent working for the World Health Organization in Geneva and later the United Nations. 'We got on like a house on fire; she was just like my old colleagues, although less than half my age,' she explains. And it would be lazy to imagine that their calls are one-way, a vehicle for Audrey to tell her old stories (incredible as they are); on the contrary, the pair discuss politics – they were fixated by the 2020 US election – film, and their shared dream of owning a chateau. 'It was so easy – one so young speaking to one so old – it was amazing,' says Audrey.

What's really extraordinary is that she didn't even know her new friend's surname until they were invited to speak about their friendship on Radio 4's *You and Yours* over a year into their calls. I mean, I once went out with someone who hesitatingly admitted after three months that he didn't know my surname, but Audrey wins hands down.

She told presenter Winifred Robinson that her younger friend was 'like a breath of fresh air'. But it was Charlotte's words that caught my attention. Hearing how Audrey's generation handled difficult situations – the Blitz, during which Audrey was a child in London, the 1952 Great Smog – had given her, she explained, a sense of hope during Covid. It made her feel that 'this too shall pass'.

It made me wish I'd had my own Audrey for some perspective on those darkest of lockdown days. It shows that you don't need a formative 'moment' to create a friendship, or even to have met face to face. There are other, more subtle ways to find mutual support, and sometimes it comes from very unexpected places – and when, as Audrey put it, you're 'not even looking'. I also loved Charlotte's aside that Audrey 'is just a single girl in London like me' – what better reminder that however old we are, we're all just human flesh seeking flesh. You can have that one for your Tinder profile for free.

Sex, actually, turned out to be at the heart of several unlikely friendship stories – one of those things it seems easier to speak about when the other person is older or younger or separate from everyone else in your life. My pal Iona tells me that she's become good friends with her neighbour, who's thirty-five years her senior. 'I was initially astonished and a bit uncomfortable that she talked to me so frankly about sex,' she says. 'How men of her own age were uninterested in adventurous sex and the only people who were up for it were much younger men, who thought they could teach her a thing or two.

'I knew she was online dating, like me, but I'll be honest – it had never occurred to me that she might be looking for sex, as well as someone to go to the theatre with. I'd put her in the same age bracket as my mum, when in fact a friend is a friend however old they are. I suppose it hadn't struck me that I could have genuine friends from a different generation, which seems very closed-minded now. I really value her experience and the fact she's at a different place in her life, and yet in many ways we're going through the same things. Online dating is pretty dire whatever decade you're in.'

Jilly Cooper's most unlikely friendship sprang out of sexual jealousy. Jilly has written openly about her insecurity as a younger woman over her late husband Leo's first wife. In a column for the *Sunday Times* called 'On Being a Second Wife' she described her all-consuming envy of her predecessor, Diana, as 'an obsession', writing 'jealousy gnawed at me for those years they'd spent together' – not helped by Leo returning from seeing Diana and telling Jilly 'she was looking very pretty ... I wanted her like hell'. Yup, that'll do it.

But when we speak on the phone, cautiously, Jilly tells me that the two women are now friends – not BFFs, but fond of one another. 'I just sent her a birth-day card, and the lovely thing is – well, the thing I love most in the world are greyhounds and she's just got a greyhound. And so she and I discuss greyhounds,' says Jilly. 'And when she comes down to the country to stay with friends, she comes over and has a drink. So we are friends, yes.'

It could be something straight out of one of Jilly's plots – we are never not titillated by tales of supposed 'love rivals' becoming friends. Though things are rarely as they seem. And while such a friendship might look unlikely to the outside world, as long as it feels normal to you both, who cares? You can't force a genuine connection, but neither should you ditch one just because it's a bit improbable. That only makes it all the more special.

With unexpected or unlikely friendships, you are making your own rules and experimenting with boundaries. Your friend might be challenging, questioning and encouraging in ways that others aren't. Under those conditions it's often easier to broach subjects you might feel a bit nervous about with your peers. Although not everyone wants to chat about how much sex they're having, whether they orgasm and how often they masturbate, even with their closest friends. Don't get me wrong, I think it's fantastic that more women are having those conversations openly. We need to normalize the fact that women enjoy sex and that we're not terrifying nymphomaniacs who need Victorian electric shock treatment. I can't tell you how reassured I felt when a friend told me about a pal of hers who sometimes gets so stressed at work that she goes to the Ladies for an emergency wank – although my version would be a packet of Mini Cheddars and an attempt to 'power pose' in a tiny cubicle, pressed up against the sanitary bin.

This, to me, is why one of the most recognizable and reassuring unlikely friendships of recent times was Fleabag's televised encounter with Belinda (played by Kristin Scott Thomas). There was something about Phoebe Waller-Bridge's thirty-three-year-old character befriending a woman twenty-five years her senior that captured what so many of my generation have been searching for – and is the reason the scene went viral.

It gave us the chance to eavesdrop on a mature woman delivering a series of warm and welcome life lessons in a posh hotel bar. About the joys of flirting at any age. That women are 'machines with parts' born with 'inbuilt pain' which only the menopause will free us from: 'Something to look forward to,' Belinda quips.

It was a moment rather than a lasting friendship, but it sparked in so many of us that longing for unexpected wisdom. As one viewer put it on Twitter: 'Just once in my life, I'd love to share a moment or two with an older woman who isn't my mum or her friends, and talk . . . Nothing sexual, just intellect.'

After all, as Belinda tells Fleabag: 'People are all we've got.'

★

I think my own fascination with unlikely friends stems from some of my earliest experiences: that email at university telling me that Agatha and I wouldn't get on, for example. There's a sort of deliciousness in a friendship that seems improbable in someone else's eyes.

It might also have something to do with Lisa, my pen pal for a decade. She lived near Brighton and I was in south London, though you'd never have known there was a direct train between us given that we met only once, aged ten, at a wedding at Hampton Court Palace. Despite the fact that we seemed opposite in every way – she was effortlessly cool with icy white-blonde hair, while I was in a floor-length brown skirt, oversized white shirt and clumpy black Dolcis loafers – we swapped addresses. That was the start of years of letter-writing. We shared stories from school, first crushes, parental and sibling woes. I can still see her stationery now and feel the excitement of a mustard-yellow envelope landing on the doormat.

Eventually, we got into universities at different ends of the country. We emailed a bit and suggested meeting but it never quite happened. I started to get the impression that she was becoming quite involved in religion and, if I'm totally honest, that made me back away a bit – when really I could have seen it as an opportunity for an unlikely friend to become even unlikelier, even if I didn't share her beliefs. It was small-minded of me. Because it can work.

Labour MP Jess Phillips tells me about her cross-party friendship with Anne Milton, a Conservative MP until 2019. The pair met during the early days of the 'Pestminster' scandal in 2017 – when a series of sexual misconduct allegations emerged against male MPs – and Anne just walked up to Jess in the House of Commons and asked if she wanted to do something about it. The two had never talked before.

'She just spoke so plainly, like one of my girlfriends would,' says Jess. 'And I was just like, "Oh, gosh, I'm going to be your friend."'

But what I found really interesting about their unlikely friendship is how they dealt with political disagreements.

'You know how we handled that? We would take the piss out of each other,' says Jess. 'I would just be like, "Oh, you would say that, you hate the poor." And the woman was a nurse, she's from a more working-class background than me. But, you know, I would just be like, "Huh, typical Tory".

'But the things we really disagreed on, that we couldn't work together on, we just wouldn't have tried. That's what friendship is . . . You don't have to get on with each other about everything. But if there's a *backs against the wall, I need you* on something, they're there. That's the way it is with Anne. She was like an oak tree that you could go and touch.'

I don't know how Anne would feel about being described as an oak, but I think it captures something essential. So often an unlikely friend is a rock or a port in a storm or an anchor when our lives feel at sea. Even if they're not older, or much wiser, they still give us that feeling of reassurance and grounding: that someone who's not like me is interested in me.

Trinny Woodall, fifty-eight, tells me about a sur-prising work friendship – the closest thing to that 'enemies who became best friends' trope I have come across in real life.

'I was on a shoot abroad, and she was the fashion editor for a magazine. And when I met her we were both very prickly around each other because I hated people choosing my clothes for shoots. So we had this friction,' says Trinny. 'Then, one day we were lying by the pool together, reluctantly chatting, and discovered we were both born on the same day, in the same year and both in the early morning. That kind of broke the ice. Then I asked why she wasn't going out and she confessed to feeling a bit tired, because she was pregnant, but not telling anyone. I said, "I'm pregnant, too, and I'm not telling anyone." And our children were due on the same day. It was so odd.'

With those first prickly feelings smoothed over, Trinny started to learn from her unlikely friend.

'She has an incredible ethic around being courteous to people and sometimes when I was on shoots and I'd be a little bit . . . when I'm at my most insecure I am the most controlling, and she understood that. So she'd say at the end of the day, "Trinny, you should go and say thank you to that person." She would remind me to be my best self, is the only way I can put it. We come from different lives – her mother was from Nigeria, she grew up outside of London and really started from scratch – but we share a passion. I respect her tremendously.'

So do unlikely friends have a superpower when it comes to teaching us life lessons? I'd argue they do – that by pursuing a friendship with someone different to you, whether in age, background, politics, career, class or whatever, you are opening yourself up to expanding your own little world and seeing it through the eyes of someone who's not exactly like you. It says: 'If I can be friends with you, then perhaps I can be with anyone.' And I'm not sure there's any more powerful message for female friendship than that.

Friendship.com

*Myth: Online friends aren't as
valuable as ones made IRL*

I am part of that strange micro-generation who can remember making friends before the internet got involved. Call us what you want – Xennials, Cuspers, Geriatric Millennials (no thanks) – we were born in the early to mid-1980s, making many of us the first lot to have a home computer and the last to reach the tender age of twenty-one without the interference of social media. We are apparently as comfortable in an analogue world as we are a digital one. Fancy.

We know what it was like to get the internet at home for the first time and have your parents go mad because they couldn't use the phone while you were online. We remember when HotBot, AltaVista and Ask Jeeves were the main search engines and the frenzied excitement that MySpace created. And if you don't know what I'm talking about? You were probably born after 1996. Congratulations.

We made friends via AOL Chat and MSN Messenger – the first inkling of the power social media might have over us – and sometimes even met up with strangers we'd befriended online. Isn't that unbelievable? I chatted to a random boy whose father was a dentist not far from where I lived, and we actually became mates. Another sat on the District Line for two hours so we could hug at my front door for five minutes, before I sent him packing because he was wearing a white Kangol hat and I thought he was a bit tragic. There were no safety checks and we had no clue that we even needed them.

When Facebook landed in the UK in 2006, I was twenty-two and working as a temp, manning reception desks in Mayfair that I couldn't have cared less about except they were paying £12.50 an hour. Most of the time there wasn't much to do. But there was Facebook – a shiny brand-new platform on which I could message Agatha and tag myself in every single photo posted by every single person I'd ever met (and which, ten years later, I'd spend weeks untagging myself from). It was all so exciting and innocent, like when my sister saw a giant python for the first time at London Zoo and poked it, oblivious to any danger and ignoring the literal warning signs.

Friendship was becoming about quantity, not quality. Adding friends was all that mattered, which is why, after every house party, you'd wake up with twenty-five new requests from strangers from the night before. We would compare how many friends we had – I'm pretty sure that I boasted over 500 at one point, when I only had about three mates in real life. I wouldn't have recognized most of my online 'friends' if I'd passed them in the street, and not just because their profile picture was from Faliraki 2002.

Don't worry, this isn't going to turn into a lament about the evils of social media – we've all read enough about that. We all know our phones aren't really our friends. But I think by now we also know that social media isn't going anywhere and new platforms are popping up all the time. But whether you use Snapchat, TikTok, Twitter, Instagram – or whatever the latest one is that I'm too past it to have heard of – when it comes to friendship, each one poses the same dilemma: how to use it to stay connected with friends and communicate in a meaningful way.

It's not always easy to avoid FOMO (the fear of missing out). We know that when we're not together, our friends are doing other things, with other people, but social media rubs our faces in it in a way that we didn't have to experience in the past. And if you've previously been cut out of friendships, it can take you to a very paranoid place.

Sameeha, twenty-seven, thinks this has contributed to her generation's feelings of loneliness: 'It's crazy because we're so immersed in social media, and we're supposed to "know" so many people,' she says. 'But our feeds are often that cliche of only seeing what people want you to see. And a lot of the time, they just want you to see that they're very popular, and have masses of people around them.'

I'm the sort of person who, as you know, has now created a 'portfolio' of friends. Different women from different parts of my life, who all complement parts of my personality. There are many different things I enjoy talking about, find funny, like watching and eating. There are friends I can get deep with and others who are 'doers'. It's a blend. Yet here's what I find really strange: on social media, it's so one-dimensional. It's like you're in a room with everyone you've ever met – and thousands you haven't – but you can only present a single version of yourself: usually the happy, high-achieving one.

'I think social media has been bad for friendship,' says clinical psychologist Linda Blair. 'The whole point is only to show one side of yourself, which is the OK side. You don't post it unless it's in a good light, and therefore it's so easy to feel inferior – and also not to feel close, because intimacy involves a balance between your bad and your good, and you're only showing your good. You're out of balance in every way: to each other and within yourself.'

And if we're not putting forth our shiniest and most successful selves, we're veering towards the other end of the spectrum and oversharing: showing off our armpit hair, or telling the world about our gynaecological issues. Yet I find that this is the side of social media I really enjoy – the busting of myths and breaking down of taboos. It's bold, brave and often very funny when we tell the truth about how life really looks beyond the Insta-veneer. And it can be powerful in the same way that making yourself vulnerable with a new female friend quickly deepens your bond. It builds trust online just as much as off.

Sometimes it can throw us off balance, though. Many of us find this when we catch ourselves sharing personal strife on social media instead of calling a friend to talk it through, or when we think that a thumbs-up emoji is equivalent to support from those who know us best. It's similar with texting. I think the brevity of our message exchanges has changed the fabric of friendship. On the one hand, it's great that you can pick up your phone during a meeting and quickly let a friend know you're thinking about her. But the depth of our communication has lost something. I'm as guilty as the next person of relying on it too much and thinking that a crying laughing emoji is an appropriate response to anything.

Emma Barnett is pretty much allergic to texting. 'If I get a message saying, "How are you?" my heart just sinks,' she says. 'I'm like, "How can I be arsed to convey this in a text? I just want to ring you." And most people don't want to do phone calls any more and that is really hard for someone who doesn't like texts. So I feel like the language of friendship now is so reductive and prescriptive to be digital. I'm very capable of texting, it's not like an old-person thing. But I just find it really upsetting how we have to have our friendships: they're not fulfilling, they're like fast food half the time.'

The benefit, she concedes, is that you can 'check-in' with someone really quickly. 'I've got a friend who's going through a break-up and I texted yesterday saying "Hey" because she was in my head,' Emma explains. 'But I didn't call her. Now, is my job done for a few days as a friend? I don't know . . . I don't think that's good enough.'

It's definitely a trap I fall into. Worse is when I

wrongly imagine that I've caught up with a friend when I've actually only seen her social media updates. It can make it seem as though you're in touch when you're actually not.

'None of these digital modes of interaction are ever anything better than a sticking plaster,' says the University of Oxford's Professor Robin Dunbar. 'They'll slow down the rate of decay. But in the end, nothing on earth – or nothing on the digital earth – will stop that relationship just becoming an acquaintanceship eventually if you can't meet up.'

Though that in itself involves about twenty messages of diary negotiation. In 'You've Got A Friend' Carole King might have sung 'Winter, spring, summer or fall / All you have to do is call' ... but in 1971 she wasn't dealing with the tyranny of trying to schedule that meeting via smartphone.

'Can you do ... ? No, how about ... Sorry, Polly has piano then ... James is away ... August? ... But it's only February now ... I've got 15 minutes on a Saturday morning in 2035, between 5.45am and 6am, any good?'

Yet despite it sounding like our phones are destroying the concept of friendship as we know it, for many of the women I spoke to, the ability to communicate digitally has been good for them. Those who have friends in other countries, or live abroad, told me how important it is for checking in day-to-day and that, when they do speak on the phone or meet in person, they don't have to recap every tiny little thing that's happened because there's already a foundation there. Some have found it the easiest way to stay in touch with a large circle, or at a particularly stressful time.

Others have actually made friends. Author Daisy Buchanan not only met her husband on Twitter (keep sliding into those DMs, people) but also her closest pal, after they followed one another and started replying to each other's tweets.

'Then a friend did a gathering of women that we kept talking to on Twitter, and loads of us met up in a bar and we just really got on,' says Daisy. 'There was one thing she said, about when she used to work in an office and every so often she'd hear a rustle and think, "Ooh biscuits!" and it would be printer paper. And I was like, "That could have come from my brain." It's really thrilling to think that was a chance connection with someone who has done nothing but enrich my life and make it wonderful.'

Founder of The Five Foundation, an organization dedicated to ending the practice of female genital mutilation, Nimco Ali tells me that she had her trust in female friendship restored through a WhatsApp group – which is amazing to me, seeing as most of us are constantly looking for excuses to quietly leave the 'Cotswoldz Hen Do Crew'.

'When you grow up in a community like mine, we're kind of raised not to trust women, in a sense, because everybody's always gossiping about each other,' says Nimco. 'So your family were also your friends. I don't think I lived outside of my cultural upbringing until I started doing my activism, and then I really began to see how choosing to be friends with people who have completely different backgrounds to you can be something powerful.'

In 2018, she was added to a WhatsApp group by a

friend who wanted to bring together women of the same age, living in London. They all began messaging as strangers, with the idea of meeting once a month for dinner.

'I always watched Bridget Jones going over to dinner at a friend's house – and I used to be invited to those things myself but didn't really see the importance of it,' says Nimco. 'But then it became something I looked forward to.

'I think because of the experiences that I've had, it's been hard to let go and be able to bring anybody into my life that wasn't family ... the FGM, but also the civil war [in Somalia] and losing people meant that I was very cagey and guarded. I also thought I had to hang out with men, because as a heterosexual woman I have to meet somebody. I used to say, "Oh, I've got loads of male friends", but it was because I thought I had to make an effort with them – and I put that over making friends with women. But I've really realized that actually cultivating female friendship feeds you in a different way. Those women have become immensely important in my life.'

To me, there's no reason that making friends digitally shouldn't work – I mean, how different is it really from meeting someone on a dating app? Actually, you can meet friends on a dating app: Bumble, which in 2016 added a section called 'BFF'. And to think that 'let's be friends' used to be the last thing anyone on a matchmaking site wanted to hear.

When I interviewed Bumble founder Whitney Wolfe Herd – who just happens to be the world's youngest self-made female billionaire – she told me about the BFF function: 'We spend hours buried in our phones trying to keep up with the social lives of people we may not even know. Envy and the fear of missing out have taken over,' she said. 'Yet we are all still longing for human connection. We want that real life experience, someone to spend time with – and we want this beyond romance.'

Whitney has many superpowers, but even she couldn't have predicted the pandemic. It was a boom time for friendship apps. A survey by the *Wall Street Journal*[24] found that a third (35 per cent) of sixteen- to twenty-four-year-olds had used dating apps to make platonic friends between July 2020 and July 2021. According to Bumble, BFF saw a 44 per cent rise in women searching the friendship part of the app in the first three months of 2021.

Turns out that finding friends on apps (there are others like Friender, Meetup and Peanut) isn't all that different to looking for a relationship. You list your interests, what you're seeking – someone to go on country walks with, a Bikram yoga fan – and choose the most flattering photos for your profile. You then go on a 'date' – worrying about what to wear and how to make a good impression. At least you don't have to think about what they look like naked.

It might seem strange to the uninitiated, but then that's what we thought when people first started hooking up online. We sneered that using an app to find a boyfriend seemed desperate, whereas now it's so accepted as a way of meeting a partner that we're starting to find the idea of pulling in a bar unusual. It's quite the turnaround. Perhaps the same will happen for making female friends online.

Dating coach Haifa Barbari certainly thinks so. She used an app to make new friends, having moved from East London to South London (might as well be another country) aged thirty-seven, after a break-up. Most of her existing friends had moved out or had babies. She needed some new wing-women, fast.

'With friends, you need chemistry and compatibility. So I approached it like a dating strategy,' she says. 'It didn't matter what they looked like and where they were from, as long as we had shared interests and beliefs. But you can only test chemistry in person, so I would accept any friend date and then, once we met in person, I would pick up on the vibe.'

Her first female friend date was with Jeanette, who was new to the city. 'It lasted about six hours and it was *just* like a date,' says Haifa. 'We walked along the river and then we went to have some pasta, and we just bonded . . . and then the idea of building a group came up.'

Haifa and Jeanette decided to go on more female friend dates and invite anyone they liked to their next meet-up. 'So what once was a one-to-one date turned very quickly into group dates. And now, we have six friends in a WhatsApp chat,' says Haifa.

And if you don't feel the friend spark when you meet up in person? 'That's OK,' she says. 'Instead of "Not everyone you meet will be the love of your life" it's "Not everyone will be your BFF" – and someone who wants to be BFFs overnight is just as much of a red flag as a love bomber. The reality is you don't know each other, and learning who someone really is takes time.'

The trickiest thing was how some of her existing friends reacted – taking it too personally. 'There's this judgement and questioning that comes when you're doing something that is different from the tribe that you already have. It comes from a place of feeling inadequate themselves: *What's wrong with me? Why do you need new friends?*'

Haifa adds that, partly because of this, she now talks to some of her new app friends more intimately than her older ones.

'I met the girls in a place of shared vulnerability,' she explains. 'We were very honest in the fact that we wanted to make new friends. We bonded over not wanting to feel lonely. And that was very authentic and broke down some of the barriers. As with everything new, people are cautious. But I think that if we can have more conversations around the fact that it's OK to reassess and meet new people then it will be the norm before we know it.'

It's not hard to imagine that the generations growing up now, with smartphones glued to their hands, might come to see the act of purposefully seeking out new friends through apps as no big deal. Eleven-year-old Juliette recently got her first phone and uses it to chat to her friends and watch TikTok videos. She's part of Gen Alpha – the first full generation to be born in the twenty-first century and one which has never known any way to manage their friendships other than digitally. Along with Gen Z (born between 1997 and 2012), they've never had to leave their bedrooms to hang out.

Juliette tells me her phone is primarily a way to meet up with someone she hasn't seen in a long time (which for her can mean since school on Friday) and that she uses it to arrange football practice. But she does concede that it has already shaken her female friendships once or twice.

'It can be bad because things can be said about people and sent to each other. Like, if someone says something about someone else in the moment and they didn't really mean it. And they might have said it to one of their really close friends, who they wouldn't have thought would say it to anyone else, but then they might post it,' she says.

'Even if you didn't mean it, they won't understand that, and so it's harder to forgive. It's harder to apologize over messages, too, as you can't see face to face what the other person thinks. So someone could be really angry at you but they could be saying that they're fine. For me, talking in real life is easier, especially if you're telling someone something important – it's better to see how the person is feeling about it.'

Yes, Juliette might be the most emotionally intelligent eleven-year-old I've ever come across. But what I found really interesting was that, unprompted, she went almost immediately to the topics of forgiveness and blame. Seems like you can be part of the first truly digital age-group and still be walking on the same social-media eggshells as the rest of us.

Merrily Johnston, twenty-two, is also wary of the

potential for misunderstandings but prefers to continue messaging, as it's 'less confrontational'. 'Face to face you might blurt out something you can't then take back,' she says. 'You can also get everything you want to say in a single message without being interrupted. The only negative would be that your friend might read it in a different tone to how you meant it and then you could both be on a different page without even realizing.'

We've all been there and felt the impact of something communicated digitally that might be taken out of context. And, anecdotally, after speaking to these young women, it seems as though they are trying to navigate those potential friendship pitfalls just as much as the rest of us.

Scarlett O'Connell, seventeen, tells me that messaging plays a massive part in her friendships. 'I think I'd feel a bit lost without it – especially because my female friends tend to use social media more,' she says. 'And because girl friendships are more complicated, you feel like you have to stay in touch with them more often.'

So Gen Z and Gen Alpha want to stay in touch regularly, understand that their girlfriends probably need more maintenance than their male friendships, and hope to avoid misunderstandings. They want to invest in their female friendships, and know that digital forms of communication aren't the whole picture.

Speaking to these young women about their female friends, it struck me they weren't saying anything all that different to those in their nineties. When I asked ninety-two-year-old Audrey what advice she'd give her younger self about female friendship, she spoke about 'toleration', which, to me, is what it all boils down to – especially when you're throwing imperfect forms of digital communication into the mix.

Not that the internet is known for being a tolerant place. 'I once had a huge row with one of my friends that resulted in me blocking her on everything and having absolutely zero contact for about a week,' admits Merrily. 'You can literally remove them from your online life and they have no say in it.'

I'm sure that, if we're honest, we've all done a little digital ghosting of friends. We've all been intolerant. You might not have blocked anyone, but have you ever seen a WhatsApp message drop into your inbox, read the first line but not opened it immediately because that would mean committing to two blue ticks and a reply straight away? Thought so. Bet you still found time to scroll through the Zara sale for an hour though.

Then there's the group issue. Don't go thinking that you're sending out a perfectly innocent mass invite – whether you choose to 'cc' or 'bcc' your friends on email is an absolute minefield. Do the former and you risk mayhem: A is furious she didn't get her own invite and was lumped in with everyone else, B can't believe you've chosen to forgive C's behaviour. D is staggered that you consider E – whom she's known since childhood, thanks very much – to be your friend. And if you bcc? Well, F won't come if she isn't sure whether she'll know anyone else, while G needs to know if the person she's avoiding is invited.

Messaging group chats are just as fraught, with contact details shared without consent and anyone left out immediately obvious.

It was this sort of digital micro-aggression that started to turn me off using social media for my personal life, not to mention the amount of time I was wasting on it. My timeline was rammed with photos of people I didn't know or care about, and whose opinions I found increasingly tedious. I spent hours untagging myself from photos and had my privacy settings turned up to paranoid. When my husband and I got engaged, I called my close friends to tell them as I couldn't stand the thought of announcing something so personal to strangers and, worse, the failed BFFs I'd left behind. These weren't people I wanted to be confronted with every time I logged on, and I definitely didn't want to stay in touch.

But the moment that really convinced me to step away from that sort of social media came one morning while I was at work. Scrolling idly through a news website, I suddenly saw a face I recognized – my old school friend Mich – under the headline 'Accidental Death'. I was stunned. Although we hadn't seen one another since sixth form, I had spotted her less than a week earlier, rushing through Clapham Junction station. I called her name, but she didn't hear me and was soon lost in the crowd of commuters. Back home, I had logged on to Facebook and caught up with her life that way: how she looked now, where she worked, who her friends were. *Ah well,* I thought, *perhaps our paths will cross again.*

A week later, I was sitting at my desk, reading that Mich had gone. She was twenty-five. Her death, said the article, which had sent me physically reeling back on my swivel chair, was the latest in a series of tragedies for her family, which I won't go into here because they aren't mine to tell. But I had been looking at her on social media only a few days earlier and it hadn't revealed any of this. It had only shown one side of a person's life; the side they wanted the world – so-called 'friends' like me – to see. That was her choice, of course, but there had been so much more to know. Now I never would.

After that, I didn't really have the appetite for Facebook, other than the occasional vital check on all my exes, their new partners, children, houses, pets and which triathlon their sister was about to compete in, obviously. Eventually, I deleted it for good after watching the documentary *The Social Dilemma*, like the cliche of a person I am.

I use, and will probably always need to use, Twitter for work but I've learned not to spend entire evenings arguing with strangers. I have turned off all notifications on my phone – a total game changer, and something I strongly urge you to do. I even pressed pause on Instagram. It was at a dinner party that I confessed to a friend how looking at 'perfect' pictures of other people's lives was getting me down. When all around you seem to be achieving more, more, more, it's impossible not to compare, even when you know the filters are masking failures. My friend felt the same. And so we made a pact: delete the app from our phones and go cold turkey. Then resist the urge to re-download it and post smugly about having gone cold turkey.

My friend lasted a week. I stayed off for almost two years. And it was mostly fine, unless you count the fact that my thumb involuntarily twitched like a tiny pink addict every time I went to my phone home screen, its muscle memory desperate to please me by firing up the now-erased app. But as the weeks passed, I started to feel less addicted to Instagram itself and more addicted to the feeling of *not* being on Instagram. I felt as though I'd clawed back some privacy. 'I never know what you're doing any more', a friend told me. She couldn't have said anything better: it was working.

So why did I eventually go back? For work, partly. And because my mental resilience had improved. I felt ready and more able to set boundaries around how much time I spent on social media – and, if I'm honest, there was also an element of FOMO. When all your friends are discussing so-and-so's latest post and sharing pictures of their own lives, on which you're missing out, you can start to feel a bit excluded. Also, because I started speaking to women who helped restore my faith in social media as a place to make friends.

Nimco Ali told me that her friendship with writer Caitlin Moran began in this way. 'The first time I met her was on Twitter and she followed me, then we met in real life at events and she actually did become a really close friend . . . it's just wild,' Nimco says. 'I have a lot of respect for her and I'm able to tell her things about relationships. Recently, I liked somebody who's a little bit older than I am, and she gave me the best advice. She was like: "Do you have enough cultural references to be able to understand each other?" And nobody had ever broken it down to me in that kind of context. That was guidance I couldn't get from any of my other friends.'

Trinny Woodall did the reverse: meeting her friend, Mia, just once when she was in Australia to launch her Trinny London make-up brand and appeared on her podcast, then developing their friendship over social media.

'I felt immediately comfortable with her. Then I never saw her again,' says Trinny. 'But we've now done some Instagram Lives together and I love her energy. Would I call her if I was in trouble? No. Is she somebody who I really respect and admire? Yes.'

I think it needs saying that it is also fine to respect and admire from afar. There is no rule that says you have to take an online friendship offline, and into real life. It's something Trinny describes when talking about the women who follow her Instagram Lives and whom she counts as social media friends – going on to tell me their names and even what breeds of dogs they own.

'It's a very different type of friendship,' she says. 'I feel a responsibility to be my best for them. I feel it's important for me to be very honest for their sake, so they've helped me be the proper me. Part of the importance of being revealing is so other women don't feel alone in what they're thinking. That's a very important part of friendship.'

It's also something that author Candice Brathwaite writes about in a book of essays called *Life Lessons on Friendship*. In it, she describes Emma – the sort of good friend who uncannily seems to know when you need a pick-me-up, who messages at just the right moments, who cares about your family and so is also beloved by them.

The kicker? Candice has never actually met Emma. 'And if I'm being honest, there's a strong chance I never will,' she writes.

The two women became friends on Instagram. Candice calls it 'one of the most genuine relationships of my life' – and why shouldn't it be? They share their feelings, fears and some of the most painful parts of themselves. I love the idea that social media can be a place to cultivate long-lasting and meaningful friendships, and it's something I'm starting to explore myself. Whether it's through public Twitter exchanges, usually trying to make one another laugh, or DMing women I know professionally but would really like to go for a glass of wine with – those small digital interactions, often more informal than real-life ones, can help speed up the process of friendship intimacy. I've messaged female acquaintances on Instagram to pledge solidarity with their natural pubic hair movement, where I might never have gone up to them in person and told them that I too was rocking the seventies look.

What is an 'in real life' friend anyway? Most of us would probably still agree that, in an ideal world, it's someone you've met face to face, but maybe it's time we got with the programme. Why should an online friend who ticks all the 'good friend' boxes be any less valuable than one made in a more 'traditional' way just because you've not shared oxygen?

Yes we have a problem with screen time, but that doesn't mean we have to accept the argument that it's ruining all our personal relationships. We don't always have to put down our phones, or shut the lids of our laptops, to spend time with our friends. Some of them are (Zoolander voice) *in the computer.* And when we're working longer and harder than ever and more stressed than the generations before us,[25] isn't it kind of a good thing that we can keep up with friendships – or even create them – online? It means that Trinny can bond with a woman on the other side of the world. It means Nimco can learn to trust.

It might have changed how we communicate, but ultimately I don't think the internet has altered the fundamentals of what a friendship needs. It boils down to time, effort, investment, support, kindness, understanding, space, celebration, commiseration, honesty – and, of course, tolerance. And if you can achieve that in your female friendships, it doesn't matter one bit whether you made them online, or off.

A Room with One's Friends

It is May 2012, and I have nowhere to live. This is not where I saw myself at twenty-eight. By now, I thought I'd be, if not put together, then at least giving the appearance of it.

By twenty-eight, Shakespeare had written three plays, Dickens was on his fourth novel, Christabel Pankhurst had been jailed twice for demanding rights for women. Meanwhile I am a junior nobody at a newspaper making less money than the price of a rented flat in London, and my only career achievement of note is a short-lived stint as Britain's worst showbiz reporter.

Seriously. I'd breeze along to whatever glamorous party or opening I'd been sent to by my editor and quickly turn to jelly. Take the UK Music Hall of Fame event at Alexandra Palace. James Brown, Led Zeppelin, Prince and Beyonce were all in attendance. Yet at the after-party, I hovered nervously by a pillar and spent a not insignificant amount of time in the Ladies. At the end of the night, my best quote came from

Davina McCall's hairdresser ('she *loves* her new length!').

Still, I carefully cut that article out of the paper and file it in my WHSmith folder – one of the many possessions that I now don't have a home for. I have broken up with my boyfriend of five years and we are moving out of the flat we share together in Ladbroke Grove, which had formerly belonged to a celebrity chef who – according to our landlady – lived in total squalor. (Obviously, I didn't bother to mention that genuinely interesting tidbit to the showbiz pages.)

Our break-up comes out of nowhere and both of us are winded by the shock of how fast things have unravelled; the vision of our future life together, the one we'd got comfortable with playing out in our heads, suddenly gone forever. It's painful, disorientating and every time I think about what lies ahead my chest tightens with panic and I have to fight back huge hiccupy sobs. Unhelpfully, London is also plastered with posters for the Olympics. Every day on the way to and from work, I am surrounded by giant billboards telling me to 'Go, go, go!' and images of stopwatches to convey that time is ticking. As if I need reminding.

It's Eve who steps in, moving me into her flat on the eighth floor of an East London tower block where the ground-floor carpet is always wet and the residents' Facebook page has just posted a notice asking 'whoever is letting drug dealers use the corridor as a hang out' to please stop. This opening of her home is an act of love. Eve is someone who cherishes her own space; she likes to come home from work and not talk to anyone for at least an hour, so intense is her job.

Plus her flat is, in truth, too small for two people who aren't sleeping together.

I worry that I've been here before; that I am walking into another situation where living with a friend will jeopardize our relationship. That we'll end up giving one another the silent treatment, or falling out. That the neediness of my broken heart in such a confined space will place too much strain on our friendship. Still, we make our own version of a home. I give her space when she whirls in from work. She puts up with my heartbreak hormones – one minute hyperactive and sociable, the next flat and under a National Trust blanket on the sofa watching *Sunday Brunch*.

We decide to have a house party for the Olympics opening ceremony. There will be Lycra. There will be views: one entire wall of the living room is glass, and the pay-off for it being hotter than the Kew Gardens' Palm House in summer is an uninterrupted view of the Olympic Park. But what this party really needs, we agree, is our homemade attempt at the Olympic rings. After mulling over the various methods available to us, we settle on papier mache. Simple, nostalgic, plus I work at a newspaper and can get my hands on all the raw materials we need.

Which is how I find myself, on a sunny Sunday afternoon, sitting on the pale-grey lino of Eve's kitchen floor in my M&S knickers as I don't want to get the gluey paste on any of my clothes, crafting an ambitiously big and very lumpy version of the famous rings. They are, frankly, dreadful. Even Gollum wouldn't have looked twice.

They are also too cumbersome to keep inside the flat, so we put them on the balcony to dry. The next morning, we get up and go to work, leaving them baking in the sunshine. That afternoon, it rains.

'Maybe they'll be OK?' Eve texts me. *'We can bring them inside and put them on a towel'.*

'Reckon they'll be wetter than Michael Phelps', I reply.

The rings are gone, melted down. All that remains is a sodden pile of gluey grey mush on the balcony. Not exactly the tribute to Team GB we had planned. After that, our cohabitation is one long mishap. Eve manages to flush her iPhone down the loo no less than three times, until I ban her from putting it in the shallow pocket of her Primark jacket from which it keeps slipping.

One afternoon, when she's out, I decide to take advantage of having the living room to myself and lie out indulgently on the sofa – legs up on the arm rest. I'm pretending to read while checking Twitter on my phone, when I hear it. A weird cracking noise somewhere north of my head. It's loud. I jump up as the shelf above me – overflowing with books, and with books stacked on top of books – falls off the wall, knocking into the similarly rammed shelf below it, and the two come crashing down onto the sofa, bouncing off and hitting the floor.

There is silence. I can't even hear my own breathing, possibly because I'm not. How am I going to tell Eve that I've trashed her flat? Worse, I'm now running late to catch a train to Birmingham, so I can't even tidy up.

I go over and over the conversation in my head on the way to Euston. *I'll pay to get them fixed. It's not as bad as it looks* (it is). *I don't know how it happened. Sorry, sorry, sorry.*

I have to run for the train and, once on board, panting, I leave Eve a voicemail (drawing evils from everyone else on the quiet carriage) saying that 'something bad has happened and can she call me back' – and which, she later tells me, was so breathless she thought I was either on the way to A & E or had committed a murder and was asking her to help bury the body.

When she finds out the only victims are her IKEA bookcases, she tells me I'm ridiculous. She couldn't care less about the shelves, only that I'm OK. It's like the invisible person who's been sitting on my chest has suddenly stood up. She doesn't think I'm a bad friend. This isn't going to make living together uncomfortable. We definitely need to buy some new shelves.

It sounds bonkers now to explain just how panicked I was that my near-death by Lonely Planet guidebooks would be the thing that curdled our friendship. But that's how I felt in the moment, with all my old fears resurfacing. That even though someone looked and acted like my friend, maybe they were just waiting for an excuse to get rid. To put me back on the shelf, had it not just fallen off the wall.

When that didn't happen, it felt like another breakthrough. It's not that I didn't trust Eve's loyalty or kindness. It was that I didn't trust myself. But perhaps I should? The evidence was right in front of me, even if I couldn't always see it: she had moved me into her flat in my moment of need; we were still speaking, and she had only tried to kill me once. Maybe, just maybe, it was time to start trusting myself to be a good friend. Perhaps it wouldn't all go wrong again.

It didn't. And when, a few months later, I nervously tell Eve that I'm thinking of moving out, she doesn't take it as a sign that I'm walking away from our friendship. Instead, she just says: 'I thought you'd have said that months ago.' She's right; we both have new partners and on the nights all four of us are there, we constantly have to dance the Dosey Doe in the hallway. It's time. Except I can't afford to rent on my own, it's far too soon to think about cohabiting with Tim, and I really don't want to move back in with my parents (I suspect the feeling is mutual).

To my surprise, an even newer friend, Rachel, suggests I move into her spare room. I say yes straight away, emboldened by the success of living with Eve and conscious that, beneath the surface, I'm not yet fully healed. The wounds caused by the end of a significant chapter, the loss of life as you knew it – your home, mutual friends and future plans – don't close over in a matter of months or even after getting a new boyfriend. You need friends to help stitch your Franken-heart back together.

Rachel has a ground-floor flat with two bedrooms. Mine backs on to her patio garden, from which I have a front-row seat to south London's most vigorous fox sex show. They are at it night after night, screaming and snorting in what I hope for their sake is pleasure, but to our human ears sounds like torturous pain. I spend an evening googling 'do male foxes rape female foxes?' but come away none the wiser (also, wouldn't recommend this search on a work laptop).

Rachel finishes what Eve started, helping to bring me back to life one 'scratch supper' at a time. It's a running joke that all she ever has in the fridge is an avocado, butter, radishes and several champagne miniatures from work events. We supplement them with sourdough and ice cream, and live off this diet for the better part of a year.

One weekend, we are invited to review a spa in the Italian hills. Tough life. It sounds like heaven: massages, mud packs, facials. Sure, the publicist has emphasized that there's also a 'detox angle' but it doesn't sound like anything we can't handle. *'Anyway, a weekend in Italy without Campari is unthinkable'*, Rachel emails, as I book our flights.

We arrive early, in time for breakfast – I'm imagining heart-thumpingly strong espresso and sweet pastries – yet are marched straight to see the spa's doctor and dietician. Even though I tell all sorts of fibs about my alcohol intake, I'm told that my internal organs are 'sluggish'. That's nothing: the doctor asks Rachel if she's pregnant.

Breakfast, we soon discover, is fruit. Oh well, there's always lunch, which turns out to be gloopy broccoli soup. The spa, we learn, has a 'no sugar, no fat, no alcohol, no caffeine' policy.

The rest of the day is spent having treatments – but instead of the indulgent pampering experience we'd imagined, we are caked in cold mud, wrapped in polythene and left to marinate. I am shivering and look like a goose-pimpled chicken leg by the time a woman in a white coat comes to unsheathe me. I imagine slipping into a bubbling hot tub to clean off, or having the mud caressed from my skin with steaming towels. Instead, I am led into what looks like a white-tiled interrogation room, made to stand naked at one end and then power-hosed down. So this is how I die, I think.

We wait as long as we can – both deciding that 4.30 p.m. definitely counts as 'early evening' – before venturing to the top floor. We have heard rumours of a bar and, praise be, it exists. It serves actual wine and chunks of Parmesan, to which we are drawn like ravenous moths to a cheesy flame.

We are the only two drinkers: either hardly anyone knows the bar exists, or else no one else is breaking their detox after eight hours. Outside the bar, high up on a shelf, I notice a row of Lindt chocolate bunnies. Not the tiny little bitesize ones, of which you can inhale half a dozen without even drawing breath. No, the full-size rabbits, which are glinting at us temptingly in their gold foil wrappers.

'How cruel!' I gesture towards the bunnies in horror.

'I suppose it is almost Easter,' Rachel sighs reluctantly.

'Easter in a *detox spa*,' I reply.

We finish our drinks in silence, shovel down some more green gruel, and are in bed with splitting head-aches before 10 p.m.

Over the next thirty-six hours, three of the bunnies disappear. Rachel swears she hasn't taken them and accuses me of turning on her in my carb cold turkey. We decide the only option is to break out. We know this is possible because we meet a Russian man named

Grigori in the bar who tells us that he is a regular, but admits to slipping out for seafood in a local restaurant when he can't take the hunger any more.

We walk around the edge of the compound, trying to look inconspicuous. Like two women out for an afternoon stroll, casually assessing the perimeter wall for a weakness. I'm not certain we're not allowed to leave, only that there's no obvious exit. The gate at the driveway where we entered the day before last – has it really only been two days? – is shut. Just as we're about to give up, Rachel spots a gap in the fence.

We race up to the shuttered door of a pizzeria. 'It doesn't open until seven,' wails Rachel. It is now 3 p.m. The tiny local town is having its afternoon nap. Even the newsagents are sleeping. We head back to the spa, tails between our legs, counting down the minutes until the bar opens. As first-world problems go, it's right up there with one's diamond shoes being too tight. It's also funny, and our ravenous delirium means that we hardly stop laughing the entire trip. It's as though we've found our own language: the shared experience and in-jokes that can't help but bring you closer.

The next morning is our last and we have a final assessment with the nutritionist. Rachel has stayed the same weight, so I am forced to believe her on the Lindt rabbit front. I have put on two kilos and am told by the doctor that I am 'an anomaly'. We buy every bag of crisps in the airport and shovel them into our mouths on the flight home, a new feeling of security around our shoulders like a cosy blanket.

★

Rachel and I live together for months before it happens. One day, the man who will become my husband asks me to move in with him. This is not as momentous as it sounds, seeing as he's been asking for months but this time I can tell – because he tells me outright – that he's starting to wonder why I'm so reluctant.

It's not that I don't want to move in together. It's just that I'm already living with someone I love. Someone who has taught me how to be a friend simply by being a friend to me.

I decide the best venue to deliver the news is the basement of Habitat on the King's Road, surrounded by piles of plush towels and soap dishes. Rachel has always loved a good bathroom interior and I'm hopeful that the calming environment might make it easier to take.

'I'm going to move in with Tim,' I blurt out, nervously running my fingers across the top of a wicker trunk. 'I'm really sorry. I adore living with you, but I think he might break up with me if we don't do this.'

We walk around a display of loo brushes in varying shades of beige in silence.

'I'll miss you,' says Rachel, giving me a hug. 'But you'll be happy.'

I leave a few weeks later, writing her a card that says 'I come, I fox shit up, I leave' on the front, with an illustration of a fox wearing a monocle and a bowler hat.

'They're having loud "missing you already" sex', she texts me later that night.

Unfriend

*Myth: It's kinder to cut off a friend than hurt
her by explaining what's gone wrong*

Imagine that you text a friend and she doesn't reply. If
she's anything like me – generally a bit rubbish at
responding – then you probably won't think anything
of it. Now imagine that she doesn't reply the next day,
or even by the following week. You message again.

'Brunch this weekend? Lemme know x'

Silence.

'Hi love, getting a bit worried about you? Brunch
can wait if things are a nightmare. Shout if I can help x'

Nothing.

'Are you getting my texts?'

You start to wonder what could be preventing your
friend from responding – a bit like when someone
you're dating stops replying to your messages, and you
decide it must be because a terrible tragedy has taken
place (or maybe it's because they like you *too* much?).
Perhaps your friend is trapped under something really

heavy. Yes, that must be it, her bathroom cabinet has fallen on top of her, knocking her phone out of her hand where she can't reach it. Or she's gone on a last-minute holiday, lost her phone on the way to the airport and the island she's staying on doesn't have the internet. Yup, plausible. But when the silence stretches so far – into weeks or months – you eventually have no choice but to accept that she has simply chosen to edit you out of her life.

Welcome to the decidedly unfriendly world of unfriending.

It doesn't have to be a big blow-up, or brutal ghosting. It can sometimes be a slow fizzle. Maybe you had a door slammed in your face, or a letter dropped on the mat telling you it was over. You could have been unfriended on social media. Possibly, you did the unfriending yourself. But it's pretty inevitable at least once in your life. The Spice Girls might have tried to convince us that friendship never ends but – as Sporty, Ginger, Scary, Posh and Baby now know all too well – that ain't the truth.

This is the truth: being dumped by a female friend can be just as heartbreaking as any romantic split. The same gut-whisking pain and bewilderment. The same waves of realization that threaten to knock you off your feet when they hit: she is not in your life any more. The same montage of memories playing in your mind: drinking frozen margaritas outside with your gloves on, the time she asked for Durex paint in the DIY shop, the way she held your hand when you needed it.

Pretty much every reason you might end a

relationship also applies to female friendship: neglect, jealousy, poor communication, a refusal to compromise. Betrayal or lies. A lack of trust, money, different values, holding someone to unrealistic standards. Not committing. Not listening. Not having respect or empathy. Any combination of these things will, over time, wear away at your compatibility, making it thin and brittle like a sliver of soap left for too long at the side of the shower. The symptoms might be the same, but the sympathy isn't. If you get dumped, everyone rallies round, offering support. We know what romantic heartbreak looks and feels like, and we want to help ease the agony. With a friend break-up? It can feel incredibly lonely.

Sometimes the end of a friendship is a good thing, of course. There's nothing childish about deciding your life would be better without a particular person in it. It can be a mature response that prioritizes your own emotional needs. What often isn't mature is the way we handle it.

Female friendships have no 'till death do us part'. No milestones when things are great, or recognition when they fall apart. We don't discuss how to maintain them, like we do our romantic relationships. It means we're lost when it all starts to go wrong: we don't know how to react or whether it's even worth trying to save. Often, we just walk away.

'Because female friendship comes with no protocol, no ceremony, no nothing, you can do whatever you want at the end,' says friendship expert Liz Pryor. 'And it's kind of embarrassing that, left to our own devices, we would walk away after such a beautiful connection with another human being, and feel zero responsibility to address it. It's so hurtful and damaging to many people's lives. It's crazy to me that it's still not talked about.'

So I've decided to talk about some of my own experiences, and share those of other women, in the hope of helping us all navigate the potentially devastating decision to unfriend – and understand that we can start to go about it differently. Because – I'm going to level with you – this chapter has been one of the toughest things I have ever written. Forget magma; beneath the Earth's crust there is a hot, swirling, liquid ball of pain, guilt and shame around the end of female friendships. I only had to tap lightly at the surface to release a river of molten emotion from almost every woman I asked. It shocked me because it's so easy to imagine that you're the only one going through these experiences, but, trust me, you're not. When *Woman's Hour* did a segment on this very subject in August 2021, Emma Barnett told listeners that she had 'never seen so many messages come in so fast. The pain of it is visceral.'

These big-girl break-ups can be so devastating that many of the women I asked to speak to me about it simply couldn't. They apologized but admitted it was still too raw. A few who had previously talked publicly about a friend break-up said they didn't have the strength to go there again. 'I don't want to make things worse,' one emailed.

When it comes to unfriending, I'm not sure it could be much worse. Female friendships end every single day, yet we know almost nothing concrete about it. I'm staggered by the fact that hardly any major scientific studies have been done to investigate the emotional impact of this heartbreak. Perhaps that's why a lot of us find it too painful to talk about. It's even more mind-boggling when you understand that the end of a female friendship could actually change the shape of your heart – and possibly even kill you.

As I was writing this book, a team at Imperial College London published research into 'broken heart syndrome'.[26] Its real name is Takotsubo Syndrome, and it is basically an abrupt failure of the heart, which weakens and bulges until it resembles a round-bottomed Japanese trap used to catch octopuses, called a *takotsubo* (unexpected). It affects roughly 2,500 people in the UK each year, mainly women, and the symptoms are a bit like a heart attack. Most recover, but it can be fatal.

It is usually brought on by heartbreak or extreme stress, but it could also be a 'sudden emotional shock', according to Professor Sian Harding, who led the Imperial study, which identified increased levels of two types of microRNA molecules linked to anxiety in the blood of sufferers.

So, given that it largely impacts women and can be caused by an emotional shock, what's to say that the end of a female friendship couldn't lead to broken heart syndrome? 'That's an interesting question. It's certainly plausible, if there is a strong emotional response,' agrees Sian, when I email her to ask.

So, according to a scientist who actually knows, it is possible that you could die from being ditched by a female friend. Something to think about next time you want to ghost someone.

Of course, you can't stay friends with everyone forever. For lots of reasons we've already covered, you might grow apart. Some friendships are destined to be temporary, linked to a particular workplace, club or hobby before fizzling out. That's normal. But what shouldn't be normal is the way women are going about ending long-term and close friendships like they're utterly meaningless – with the other person left devastated and in the dark. It's like being found guilty without trial, and not even knowing what you've been charged with.

Psychologist Terri Apter thinks it's down to women being sold that fantasy of perfect female friendship – one where they both get along all the time and see eye to eye on everything. 'It's a myth that good friends never argue,' she says. 'So when they do have conflict, they either bury it or think, "I feel this conflict, therefore it isn't a friendship and I have to leave it."'

When a friendship starts to wobble, we don't know what to do. We see it as a failure. But what we definitely don't want to do is talk about it. Forget that very sensible option. No thank *you*. Much better to bottle it up, secretly brood over the thing your friend has done to upset you without telling them, and then – when they do it or say it again entirely unwittingly – snap and walk away. Good, glad we're all agreed on the most adult way to handle this.

Women are socialized to want to smooth things over – we are taught from a young age to be pacifying and gentle. And we're just so very good at it. So we allow the comment that caused offence to go unchallenged. We ignore one-up(wo)manship. We let unspoken resentment, jealousy, guilt and hurt build up until we're internally furious, and furious that our friend can't see how furious we are with them, even though we haven't shown them our fury. We're too busy hiding it, furiously.

It all means that we are more inclined to reach that 'final straw' moment and end a friendship without an explanation. To pull up the drawbridge, drain the moat and change the castle locks without a word about why to our now ex-friend. And women are, according to the experts, far less willing than men to give their reasons. We want to avoid confrontation and we don't want to give them a chance to defend themselves. It's this I find troubling. The way so many women are left feeling guilty, ashamed and blindsided. The impact can last for years and can be, as one woman put it to me, 'worse than divorce'.

Georgie's account of friendship heartbreak made me cry. After having a baby during lockdown, she was desperate for her friends to meet her son in their garden when restrictions started to lift. But one close friend, herself pregnant, refused, saying she didn't feel safe.

'I knew I had to accept her decision, but the more I thought about it, the angrier I became,' says Georgie, thirty-seven. 'I knew she was still going to the supermarket and on a staycation, but she wasn't prepared to meet my baby. I obviously went on about it so much that my husband called her to tell her I was upset. She asked why he was making things so difficult. I couldn't believe it. I still can't. It probably hurt more because I was already so angry about having a baby during lock-down. My birth and postpartum was just not what it should have been.

'The only way I am able to come to terms with it is to listen to my psychologist when she says that people weren't behaving as they usually would during the pandemic. But I can't get past her not talking to my husband and trying to figure out a way to meet. So I just told her that I needed some time, in the hope that I could eventually let it go. She said if I wouldn't talk about it now, then our friendship wasn't aligned. We've had no contact since. I just needed the anger she caused to be out of my life, and so I needed her out of my life.'

It was Georgie's recollection of how it felt physic-ally that brought tears to my eyes – and will resonate with anyone who has said goodbye to someone close.

'Until this happened I probably wouldn't have used the term heartbroken for a friendship, but it hurt the way a romantic break-up would,' she explains. 'I was literally cry-shouting that she had broken my heart. I'm not sure I can explain the physical feeling accu-rately, but it felt like I needed to scream it right from my stomach and that it hurt my insides on the way out. I would compare it to times of grief. It felt like I couldn't control my emotions at all.'

Full disclosure: I haven't covered myself in glory when it comes to breaking up with friends. Ghosting wasn't a thing in the noughties, but that's what Agatha and I did when we stopped inviting another girl to our post-university meet-ups. What we should have done was to talk to her and tell her we felt like she was always looking over our shoulders for a better offer. There were good reasons for walking away from that friendship, but there was also a good way to do it – and we didn't take it. We just dropped her, although it must be said that she never showed any signs of wanting to be picked back up.

That's often the truest test there is when it comes to a friendship that feels one-sided: to stop making approaches and wait for the person to contact you. It's a risky game, however, and one you've got to be prepared to lose. One woman I know did just that with a former university friend who seemed to drift and lose interest in her life after moving to London. 'For her birthday, she planned some drinks at her flat before going to a bar,' she says. 'My boyfriend and I were already going to another friend's birthday, so said we'd meet her at the bar. She never showed. We waited for two hours before calling it a night, and she didn't apologize. I felt it was the last straw – it was pretty obvious she didn't value our friendship. So I decided I wouldn't contact her unless she contacted me first. And she never did.'

It's astounding, really. We're prepared to let an important friendship flounder through – what? – laziness or irritation that your friend went to another birthday first? (Although everyone knows you attend the best party last.)

'We can go out with a guy three times and if we decide we don't like him, we say, "Hey, sorry, it's not you. It's me." We say, "I'm moving." We lie. We do *something,*' says Liz Pryor. 'And yet, you could be friends with a woman for twenty years and still not feel compelled to say anything. We don't do it. We just disappear.'

A few years ago, I had a friend who wanted to have after-work drinks. '*I finish at 7pm, meet then?*' I messaged her. '*Oh, that's a shame, I finish at 5.30pm*', came her reply. She was surrounded by the capital's best museums, shops, parks and pubs, but apparently couldn't work out how to pass an hour and a half. That should have told me loud and clear, as if she were standing next to my ear with a megaphone, bellowing 'You are not worth ninety minutes of my time.'

We did manage to meet up one Saturday afternoon and while walking along the pavement I suddenly felt a hard, cold thud against the back of my skull. Not the penny dropping, alas. At first, I thought someone had thrown a stone at me, but, putting my hand back, my hair felt wet. Was I bleeding? Oh god, please not dog poo.

No, my friend said, laughing – I had been egged. She'd seen a group of boys running off. Wasn't it hysterical? Side-splitting. I can't think of anything funnier than being pelted with chicken bullets on a London street at 3 p.m.

The egg reeked. I twisted this way and that, trying desperately to remove tiny bits of sticky shell and slime from my clumped locks, which had been perfectly straightened with my GHDs only that morning. But my friend didn't offer to help, or seem to even notice, just going back to talking about herself. That small unsupportive act seemed to represent the cracks in our friendship. When I got home and washed my hair – and no, contrary to the myth, I can confirm that albumen doesn't make it softer or shinier – I decided that I wasn't going to keep making the effort. If she messaged me then I'd reply. She never did.

(Footnote: We recently bumped into one another in a local park. I heard her screaming 'CC! CC!' as bemused families turned around expecting to see a Spanish woman having a paddy. 'Let's go for a coffee!' she said, as we swapped numbers. That evening, I messaged her saying how nice it would be to have a cuppa. Guess what? She didn't get back to me.)

In some ways I was grateful to find out when I did. I spoke to Alice, sixty-seven, who put up with a self-absorbed friend for years. 'She was a friend to me on her terms. Everything was about her and her family, and I was never asked about anything to do with my life,' she says. 'She constantly bragged about her children being the brightest on the planet and her home being the most stylish. She offloaded her problems but didn't want to hear mine. I began to feel used, so I gradually became unavailable and the friendship fizzled out. It sounds harsh, but I was relieved.'

Alice's story made me think of *Motherland*, the painfully well-observed sitcom about school-gate mums. The show's best-worst friendship is between Alpha mother Amanda – polite on the surface, poison flowing through her veins – and her right-hand woman, Anne, who listens to her boast about her perfect life. There's a monstrous exchange in which Amanda manages to both belittle and gaslight Anne in front of all their friends.

AMANDA: How long did you work at Greggs, Anne?

ANNE: I never worked at Greggs. I was head of product development at GlaxoSmithKline worldwide.

AMANDA: Why did I always think you worked at Greggs? Are you sure?

ANNE: Yes.

AMANDA: I can't picture you working in an office, Anne. I see you with cakes and puffs. Really, not Greggs?

ANNE: No. I've been there once or twice but more as a customer.

It might be an extreme version, but we've all seen that sort of power-trip friendship up close, or else been in it ourselves. We recognize the dynamic (and every viewer is rooting for Anne to end their friendship).

Joanna Morris, fifty-six, from Surrey, certainly understands what it's like to experience such an imbalanced friendship. It's been a decade since her best friend of thirty years ghosted her. Yet, when we speak over the phone, she says that she is 'shaking even now' as she tells me what happened. Her story begins in the same way as so many of our female friendships: they met at school, were close as teenagers, lived together in their early twenties. Joanna was her friend's bridesmaid. Their husbands became friends and they had children around the same time. Everything seemed great. Then her friend moved abroad for work.

'They'd been there for about a year, when I got a phone call saying she was coming home and could she stay with me,' recalls Joanna. 'She was leaving her husband and said her marriage was over.'

'Her family came back and it was all a bit messy. Then she decided to move in with a new guy. It was like she wanted to create a family unit again, really quickly. But I don't think he could cope. Over the next few years, they split up so many times and every time, she'd call me, and I'd go over. I remember walking out of restaurants and leaving another friend at my house, to make sure she was all right.'

On one of those occasions, Joanna told her friend that she shouldn't take him back again – and that's when everything started to change.

'I said, "What sort of an example are you setting for your son: that he can do this to a woman? And your daughter: that as a woman you can let a man do whatever you want to you?"' says Joanna. 'She didn't blow up at me, but she did go cool. She didn't respond to my texts very quickly. And then she just stopped. To this day I still don't understand and I'm still really hurt. I just thought we would be best friends forever.'

This lack of clarity over precisely why one friend has cut off contact is what drives Liz Pryor to despair. She regularly speaks to women who have ended a friendship and tells me they often justify it by saying, 'I really couldn't tell her. It would hurt her so much.' 'But what they don't realize is that by not saying anything at all and leaving a woman hanging – in purgatory – it's hurting her twice as much,' adds Liz. 'In the end, it's grossly selfish because it's disguised as compassion.'

So what do the initiators themselves say? I spoke to

many women who had ended friendships and it might not surprise you to know that most of them said they still felt terrible about it. Take Aisling O'Leary, twenty-nine. 'We met on a summer abroad and ended up living together, and then I was like, "Oh no, you're from a very different part of my life, I actually don't see you fitting in now" and I just completely cut them off,' she says. 'Thinking back, it was so cold. It was awful. I just didn't respond to any of their messages. I don't think it gets acknowledged enough that it's OK for people to just sit in one part of your life, and for that to be that. But it was very harsh.'

'My husband is much nicer than I am and likes everybody,' explains Tina, forty-nine. 'But we left my friend's house and he just went, "I think she was really unpleasant. If you want to see her it's fine, but I am never coming again." It was the first time in our whole relationship he'd ever said anything like that. I just thought, "He's actually right." After that I totally ghosted her. She is so dramatic and I just couldn't cope with the scene. I couldn't be bothered. I just thought it would be so draining and I didn't have it in me. But I do feel guilty about it. I also live in absolute terror of running into her in Marks and Spencer's and thinking, "Oh god, now I've got to deal with this."'

That's the truth, isn't it? That many women who dump a friend just can't be faffed with a showdown, however bad they might feel about it. When we say, 'I can't handle your drama', what we really mean is 'I don't want to have to deal with your emotions.' We are generally quite conflict-avoidant. I'm no better. Like Tina, I am married to one of those annoying men who gets on with everyone. You know the sort – at the end of every social situation, he'll smile and remark how nice the other person is. You have to be pretty awful for him to object. We had been together for two years when he pointed out that a friend of mine was, in his words, 'the most self-obsessed person I've ever met'. It felt like a slap round the face with a wet flip-flop.

'How dare you speak about my friend like that,' I said.

'She never asks you anything about your life, and she has never asked me a single thing about myself,' he replied. 'It's rude and it makes me not want to spend time with her.'

I said something mature, like 'Well, don't then.' But later, turning his words over in my mind, I had a feeling he was right. When was the last time we had talked about anything other than her? After that, I slowly but deliberately began to drift. I found that I was quietly relieved.

One rare woman who did tackle the end of a friendship head-on is Radhika Sanghani. Her experience sadly stands out in my research because she apologized to her former friend and they had a 'closure' conversation. Her pal knew not only what was happening but why.

'I tried to drift from a friend,' she says, 'but she emailed and was like, "Can we talk about this?" So I told her, "I'm really sorry, I just don't feel like we have as much in common any more. And sometimes when I see you, I find it hard for these reasons." It felt horrible and she was really hurt. All I could say was, "I am so sorry. I personally wish you all the best. I just think this friendship isn't good for me." It felt like a romantic break-up and no one likes breaking up with someone – it's painful.

'It sounds dramatic, and I think my mum, who's from a different generation, would think it was so weird,' she adds. 'But it means that I have really high-quality relationships with the friends I do have.'

In her book *You're the Only One I Can Tell*, linguist Deborah Tannen sums up the two sides of that 'why' in the unfriending story: 'Women who told me they had been cut off . . . almost always said they didn't know why. But women who told me they had cut off a friend could always tell me why,' she writes. That pulled me up sharp. Is it really always so clear-cut? Could there be friendships in my past where I think we just grew apart, but the other woman considers herself to have been unfriended? Or vice versa?

Sarah and I became friends in sixth form. We both liked indie music, Malibu and pineapple juice and wore those wide-legged jeans that soaked up puddles. Throughout university, we emailed and saw one another during the holidays – usually for a Pizza Express with a side of dough balls, quite extravagant on a student budget. When she moved abroad for work in her early twenties, we never lost contact and when her love life became complicated, I remember sending messages of support, hoping dearly that it went her way. So what happened? I thought I knew, but a trawl through my inbox turned my version of the story on its head.

The romantic turmoil did right itself: Sarah moved back to London with her boyfriend and they got engaged. There was a hen do, involving a treasure hunt, penis straws and not a bit of eye-rolling, as hers was the first hen I'd been to and I wasn't the jaded crone I am today. The wedding was to be abroad, and I ummed and ahhed over going. Looking back, I should have politely declined from the off as I couldn't afford it and wouldn't have known anyone else there, something that felt very daunting at the time. But I stalled. It just seemed so young to be getting married, in a different country, and to a man I barely knew. I felt as though she was abandoning our friendship now that she'd got the guy – which wasn't the case at all. But I didn't want things to change and didn't want to admit that they already had. In the end I didn't go and, to my shame, I don't recall sending a gift, though I desperately hope that's just my shoddy memory. I'm convinced that I at least wrote a card. I must have.

In my mind's eye, this is where our story ends. She was upset, I felt bad and we didn't clear the air. But when I look back through my emails (shout-out to still using the same Hotmail you've had since 2001) that's not the case. I invited Sarah to various things after that, including my thirtieth. She and her husband didn't come, but in her last email she wrote: 'Would be lovely to catch up sometime, let me know if you fancy it.' As far as I can see, I never replied. So, did we drift? Or did I end the friendship with my silence? Is that how she's always seen it? The truth, I hope, is probably a bit of this and that, topped off with a large dollop of immaturity.

'It's never one thing,' says Liz Pryor, reassuringly. 'It's an accumulation of behaviours that bother somebody – you drink too much, you're always late. All of those things that we don't address because we're so "nice", right? I mean, we're on to our husbands or boyfriends in a heartbeat for any bad behaviour, but with our girlfriends we're much more "generous". We think we're compassionate and understanding, but not really, because after several years and all of that accumulation . . . one little thing is the straw that broke the camel's back.'

I'd never pull my friends up on the sorts of things I do with my husband (although I've never noticed my pals walk over to the empty dishwasher and leave their dirty plates next to it). It's not that I wouldn't feel irritated by a friend, it's just that I wouldn't necessarily vocalize it. But if we're going to treat our female friendships with as much care and respect as our romantic relationships, don't we owe it to them to speak up? To have those awkward conversations, as I should have done with Sarah?

'It's weak and not courageous to have any experience with a dear friend that hurts you and then for you not to address it,' adds Liz. 'That's not being nice. That's being stupid. Because over time that is going to lead to the ending of the friendship.'

Roma, fifty-three, did address it. She was fed up with a friend constantly being late – not just five minutes, but an hour or more every time. It began to feel, she explains, like a lack of respect for the friendship. On the brink of ghosting her, in the end she forced herself to confront her friend – telling her how angry she felt. Her friend started to cry and explained it was a symptom of other issues she'd been avoiding that had nothing to do with Roma. It ended up bringing them closer as they navigated her friend's problems, and years later Roma is so relieved she didn't walk away from an important friendship for the sake of having a hard conversation.

Aisling O'Leary went one step further. She and one of her oldest friends had friendship therapy after they ended up living in the same city for the first time in years, and struggled to work out how to physically reintegrate their friendship into their new lives.

'Our friendship was in a very weird place,' she tells me. 'The communication wasn't great and I needed to take a more active role. I was letting it slide.'

It sort of makes sense. If your long-term romantic relationship started to go south, you'd try to work it out – assuming it was worth saving. You might well have couples' counselling, if you could afford it. So why not with a long-term female friendship? After all, it's just as emotionally intimate and important, and plenty of the same issues arise: co-dependency, communication and commitment.

Admittedly, googling 'friendship therapy' doesn't turn up many options. Just one example of how far we are from seeing it as a thing: Aisling tells me about two women she spoke to who had been struggling with their friendship and decided to have counselling. But the first therapist they saw? He questioned their sexuality and tried to convince them that they were secretly in love with one another.

Friendship therapy was, Aisling admits, incredibly

challenging, so much so that her friend hasn't told anyone about it.

'It's really uncomfortable and confronting,' she says. 'But it allowed us to air a few things that might not have been said otherwise. You can get away with not saying a lot in a friendship, but in that space you have no room to hide. Which can be quite freeing and also really scary – you know that there's no going back.'

*

Could this become the age of the unfriend? I ask not only because of the tsunami of tears that hit me when I spoke to women about this, but also because of what we've collectively been through. Just as the pandemic saw record numbers of couples file for divorce, so friendship fissures appeared among those with whom you thought you shared a set of common values. Be honest: how many of you have seen something on the timeline of a friend in the last few years that's made you take a deep breath?

A survey in April 2020 by US marketing agency Digital Third Coast[27] found that 24 per cent of people had argued with someone on social media over Covid and 20 per cent had unfriended a friend over the disagreement.

However, it's not always as easy as just clicking 'unfriend'. According to academics at the University of Colorado Denver, unfriending someone on Facebook can have real world consequences.[28] They found that 40 per cent of people would avoid in real life anyone who had unfriended them online, with women less tolerant than men.

When Sophie Mumford, forty-one, decided to remove herself from a WhatsApp group, the real-life impact was immediate and frankly incredible. It was at the height of the pandemic and she was struggling with three young children and her mum's dementia. I mean, I don't know about you but I can find the sheer volume of messages overwhelming when I don't have anywhere near that much on my plate.

Sophie chose to leave a few groups at the same time, one of which contained school mums whom she'd known for years and described to me as good friends. She wrote a message: *'You're all fabulous but I'm slightly overwhelmed and struggling to cope with WhatsApp at the mo . . .'* pressed send and then exited the group, as well as several others, thinking that her friends would be supportive. Most were.

'They were the only group that took it personally,' she says. That's an understatement — without a word, most of Sophie's mum-friends unfollowed her on social media and never attempted to speak to her in person.

'I just found it incredibly odd,' she says. 'Our kids were in the same class. We had holidays planned together. And when you're deleted like that, you don't know why and you don't know how to move on from it.'

In the end, she decided to do nothing and accepted having lost her friends. 'I think it is more awkward to confront things and I was sort of hoping they might come to me. One of them did and said, "I'm sorry, I overreacted and I felt that when you left the group you didn't want to be my friend any more." And I was waiting for that response from the others. But it just didn't happen.'

So what can you do if you've been cut off and left in limbo? The harsh truth is not a lot. Liz Pryor suggests writing a letter, which you never send, laying out everything that you would say to your former friend were you to get the chance. And I say former friend deliberately, because this is all about acceptance. You can't win someone back if they've chosen to walk away.

'Write a letter, talk about the friendship and tell the truth,' advises Liz. 'Say "I don't know what happened, it's evident that we're not friends any more, so I saw it as important for me to say that this is over." Call her out and say "I'll have the balls to do it. We're not friends now." And somehow that does seem to bring empowerment, because you can only control so much . . . you can only control you.'

It might sound like a cliche, but I like the letter-writing idea – or it could be an email – as it allows you to have the last word. That might also include deleting your former friend on social media, or having an imaginary conversation with them out loud in the shower and saying what you need to say. Then draw a line.

The key is to not let yourself slip back into old patterns, as I almost did with my egging friend. Or with Ana, whom I contacted online after she posted that her father had died. Having spent a lot of time at her house as a teenager, I sent a brief message of sympathy; she never replied. Perhaps she felt I was intruding on her grief. Possibly I should have known better than to expect a response. It helped me to finally accept that, twenty years after she ended our friendship, she definitely doesn't consider me part of her life. It taught me that her opinion of me – in fact, the opinion of anyone who doesn't know me now – isn't important. Nor is it fact. It's just one person's take, and maybe it's a bad one.

The last and maybe the most important way to blast your friend-dumping pain into the past is to talk about it. If it were a painful romantic split, you'd tell your friends how it was making you feel. This is no different. Any intimate relationship in your life that comes to an end deserves to be recognized and mourned. But this is only possible by bringing it out of the darkness. Shame can't survive when it's exposed to the light, so don't let yours fester in the shadows. Talk about it, normalize it, trust your other friends to support you – and not to think you're being petty. Because if there's one thing I've learned it's that unfriending has happened to almost all of us. It's high time we started telling each other about it.

Funny Friends

Myth: Women don't do banter

According to Robert Provine, the late psychologist from the University of Maryland, we laugh the most in life when in a social setting, with our friends. In his book *Laughter: A Scientific Investigation*, he found that we're thirty times more likely to laugh at something when we're in company. The key, he concluded, isn't the joke or conversation itself but the presence of another person: laughter is how we communicate and show someone that we like or 'get' them. It's the glue that helps bind us together – and nowhere is that truer than in female friendship.

It's a deeply unfunny myth that women have to be hammered on Prosecco or Chardonnay to have a proper laugh. The depressing stereotype is that the only way we can have anything approaching the sort of 'banter' we're used to seeing in male friendships is at a drunken cackling hen party.

'It's that pervasive "wine o'clock" attitude for women and how we can only bond over a bottle,' says Emilie McMeekan of *The Midult*. 'Actually the funniest nights of my life have been sober around a kitchen table.'

While humour in friendships between men can be more obvious, that doesn't mean it isn't just as potent and just as hilarious between women. We have amazing, brilliant, pant-wettingly funny banter – although we'd probably never call it that – in our friendships. We laugh more than we cry, moan, bitch or whine. We can be raucous. It just doesn't really get talked about in the same way as 'lad bants'.

Want proof? A major study led by the University of California (UCLA) in 2016, which looked at laughter in twenty-four different societies across the globe, found that groups of female friends laugh together more than male or mixed ones.[29]

'We always have this idea that sense of humour is a male attribute and that women don't really have it,' says evolutionary anthropologist Dr Anna Machin. 'But the great thing about a female friendship is that you can go from having these really intense intimate conversations to just being silly. Women have bantery conversations all the time.'

It's why so many of the women I interviewed used the word 'laugh' when describing their female friendships to me:

We still laugh about it now.
We roar with laughter.
We spent so much of every day laughing.
They make me laugh until I ache.
It helped to laugh at myself and each other.

So what are we getting out of all this laughter? Closeness is one great big benefit.

'Humour is one of the main things for me, in terms of forging a connection with another woman. That just surpasses everything else,' says Sameeha, twenty-seven. 'It's the most magical thing if you get each other's jokes. And there are so many unsaid things that go into humour. It's like another language and, for me, it's by far one of the most connecting things about a friendship.'

That feeling you're on the same wavelength with a female friend, that you watch the same sitcoms and laugh at the same things, can go such a long way to cementing a bond. For me, it means that I think warmly of them when I see something I know we would both find funny – immediately imbuing the friendship with positivity. And it can be sad when the opposite is true. I remember meeting a woman who was, on paper, perfect friend material for me; someone I was keen to get to know better and felt sure would be on my wavelength. But after getting together for drinks and dinner a couple of times, I started to feel differently. There wasn't much laughter and whenever I made a quip to lighten the conversation, she reacted earnestly. We just didn't get each other's sense of humour and that, to me, meant we were never going to be able to fully relax together or open up.

That's OK. Our sense of humour doesn't have to appeal to everyone; you don't have to justify what you do, or don't, find funny. It just means that when you meet someone who shares your taste, it's powerful and means you don't have to hold back.

What's more, it actually shows in *how* we laugh. According to the global UCLA study, women laugh differently with female friends than with strangers. When we're with a woman we don't really know, our laugh is more likely to mimic theirs. When we're with a friend, it has greater variations in the pitch and volume – it's spontaneous, genuine and full of excitement. We let go, basically. I can't think of anything more joyous. It's the sort of laughter where you only have to say one word to bring back a memory so potent that it gets you hooting. I only need utter the phrase 'dirty bitches' to Agatha to have us both wiping tears from our eyes at the memory of an appalling campsite in Shropshire, owned by a couple who wouldn't have been out of place in a Julia Davis sitcom and who, on our last morning staying there, screamed those words at us for not getting out of the shower block fast enough.

It's somehow even better if no one else gets it. Izzy messaged me a few months ago, saying *'Turns out it's really hard to explain Mr Crouton'* – an in-joke we've had since our teenage days, when I once dropped a crouton from a bowl of soup. 'Oops, missed a crouton!' Izzy said. 'Who's Mr Crouton?' I replied, genuinely confused. See, it's just not funny to anyone who wasn't there – but to us it's one of the most hilarious moments of the last thirty years.

The other thing that women couldn't wait to tell me was absolutely key to their female friendships was piss-taking.

'Mocking is my love language', as one of my friends

says. And isn't she right? As much as I want us to mark our friendship milestones, tell our pals we love them and not dump one another quite so brutally, I feel as though the more serious side of female friendship can sometimes eclipse the pure joy of ripping it out of one another. I always lose it when I think about my friend Cecilia – a very sophisticated and accomplished woman – in a classic car and halfway to her own wedding, when she realized that she'd forgotten to brush her teeth. Beautiful ivory gown, face of immaculate make-up, tousled hair, last night's garlic breath. And we won't ever let her forget it.

'There's plenty of laughter in female friendships. The idea that we just sit around weeping and doing tapestries together and talking about our hormones – well, there is an element of that out of necessity, but it's never been more than 10 per cent of what women do when they get together,' Jane Garvey tells me. Her friendship with her podcast partner Fi Glover is, she adds, based on sparring. 'She takes the piss out of me and I take the piss out of her, but we also support each other. That mocking side of female friendships is so prevalent but it's just not really spoken about in the same way as the awful "banter" is always talked about in terms of male friendships.'

As Dr Anna Machin puts it: 'You really know that you can rely on someone if you can take the piss out of them and they still love you. That's a sign of real closeness.'

'Our love language is to take the piss out of each other,' agrees MP Jess Phillips. 'If somebody has made even a minor infraction, like thirty years ago, that will be brought up every single time we're together. One of my friends is slightly posher than the rest of us and she once said "strawbs" and there will never ever be a birthday card, there will never ever be a day where we are together, where we don't take the piss out of the fact she said "strawbs". Once.'

The truth is: we are masters of mocking our own lives and the messes within them – from the tiny and insignificant to the tragic. It's why some of the best conversations at house parties are so often in the kitchen with other women. It's why some of the best books by women are those that capture the absurdity of our everyday existence.

'Women are so brilliant at skewering daily life and the humour in the everyday – the tiny touch-points of crises that are so funny,' says Emilie McMeekan. 'If it wasn't all so fucking funny we'd all throw ourselves off a cliff. And nobody makes you laugh [about it] like your female friends.'

An ability to raise an eyebrow at our toughest times is one of the strongest things that binds us together. As Dolly Parton says in the 1989 female-friendship film *Steel Magnolias*: 'Laughter through tears is my favourite emotion.' Women are really good at absorbing life's blows in that way and seeing the darkly funny side; using black humour to help us cope with everything from divorce to death. Not to mention our bodily functions. So much of being a woman is having to deal with that, it would be unnatural for us not to turn it into the source of humour. I have endometriosis, which is painful and often debilitating. It means that for a portion of each month I experience chronic, doubled-over-on-the-bedroom-floor levels of pain. The lack of knowledge around it is horrifying: one in ten women suffers, but it still takes an average of seven years to get a diagnosis, usually after having your inside-scraping agony dismissed by disbelieving doctors. It's seriously unfunny, but that doesn't mean I don't joke with my friends about having a cold condom-covered dildo camera popped up there (the technical term, I believe). We have to laugh about this stuff with other women, otherwise it would all just be too hideous. As fellow endo sufferer Emma Barnett says: 'If you've ever helped someone put a tampon in – or get one out when it's stuck – you know how to be silly.'

I'll always remember Cecilia telling me about giving birth to her daughter, describing how one minute she was squatting like an animal in the woods and screaming her lungs out – 'it was primal' – and a few minutes later she was sitting up in her hospital bed eating white toast and jam from a china plate, with a cup of tea. Something that life-changing and surreal just *is* bloody funny.

Linguist Deborah Tannen recalls a story about how her group of friends once spent an entire evening dissecting how each of them folds the loo paper before they wipe. It became so in-depth that the host went to get a roll, so each of them could demonstrate their technique. 'I remember this evening because it was so funny – and so intimate,' explains Deborah. 'The effect was a precious element of friendship: reminding each other of our shared humanity.'

I bet you've had a ludicrous chat just like that with

your female friends. I certainly have, from whether it's normal for them to do your bum cheeks when you get a bikini wax to whether it's OK for your husband to call pessaries 'botty poppers'. Mine and Agatha's favourite game to play has long been 'Desert Island Dicks' (patent 2004). You don't really need me to explain the concept and, frankly, I'm sure any truly dedicated Radio 4 listener will already have considered which eight men and their appendages they'd like to be cast away with. It's the sort of chat we all have – where you suddenly think that if anyone else could hear you, they'd probably be reaching for the straitjackets.

Laughter is one thing that film and TV often get right about female friendship. *Broad City, Parks and Recreation, The Bold Type, Booksmart* – they do at least show women finding one another hilarious and the bizarre humour that is a big part of our lives. For me, though, maybe the most relatable scene is Bridget Jones's attempt to cook dinner for her friends on her birthday. Her Borough Market flat, apparently paid for on a publishing assistant's wage, might have been a stretch of the imagination, but her feast of blue soup, omelette and marmalade, and her friends' reaction to it, is just bang on. After a pause, they collapse into hysterical laughter at her expense, over which she can't help but join in. She has cocked up in a way they know, understand, love and feel totally comfortable teasing her about.

That sort of genuine laughter is actually good for us, releasing endorphins, our happiness hormones. And it can also help us open up. According to a 2015 study by Professor Alan Gray at University College London, laughing with another person makes you more likely to share secrets with them.[30] This could be, he concluded, because endorphins help us combat negative thoughts and make us more outgoing. Despite the fact that he tested this theory by making his subjects watch Michael McIntyre videos, it makes perfect sense. Laughter is a bonding activity – if you want someone to spill the beans, just make them giggle.

Author Nell Frizzell can relate to this: if she sees a glimmer of a shared sense of humour with another woman, she admits, it makes her want to fully commit to them as a friend. 'If someone has the same sense of humour as me, I think I can say anything I like to them, and we will be incredibly close forever,' she says. 'All my boundaries completely drop to the floor. And it's not true – we're not best friends just because we laugh at the same thing.'

I'm so guilty of that. There are also women I follow on social media whom I find hilarious and because their jokes and asides are 'so me', I pretty much think of them as friends and occasionally reply to their stories, instantly regretting my overfamiliarity when I do. The most mortifying is often at women's events. You're all sitting in a room together, sharing moments of vulnerability, challenges and failures, and some laughs. Then after the talk? You giddily feel as though you've all known one another for years, which is why I end up doing things like calling Dame Helena Morrissey 'mate'.

When it comes down to it, the whole thing is a sort

of vulnerability balance: you want to share intense emotional intimacy with your female friends, but you also want to wet yourself laughing with them.

Daisy Buchanan says that she is more aware than ever of achieving that equilibrium in her own life. 'When we talk about being a good friend, it's like "You're always there during the bad times." And I have friends who have been so kind to me during dark times and I'll never forget it,' she says. 'But I just want my friends to be fun, jolly and lovely. Therapy changed my priorities in friendships and really brought home to me how I want them for the good times and to celebrate with.'

The truth is: subtly and without either chest-beating banter or Prosecco, our friendships with other women are *already* thriving on laughter. It's just more likely to be over a cuppa, strolling in the park, via a video call, around the dining table or in the car on the way to your wedding than in the locker room.

Laughter is a tonic and it's your friends who can often pick you up when you're feeling anxious, down, or as though you don't want to talk to anyone at all. Their humour – whether gentle wit or brutal teasing – is the glue which holds us together and means we experience the sort of side-splitting moments that stay with us, and bring us joy, down the years.

Jilly Cooper, a woman who has made me laugh so much, said something that has stayed in my mind ever since. When I asked what she considered to be the most important trait in her female friends, she told me her favourites were 'always ones that make you laugh'. And when I asked Jilly if she thought she was a good friend, she replied simply, 'I hope I make them laugh.'

Funny, maybe that is the key to it all, after all.

Family Friends

Myth: You can't be friends with your relatives
(especially your annoying little sisters)

Ah, sisters. Whoever said they couldn't be the best of friends? Well, maybe not in September 1997 when, aged thirteen, I furiously wrote the following in my diary in orange highlighter (and you *know* it's serious when someone uses the tip of a highlighter pen to drive home their point):

'R and F are making my life hell. They dob, sneer, laugh at me and kill my Tamagotchi.'

Oh and a couple of weeks after that: 'My sisters (brats) actually opened, actually sat and read YOU my precious diary. I can never trust them again.'

I remember the feeling of betrayal flooding through my veins, and pushing my diary even further under my mattress after that.

These days, the photograph on our 'Sistas' WhatsApp group shows the three of us in the garden under a pink and white parasol. We are all wearing 1980s puff-sleeve party dresses with Peter Pan collars, our brown hair in pigtails hanging below our fringes – lovingly but haphazardly trimmed at home with the nail scissors by Mum and which went all the way back to our ears like a frontal bowl cut.

We look so sweet and happy. But back then, I'd never have thought I could be friends with my twin sisters Felicity and Rosanna – three-and-a-half years younger than me, and ten times more annoying.

I was cross that their names made them sound like Flower Fairies, romantic and mysterious as though they belonged in a Christina Rossetti poem, while mine made me sound as though I should be holding a clipboard. (Actually, I still feel that way.) After Mum and Dad, they were the people I loved most in the world, but also the people whose upper arms I wanted to pinch so hard it made them cry. They were the two little people I'd have done anything for, but whom I wanted to send to the orphanage if they so much as breathed on my Sylvanian Families. There was never a private moment; always someone trying to get into the bathroom while you were sitting there perfectly happily reading a book, a red loo-seat-shaped welt forming on your backside. There was always a sister trying to look through the keyhole into your bed-room, or getting in the way when our much older brother, Tim, came over – sometimes with gifts from his grown-up holidays to places that weren't even in England, and always with stories to tell about going to see bands or his latest girlfriend.

So how did our relationship change? And can you really be 'friends' with your family? Anthropologist

Robin Dunbar explains that it all comes down to something called the 'kinship premium' – basically blood is thicker than water. You can't shake your relatives off as easily as you might a friendship, meaning we cling to each other throughout life like biological barnacles. Even better, you can take your family for granted and they'll probably still like you.

'Kinship relationships are kind of odd. They can become – and very often do become – genuine friends; it's down to the individuals concerned. But there's very clearly this kinship premium that makes family members more reliable, for less effort, than conventional friends,' he says. 'It seems to make family, in general, more willing to put up with your foibles and still be the cavalry riding over the hill. That's true right the way across the range of your social network – close family are better and more reliable than close friends, and distant family are more reliable than distant friends.'

But that doesn't mean you're destined to become friends with your immediate family. And, certainly in our younger years, we're more likely to use them as test runs for friendship than see them as the real thing.

Sibling relationships, if we have them, are our first attempts at making friends, before we start school. They set the tone for our future friendships. My template was, and still is, that of the classic eldest: the one who felt she had to be first in everything, just by accident of birth. To set a good example – as I was always being told by my parents – by getting the grades, going to a good university. The trailblazer who fought every battle so that my sisters might have a slightly easier path through puberty. If you have siblings, whichever birth position you're in, you've probably heard the firstborn tell that (true) sob story.

Twins bring a different dynamic to being the eldest. The sense of displacement you feel in no longer being your parents' sole focus is a double whammy. You have the great responsibility of being the big one, but the great power that comes with it is easily undermined by the fact your sisters are a team. They shared a womb. Your sibling superiority is diminished by their numerical advantage. You only need to watch *Sister, Sister* to see how Tia and Tamera are more powerful together than apart.

Linda Blair, author of the book *Siblings*, confirms that your birth order does matter, and that I haven't got a giant chip on my shoulder.

'The first sibling in the family is most likely to be in a more caring role than the others, because they want the attention back from their parents that they lost when this troublesome baby came along, and they learn quite quickly that one of the best ways to do it is to help,' she says. 'Middles are the negotiators. They learn how to smooth the waters, how to get on, how to make things work. The youngest is impatient and relies on the others to look after them and to sort things out. That's a very broad template and it doesn't mean you have to become that – but it's the most likely picture.'

As we all know, one of the main compensations for being the eldest and having your perfectly nice little life spoiled by younger siblings is getting to pull rank when putting on plays for your parents. I always landed any role I wanted, probably because I was also the casting director, scriptwriter and choreographer. Cinderella? Belle? Dorothy Gale? Me, me and me. My sisters played the Ugly Sisters, the Beast, Quasimodo or whatever supporting role I demanded of them.

I suppose this could be one of the reasons they liken me to Claire, the big sister in *Fleabag*: controlled, terrified of failure, tight-lipped. Hungry to set a good example and exasperated when her younger sister doesn't follow it. My WhatsApp is full of hilarious messages saying things like 'Nice to see you won a Bafta' and GIFs of the disastrous asymmetrical haircut that makes Claire shriek 'I look like a pencil!' sent every time I mention I'm going to the hairdresser.

It's the sort of thing my female friends might do, but turbocharged. Delivered with the absolute certainty that, even if they annoy you, it doesn't really matter because you're sisters and bound by something unconditional. But siblings can provoke strong emotions in a way that female friends often don't, because you know one another's touch-points and you're not afraid to use them. That's how you got attention / a reaction / your sister in trouble with your parents as a child. It's how you won arguments or brought her down a peg or two.

In her 1978 book *How to Eat Like a Child, and Other Lessons in Not Being a Grown-up* Delia Ephron wrote a chapter called 'How to Torture Your Sister'. One of four girls, the eldest of whom was superstar Nora (writer of classics such as *Heartburn*, *Sleepless in Seattle* and *When Harry Met Sally*), Delia probably knew a thing or two about being torturously in your sibling's shadow. I love the stories she tells: about saving your doughnut from lunch and then eating it gratuitously in front of your sister hours later; telling her there's an invisible man under her bed; sitting in the room while she's on the phone and mimicking her conversation; persuading her that she's adopted.

I'll bet you had your own versions. I'd feed my sisters cups of toothpaste mixed with tap water claiming it was good for them, and would creep into Felicity's bedroom at night, because I knew she was scared of vampires, and pretend to be a Dracula-esque monster called a Dakeela. I can still hear her screams occasionally in my daydreams. Happy times.

There were two things that acted as a peace treaty. The first were our BBC *Chronicles of Narnia* videos, recorded off the telly and fuzzy with years of watching. We warbled the opening music. We fantasized about silver boxes of Turkish delight. And we were as one in our fury towards our dad, Howard, for having recorded the 1994 Christmas episode of *EastEnders* – the one in which Sharon and Phil's affair comes out – over the second half of *The Silver Chair*. (This is the same man who taped the 1988 FA Cup final over my nursery nativity.)

Another was our holidays to Cornwall, or 'Cornie' as Dad called it, staying on a farm that came to feel like a second home. Each summer, we'd set off on a drive that according to Google Maps should have taken four hours forty minutes, but which the Family Cohen made last around eight – piling into our beloved blue Volvo estate that, when we eventually sold it years later, was used to run drugs around Lambeth and appeared on an episode of *Crimewatch*.

To pass the journey, my parents would put on our favourite cassette: an Enid Blyton story about a thief named Slippery One, who terrorized a village until he was caught by the local policeman with the immortal line – uttered in a Yorkshire accent – 'Slippery One, your slippery days are over.' We used to shout it out loud, squealing with laughter, any sisterly bickering forgotten and the holiday ahead hoving into view.

We could also be united behind a cause. If my parents ever suggested selling our childhood home, we became a trio of lawyers for the defence, arguing passionately that moving was a terrible idea and threatening to stage a protest on the garden path should any estate agents be spotted (this is presumably why they still live there now).

But we didn't consider ourselves friends. We had our own friends at school and sisters were, at that stage, to be taken for granted, ignored, resented and goaded, as well as loved, cuddled and bossed around. As psychologist Terri Apter puts it: 'You know how to tease them, how to insult them, how to control them ... There's great closeness and also constant competitiveness over just about anything.'

Growing up with sisters means having a sense of comparison culture in your home all day, every day. As we heard earlier, women and girls are encouraged to regard each other as competition. To judge one another's bodies and our own. To see other women as rivals for men, jobs, friendships. It sets us up to tear one another down and it holds us back from bonding as fully as we might in those younger years. It turns us into our own worst enemies, as well as each other's. And just like female friendships, it means that our sister relationships ebb and flow.

'It's a bit like dodgem cars, where you come close and bump into each other and then go apart again,' says Linda Blair. 'Absolutely you can be the best of friends, but that often doesn't happen until you're all grown-up, because then the competition element is diluted, and you have greater individuality.' Basically, as you develop your own interests, friends and career, you don't care so much about having what she's having. Suddenly, you are surrounded by your own network and have created a world independent of your family, which can help relax that sense of sibling rivalry.

It makes me wonder how on earth sisters like Venus and Serena Williams – who pursued exactly the same career and have not been independent of their family – managed it. In interview after interview they've claimed to be best friends and yet their entire lives have been about competing in the public eye. Venus appeared on the *Goop* podcast with Gwyneth Paltrow in July 2021, to explain:

'Growing up, my parents told us that your sisters are your best friends,' she said. 'That was the rule. So that's what we did and I like that because now we're even closer . . . There's always someone you can call, there's always someone there for you.'

I just don't know that if my parents had told us to be best friends that we'd have snapped into action and made it happen as children. But maybe that's why none of the Cohen sisters have won a Grand Slam despite growing up in the shadow of Centre Court.

Literature is also full of sisters who compete, disagree, betray, proclaim to despise one another and yet who love each other's bones. The Bennets in *Pride and Prejudice*; Meg, Jo, Amy and Beth March in *Little Women*; Pauline, Petrova and Posy Fossil in *Ballet Shoes*; the Ingalls of *Little House on the Prairie*; Jessica and Elizabeth in *Sweet Valley High*. If I'm honest, I often find these fictional sister relationships a little one-dimensional and predictable. There's a wise and patient one, a trouble-making one and a butter-wouldn't-melt one. In truth, we're capable of being all those things at different times. Just as with female friendship, the sister bond is dramatically over-simplified.

Austen perhaps came closest to the reality, particularly I think in the relationship between Elizabeth and Jane Bennet who, as friendship historian Professor Barbara Caine puts it, 'have to manage their family and manage their impossible mother, but they have a confidential relationship that gives them both enormous amounts of strength'.

Daisy Buchanan, one of six sisters, points out how hard it can be to forge those individual connections when you're part of a larger sister dynamic.

'Something that I worry about is because we're such a gang – and I think this happens in friendship groups as well – it's really hard for us to have separate relationships with each other,' she says. 'Getting to know each other outside the context of the gang is really rewarding, but I wish there was more time to be able to have unique relationships with them. If I was to ask them whether they felt that I was a distinct friend or just part of the jumble, I don't know what they'd say.'

Honestly, I don't know what my own would say either. Even though at this point, all in our thirties, I consider them friends as well as my little sisters. Only they're not so little now, being old enough and clever enough to run their own lives. If they come to me for advice it's usually just an approving nod of my head they're actually seeking; reassurance rather than actual guidance. We do talk about our worries – to an extent. There's still a part of me that holds things back, though; ever the big sister who doesn't want to burden the two people in the world to whom I'm supposed to be a role model, even if the hat no longer fits on what they never fail to remind me is my tiny pea head.

In any case, they have their own close female friendships; women who know them in a way I don't and whom they'd turn to as confidantes before they'd come to me. As do I. (Which is why, at my hen do, their jaws fell open as one of my friends told them about the time I went on a date with a well-known singer that ended with us eating Harrods steak while sitting on his kitchen floor.) Yet I don't think that having close female friendships has impacted my relationship with my sisters – in some ways it has helped.

Let me explain.

We were in our twenties before we started to become closer – shocked into it, I think. One March afternoon in 2015, Mum was rushed to hospital with sepsis, twenty-four hours from death, we were later told, and spent weeks in intensive care. That whole time is a blur. Visiting her every evening after work, getting home late after being gently asked to leave by the nurses and crying my eyes out while my husband held me. The tiredness, the worry, the fear. The constant brain-churning: what could I take with me to cheer her up, or bring comfort? Did my face betray my feelings? When could she come home? Was my dad coping? Was she improving? All this was made easier by knowing my sisters were feeling the same way. Just a text saying 'love you', and the knowledge they too were messaging, calling, worrying, visiting like I was, loosened the pressure valve. It brought home to us that someday, maybe even someday soon, we were going to swap roles with our parents and have to look after them. It's a sobering moment when that realization dawns and you try to push it to lurk in the outer reaches of your brain.

Two years later, I was on the train to work after having viewed Loughborough Junction's most eccentric flat during my lunch break. Having lived together for two years, Tim and I were hoping to buy our first home and it wasn't going well. So far we'd seen more than forty mostly awful places, including one where the estate agent managed to lock us in and we had to climb out of the window. This latest flat had been no better – the tenants had refused to let us in and when we did finally manage to gain entry, one of the women had refused to let us see her bedroom because her ankle was in a cast and she hadn't got any clothes on.

Deflated, I was on my way back to the office, when Mum called. My brother Tim, she explained, was fading and she and my dad were on the way to Scotland. Although he'd had cancer for some time, I don't think the hard reality of it had hit us until we'd seen him just a few weeks earlier, over Christmas. Before then, there had always been something that seemed to keep us positive, despite the gruelling hospital visits and rounds of chemotherapy he had endured: a medical trial, a successful operation, his downplaying of how bad things really were.

Now, he seemed to have aged prematurely – my tall, skinny brother who always turned up at our house when we were kids wearing a leather jacket and a silver hoop in his ear like Damon Albarn. Who would tell me how the bass at the Prodigy gig had been so loud he'd thought the balcony he was standing on might collapse. Who had briefly moved in with us when we were children. Who'd married the woman of his dreams ten years earlier, under an ancient tree in Inverness, and encouraged me to dance ceilidhs all night on a broken foot. Who had two wonderful children; one boy and one girl. Who still had his group of close friends from school. Who'd once been to the top of the World Trade Center. Who was obsessed with *Star Wars*, Arsenal, collecting old records and buying ludicrous cars, including a Hummer. A couple of days after that phone call, he was gone. Aged forty-eight.

This might be a book about female friendship, but my brother's death taught me the hardest lesson of my life when it comes to my sisters: how important it is to cement our relationships now. That it's not enough to imagine that, one day, you'll be the only ones left who remember your parents and that this simple fact will bring you closer. Because you can't count on it and to imagine you can is a fool's errand. I did and now I'll never have the adult friendship with my brother that I imagined was written into our futures.

In many ways, we're all still coming to terms with it and we're not a family of talkers. But it has created a shift. We started to need one another as sisters but also as equals, ploughing the lessons we've learned from our close female friendships over the years – the subtlety of language, empathy, compassion, the unspoken acknowledgement of support – back into our sibling relationships. It's still a work in progress, but it means so much more to us now than ever before.

'It's enormously important, the relationship we have with our siblings – more important, probably, or at least as important as the ones we have with our parents,' says Linda Blair. 'Those are the longest relationships of our lives. Our parents die before us usually, so our siblings really matter. And the great advantage of sibling relationships is you can't get out of them. That may not sound like an advantage, but it is . . . because you can't divorce your siblings, you've got to sort something out.'

It is of course important to acknowledge that families have all kinds of complicated dynamics and no-go subjects. Truthfully, you might never be friends with your siblings, cousins or parents. You might be close one year, estranged the next. Your family ties might not ever mature, or matter.

Sister estrangement, Terri Apter explains, is usually the result of a long history of insults, rejection or put-downs. 'But one of the most vehement quarrels between sisters has to do with different stories about the family that they tell. They might both remember that something happened, but have a very different take on it. And there can be a lot of fractures over that: "you're betraying my family with your memories".'

'What causes all kinds of relationships to fail in the end is the amount of crap that you throw at them through negligence or just without thinking,' adds Robin Dunbar. 'But family in general is kind of more prepared to put up with more. They're held in place by this interlinking spider's web of relationships. Still, there comes a point where it's just too much and, like romantic relationships, they fracture totally and irreparably.'

★

So many women I interviewed told me that their friends were their family. Sometimes because they didn't get along with their parents and siblings, sometimes because they simply weren't close and had actively sought out friends who could offer the same sort of support system.

'There's an awful lot of people for whom their family is their friendship group,' says historian Barbara Caine. 'And I think women have the freedom to do that now, which they wouldn't have had before. You're financially independent. You may get on reasonably well with your parents and siblings, but you might just feel you don't have that much in common. And you're no longer in a situation where it's expected that's where you will spend your time and where your emotional energy will be directed.'

The term 'chosen family' originated in the LGBTQ+ community, which saw so many people rejected by their biological families and so seeking that connection elsewhere. Theirs was a bond based on a shared identity; something that is still vital today. A study of teenagers in Illinois in 2013[31] showed that a 'chosen family' was still their most important outlet for discussing issues around sexuality, with networks of friends being most crucial for transgender, gender non-conforming and genderqueer teens.

Abbie Naish, whom we met in 'The Friendship Gap' chapter, grew up thinking that as a lesbian she would never have children, so always recognized the importance of friends in her life. 'Back then I thought, "I'm gonna need a lot of other people around me, I need a chosen family,"' she says. 'That's been a huge part of my life, thinking, "Who's going to be there for me when I'm really old? Is it going to be friends?"'

In recent years, however, the term 'chosen family' has been co-opted to mean, simply, your people. Your 'ride or dies'. Anyone who can meet the needs that your biological family isn't able to. In my research, I've come across it used to describe groups fighting addiction, networks of single mothers, refugee communities who have been forced to flee their homes, charities who provide Christmas lunch for women in domestic-abuse refuges, as well as groups of hipsters living in Brooklyn lofts.

'It certainly is becoming a very powerful thing that you have this group of people you have chosen who are much more to you than your biological family,' says evolutionary anthropologist Dr Anna Machin. 'You can be your true self and you're not judged by your chosen family.'

And as we're reaching the markers of adulthood later – if we choose to do those things at all – so the role of a chosen family that won't judge you for not 'conforming' is taking on more importance in our lives. Increasingly, that means our female friends, the women we actively choose to have around us, spend time with, expend emotional energy over, might just end up feeling like sisters themselves.

*

If you're fortunate enough to get along with your mother, would you call her a friend? It's possibly the trickiest question when it comes to female family friendships. However close you might be, does the basic fact that you're mother and daughter – with one of you having an unknowable past; the other likely having an unknowable present, unless you tell your mum every single thing – place a barrier between you?

I am close to my mum, Jane. After all, she has everything I look for in a female friend: kindness, thoughtfulness, endless interest in my life, a car. But she's my mother and has been on the planet a lot longer than me. She had an entire life before I existed; one I only really know a little about. I am lucky that we speak a couple of times a week, at least. She is the only person I can wang on to about my passion for *Who Do You Think You Are?*. We've spent hours plotting her family tree. We discuss art, books and her awful taste in romantic comedies – do not watch *Surviving Christmas* starring Ben Affleck, I beg of you. She is my dearest friend (sorry Dad, female friend) but she's also my mother and so . . . not perhaps a friend in the truest sense?

'I think that the mother–daughter relationship is not quite a friendship,' says Terri Apter. 'People sometimes say, "I'm good friends with my mother" and that suggests it's relaxed. You can reveal your feelings, your problems, your thoughts. Many people can't do that with their mother though – they're worried about being judged, they're worried about their mother's anxiety. They don't want too much revelation from their mother – not only because it's a burden if it's not going well, but also because it's a bit icky if it involves personal feelings. Yes, they accept they're sexual beings but they want to keep that knowledge at a little bit of a distance.'

That escalated quickly. But it sort of gets to the nub of the mother–daughter friendship issue: they aren't your peers, with all those shared current cultural references and experiences that can get you so far. They aren't age-gap friends, with whom you can speak openly and freely about your interior life. Where do they fit into the picture?

'My mum tells me I'm her best friend but she is not

mine – she's my mother, which is different,' says Kate, thirty-two. 'I've got lots of friends and don't need another, but she's my only Mum. I think friendships were different for my mum's generation; she got married, moved and made friends with other parents – but not the sort of deep friendships I have. She doesn't have anyone to speak to about her problems and worries, so she tells them to me – of course I support her but I'd love it if she had friends, too. There is this bit of loneliness within her that I think comes from the lack of true friendships in her life.'

My friendships are also different from my mum's. She's always had a couple of close childhood pals whom she stays in touch with, and there were several school mums, but her circle was quite small when we were growing up. It's only as we've moved out, and her obsession with Pre-Raphaelite art has become almost a second career, that I've observed with pride her ability to move easily in rarefied circles and make new friends, including the closest female friendship of her life.

'Any reflection on your mother as a friend to her friends usually comes in early adulthood and up to middle age,' says Terri Apter. 'You see the fluctuation of friendships, you see them come and go, you see the delight and the pain that they often cause, and then you think, "Gosh, my mother would drop people if she didn't think they admired her enough" or "My mother put her friends first".'

That, psychologist Linda Blair thinks, is the key to a true mother–daughter friendship: that your mum can almost treat you as she might one of her friends.

'But it takes a really long time,' she says. 'Your mother has to be the kind of person that lets go and sees you as a person and doesn't need to analyse you when you're together. It's mostly up to the mother and not the child.'

For me, that's the essence of any family friendship – the ability to see you as others do; objectively and as your own person, rather than the sister who used to boss you around, or the disciplinarian parent. If you can get to a place where you know all these things about one another, but you're making an effort to find out the new – to not pigeonhole or constantly pick over the past – then you might just be able to bond with your family in a way that has those important elements of genuine friendship: respect, space and openness – something that goes beyond the dutiful promises of being there for one another because of the DNA you share.

And sometimes, even if they read your diary and killed your Tamagotchi, family friends can turn out to be the unlikeliest of them all.

Old Friends

Myth: If you haven't got any long-lasting friendships, it's too late to make them

It is 7.45 p.m. on a Sunday evening and I am refreshing my inbox for the tenth time, when it appears. The response I have been worrying about for two decades. That's how long I have waited to say sorry to my oldest friend for something I did when we were teenagers, and which has gnawed away at the pit of my stomach ever since.

Click. Open. It's short – that might be a good sign? I scan straight to the end of the email to see if there are any kisses and accidentally read the last sentence first.

'I'm not sure you've got anything to apologize for, but thank you anyway!'

I flop back in my chair, stunned. I don't know what I expected – but it wasn't this.

The thing about old friends is that they aren't supposed to throw curveballs. In our minds, they are rocks of loyalty, love and security. Pure nostalgia in human form. They know where you came from. They call your mum and dad by their first names. They remember your teddy bear and can still recite your home phone number. They are survivors in a world that so often undervalues the power and importance of friendship.

It's why we can so easily take them for granted: putting newer friends who we think require more attention ahead of older ones; sliding into set patterns of behaviour; or keeping them in boxes, resenting it when they do anything that doesn't conform to our set-in-stone picture of who they once were.

This is one of the few facets of female friendship we do tend to romanticize: 'Make new friends, but keep the old. Those are silver, these are gold.'

It's an on-screen favourite, too. The Hollywood message when it comes to old friends is that you can take them for granted and give them food poisoning (*that* scene in *Bridesmaids* . . .) but still come back together when it counts. You will stick by one another till death like Thelma and Louise or maybe even beyond it, *Death Becomes Her*-style.

For me, one of the truest fictional portrayals is in Elena Ferrante's Neapolitan novels – the sort of books you miss train stops reading – which tell the story of a sixty-year friendship between Lila, the more rebellious and spirited of two girls, and Elena, who follows a path to academia out of their violent Naples neighbourhood. They endure all the ebbing and flowing – in their case love, estrangement and passion – so many of us can recognize in our own old friendships. Clearly it's a narrative that resonates, since the books have sold more than 15 million copies and been translated into forty-five languages. The language of honesty and truth about long-term female friendship is universal and many readers, this one included, felt as though the characters were old friends of their own by the end.

In a column for the *Guardian* in April 2018, Ferrante noted that 'The Italian word for "friendship", *amicizia*, has the same root as the verb "to love", *amare*, and a relationship between friends has the richness, the complexity, the contradictions, the inconsistencies of love. I can say, without fear of exaggeration, that love for a woman friend has always seemed of a substance very similar to my love for the most important man in my life.'

Amicizia: a delicious pizza-topping of a word that captures the true romance deep within our old friendships – trust the Italians to come up with that one.

I've known some of my female friends for almost three decades. If I were marking that impressive milestone with my husband, we'd be popping champagne corks, exchanging gifts, and dancing around the living room to our favourite records. Nurturing a romantic relationship or marriage is a different challenge; but is keeping a long friendship going any less of an achievement?

Let's face it, life has a way of throwing unwanted milestones at us relentlessly as we get older – the menopause, making a will, the first time you have a 'fall' as opposed to just tripping – so isn't it about time we started making our own happier ones, too? The traditional gift for thirty years of marriage is a pearl – something that starts as a bit of grit and slowly matures into a rare and precious gem. Why does that sentiment not apply to our old friendships, too?

When Izzy and I had been friends for ten years, we marked it as any pair of wild and single nineteen-year-olds would: in the Marks and Spencer cafe. I remember sipping a cup of tea and nibbling a giant chocolate-chip cookie, toasting our mugs to having been in one another's lives for a decade. It's the only time in my life that I've done anything approaching that with a friend; acknowledging out loud the years we've spent together. Then boyfriends came along and our friendship anniversaries were replaced by candlelight (OK, striplight) meals with boys at Cafe Rouge. Why do we sideline our friendship anniver-saries in this way? It just didn't occur to us to go out for a PG Tips to mark fifteen, twenty or twenty-five years. But I wish we had at least remembered them.

I get that for some this might all sound a bit too 'perfect', like the BFF myth itself.

But for me longevity is only one factor in a friend-ship feeling 'old'. Sylvia Plath had another criterion, writing: 'There is nothing like puking with somebody to make you into old friends.' Anyone who's held a mate's hair back as they projectile-vomit will know what she was talking about. Sometimes closeness and the sense that you're 'old friends' can come from a bonding experience and has nothing to do with hav-ing been to the same primary school.

Professor Robin Dunbar can't say for sure what makes someone into an 'old friend', but he tells me, 'I suspect it has to do with the time of life when it happens [you become friends], for example university when you did a lot of drinking, singing, dancing and late-night crisis talks – all the things that trigger an endorphin hit, and so reinforce the relationship.'

The assumption being that if you do enough of these things, the friendship can feel 'old' regardless of how much physical time has passed. It's like Shasta Nelson's theory of a 'best friendship' being about quality and not quantity. Under that definition, we probably all have someone we could call an 'old friend' or who might yet become one. And just because someone is an old friend on paper, it doesn't always mean they're your most intimate. In her research, anthropologist Dr Anna Machin found that shared history can actually have a negative effect on how close female friends are, suggesting that how much emotional intimacy you have *right now* is more important. Shared history was more vital to men's friendships, which explains why my husband and his mates are constantly talking about the triathlon they did back in 2016.

It might not surprise you to know that Jilly Cooper – who has a rare talent for making anyone feel like an old friend, flattering me down the phone and inviting me for lunch (just booking my train) – is also a pro at keeping up with them all. For her, laughter and gossip are key to maintaining old friendships. 'As soon as you get together again you say, "Oh gosh what happened to so and so?"; "Did so-and-so marry?"; "Oh the marriage has broken up, oh gosh how awful",' she says. 'Three girls I knew at typing school when I was seventeen – and I'm eighty-four now – turned up to lunch the other day and it was really just instant giggles as soon as they arrived. You just pick them up again like a tennis ball and have lovely fun with them.' (Of course, adds Jilly, 'dogs have always been my best friends, too'.)

During the pandemic, she sent seventy Valentine's cards. 'I wrote, "Cruel Covid keeps us apart. Please remember you still have my heart,"' she laughs. 'I sent that to lots and lots of my old friends, right back to the girls I used to share a flat with. It was lovely sharing a flat with girls because you're just a pack of hounds hunting for husbands and so we had so much in common.'

I love the romance of writing cards to friends like that; it's thoughtful and old-fashioned in a way that cements your friendship as meaningful. I have a pile of cards and postcards that Izzy has sent me over the years; a tangible reminder not only of our longevity but of the effort we have made.

I have a clear memory of seeing Izzy in the playground for the first time, aged nine – her uniform box-fresh, a look of shy anticipation on the face that I would come to know so well.

For six years, we spent every Saturday together – at first devoting hours to stringing conkers for knuckle-throbbing battles and playing board games; later trawling Kingston upon Thames high street for inflatable aliens and velvet chokers. As teenagers, we were allowed to catch the bus there by ourselves and spend the day without any adults – now that's an endorphin-releasing bonding activity. It was a military operation: Topshop, Tammy, C&A's Clockhouse range, Madhouse, Hennes. Then HMV, Woolies, Tower Records. Quick flick through the posters in Athena.

We would 'do lunch', which meant a Boots Meal Deal, with a flatbread wrap so dry you could have worn it as an espadrille, eaten in the graveyard. If we were feeling flush, we would head for the mother ship: John Lewis. There, in the top-floor cafe, we would queue for the one thing we could afford – a bowl of lentil soup, with a roll, butter and as many croutons as you liked. We felt devastatingly grown-up.

A Saturday evening at Izzy's involved a curry. At mine, it was Mum's pasta bake and listening to cassettes of the Top 40 recorded off the radio. We went on summer holidays together and came to think of each other's homes and families as an extension of our own. Apologies to my husband, but they were the happiest times of my life – even if I didn't realize, back then, just how lucky I was.

Speaking to women about their oldest friendships has also been one of the great joys of writing this book, particularly how many wanted to share their 'origin stories' with me.

'How did you meet?' is a question every couple is asked, right from your first teenage love. But it's not something we tend to lead with when it comes to friends. And it's weird because we *adore* origin stories. We like it when something comes out of nothing – and what better example of that is there than friendship?

The problem, I guess, is that female-friendship stories don't tend to follow the same dramatic arc as those of romantic love, or rags to riches. They are often stop-start in a way that would annoy the hell out of any Hollywood scriptwriter.

Paola, twenty-eight, told me about meeting her oldest friend – a memory that makes her cringe, but that is just the sort of unique female friendship story I think we should be celebrating in all its embarrassing loveliness.

'It was my final year of university. We vaguely knew each other from hanging around with the same people, but had never really spoken much,' she says. 'One day we discovered that we'd both recently been heartbroken. We left whatever fun event we were at to go and wallow. And I mean *wallow*. We sat on her bed for the rest of the afternoon, curtains closed, feeling sorry for ourselves. This kind of behaviour went on for a whole term and for more time after than I am prepared to admit. Just to be clear, these boys weren't even our boyfriends. That's what is so cringeworthy. They were both a very brief series of drunken incidents. I'm pretty sure they weren't spending their time together analysing everything we'd ever said. Somewhere, I still have letters we sent each other over the summer (we wallowed via every available channel) and I think it will be at least another twenty years until I feel comfortable reading them.'

The silver lining to trawling my own inbox for research purposes for this book has been that it's helped me to understand that I have more old friends than I realized. Izzy. Marie, whom I've known since we were twelve. But also Agatha, whom I've known since the age of twenty-one and Eve, whom I met at twenty-two, now count as old friends in the most traditional sense. When did that happen? Those women are now irreplaceable in my life. As Jane Garvey put it to me: 'You can't acquire old friends – you've either got them by now, or you haven't.'

Though … I question whether that's actually the case. Helge Rubinstein, at ninety-one, tells me that she has made 'old friends' much later in life, with people who were mere acquaintances years ago suddenly taking on a more important role.

'At this point in my life, my friends keep dying. It's awful,' she tells me. 'It's like one's whole background begins to crumble. One is always looking around to see if there are any more there. So I'm making, not new friends, but old friends. People you knew and might have had dinners with, but you didn't know well, have become friends. And that's a weird, but rather nice process.'

I had been hoping to interview Helge along with Shirley Williams, the liberal politician and her best friend, but sadly Baroness Williams died in April 2021. What Helge describes to me is how the two women managed to keep their friendship alive for more than seventy years – from meeting at Oxford to sharing a flat in their twenties and then, extraordinarily, cohabiting for about fifteen years in a large house in Kensington with their husbands and children, and travelling together in their later years. So what was their secret? Helge attributes it simply to not demanding too much of one another.

'We just took each other for granted – by which I mean that I knew she'd be there for me if I needed her and vice versa. We took it for granted that it was all going to be OK,' she says. 'We got closer and less close; it moved backwards and forwards. But there was never an idea that we might fall out. It never occurred to us. We assumed we would be fine together.'

Simply, the two women never put any pressure on their friendship. 'It was good when we were together, and when we weren't together that was OK, too,' says Helge. 'It wasn't like a lot of friendships with girls because we didn't analyse ourselves together and maybe that was a good thing. Even when we were living together, we had very separate and independent lives, so there was never a clash or competition. I've never had a sister. But it's what I would expect a sister to be – that you were close but you could leave each other alone.'

That doesn't mean that they didn't nurture their friendship. Helge tells me how she supported Shirley when her first marriage broke down. 'We didn't have very intimate conversations about it. But I just thought, "*What can I do to make it a bit easier?*" Or "*What's the best way around this one?*" and we spent quite a lot of time together,' she says. It's the sort of 'keep buggering on' attitude to old friendship you'd expect from the wartime generation. But I think it also captures something that many of the oldest friendships have: the ability to just let your friends be. Yes, I am my own cheesy Beatles-inspired Instagram quote.

As Christine Webber, seventy-four, explains: 'I've

got one friend who I met in the 1960s, and we ring each other every week. She lives in the north of England and I live in Suffolk, but it's a friendship where you don't have to explain much – you don't have to explain who you are ever,' she says. 'I think that's important, because there are times when you just have to "be" ... who you are as opposed to what you've become.'

That doesn't mean you should take your old friends for granted; it's more that you're able to step back and let your friend grow or have space when they need it, but remain ready to step up when life demands. And deep down, whatever changes they might have gone through, they can just 'be' in your company; stripping away the layers and labels that life puts on us and getting back to something close to where it all began.

I imagine it a bit like those painted wooden nesting dolls. At the heart is the smaller person (perhaps literally) you were when your friendship began – and it's actually really comforting to think about that and know you have someone who can pop you back into that nostalgic cocoon. Someone you can randomly message saying, *'Remind me what colour your pencil case was at school?'* or *'Your mum's Christmas cake – does she add marzipan all over or just on top?'* The outer layers are those that adulthood has put on, each one expanding upon the last, helping you to grow, but not replacing the one before; just adding to it. All those layers remain beneath the outer shell and your oldest friends can peel you back right to the original little doll you are at heart.

The tricky thing is to not keep your oldest friends in that tiny box. If you've known someone since you were very young, it can be hard to see them any other way than the twelve-year-old who declared they were never getting married. That can mean you feel resentful when they do change or behave in a way that doesn't fit with your preconceived notion of them.

'I have friends I've known since I was four and I'm now thirty-five,' says Pandora Sykes. 'And I really value loyalty. But I know that can be dangerous because if you have friendships that you've been in for a really long time there can be that feeling of kind of being stalled – when you can't be who you want to be. You might want to be someone else at twenty-five to who you wanted to be at fourteen. I feel particularly lucky because we've all allowed each other the room to grow. We're not possessive friends. I've learned so much from them. I am who I am because of who they are.'

I love that sentiment – it reminds me of one of my favourite friendship sayings: 'You can't become yourself by yourself.' That's where old friends are so vital in helping to shape you, but not demanding you stay that same shape forever. 'How much do you think friendships change our lives?' Elena Ferrante was asked by a *Guardian* reader in 2021. 'A friend doesn't change us, but changes in her quietly accompany changes in us, in a continuous, mutual effort of adaptation,' she replied.

When we talk about nature versus nurture, certainly in childhood, we tend to mean the influence of our parents, as well as the social environment, class and culture in which we are raised. The nurture angle goes something like: it's your family and your upbringing that shape you. But what also shapes you are the friends you interact with from the age of four or fourteen or twenty-four, all the way up to now. They are there for the big milestones your parents don't need to know about: your first crush, your first kiss, the first time you throw up from drinking too many orange Bacardi Breezers. Perhaps they are just as important in nurture as your parents; maybe more in some ways. 'My oldest friend slept with someone for the first time when we were thirteen,' Kat, thirty-six, told me. 'I went home and wrote about it in my diary as this massive thing that had occurred in both our lives. It was like it had happened to me and I still think about it like that now'.

The lines can blur when it comes to factoring in new relationships. Maybe Justine Tabak has the right idea. She and her friend of fifty-seven years keep their friendship and their relationships apart.

'Unlike some of my other friends, where we'll have dinners and get our partners around a table ... our friendship is quite exclusive to that. So I'm not at her dinner table with her partner, and I don't take my partner. We don't do social things together, we keep our friendship quite separate,' Justine says.

When they were younger, she explains, they had boyfriends who were perhaps a touch jealous of their friendship. 'Certainly in my twenties and thirties ... I sometimes had to be very careful because they might think, "Why is she speaking to her about this and not me?",' says Justine. 'So I've learned that I've got to be a little bit careful in relationships, I mustn't put her first. And because she's such a good friend – and because she was divorced and I was separated – we both recognized that sometimes some of what we've invested in each other should, possibly, have maybe been invested more in our relationships.'

Justine tells me that their choice to keep their friendship separate was subconscious; something she hadn't even thought about until we spoke. It shows just how easily we can fall into set patterns of communication with our old friends. And how self-conscious we can feel about them sometimes. After all, it takes trust to pour decades of time and energy into a single other person to whom you have no legal or familial obligation, and when your bond will most likely be trivialized in society by comparison to your romantic relationships.

Does a tiny part of us see our old friends as 'baggage'? In the same way that you wouldn't necessarily put on Tinder that you have three cockapoos and a pet snake (definitely second date information), you wouldn't mention, probably for a while, that you had a friend of several decades who is as important to you as any partner would ever be – and whom you'd turn to first in times of trouble, as we so often do.

'I find that old friends get in touch when they are experiencing something dreadful happening in their lives and they need the support of a friend who they know they can trust and are able to speak freely with,' agrees my mum, Jane. 'If we can still pick up a phone and have a supportive and uninhibited conversation, then that surely must be a continuing, meaningful friendship. If we still think of our female friends when we are seeking a comforting conversation, no matter how many years have passed by, then it is still a true friendship.'

★

One area where old friendships can stumble is when it comes to making excuses for them. We tend to hold new and old friends to different standards. Think about it – when you make a new friend, it's often because you hold a shared world view. With childhood friends, that can be turned on its head: because you came from the same place, you *assume* that similar values exist between you and don't interrogate them in the same way. And if they behave badly, you can justify it because you 'know why they're like that' and what challenges have made them into the person they are today.

Memories can obscure morals – unless they're forced down your gullet, that is. A 2014 study by Christopher Sibona at the University of Colorado[32] found that we tend to delete old school friends on Facebook before we delete any other type of friend because of their polarizing opinions. Newer friends we only tend to delete if they annoy us IRL. As my friend Paola puts it: 'The newer friends that have stuck for me are the ones with whom I have similar core values. We largely feel the same about stuff that really counts – which is actually not a standard I hold my childhood friends to at all.'

Are you happy with the balance in your own life?

Stop and think about it. Rest this book on your lap for a moment. Do you treat the old and new differently? Are there things your old friends do or say that you'd never let a more recent pal get away with?

Here's the thing, though – I don't know if I want my old friends to hold me to lower standards. That's surely the first step on the road to resentment. Old friends are the ones I want to tell me bald truths, horrible though they are to hear. Agatha once called me up and gave me a bollocking as I was walking out of Oxford Circus Tube station. I remember standing outside Liberty, a hot red flush blooming on my cheeks, as she said the sentence that still rings in my ears today: *'We're not bloody kids any more. You can't just go around snogging anyone you want.'* In that instance, I concede that she had a point. Though it stung, I respected Agatha's honesty. I'm glad that I have old friends who care enough to deliver me a shit sandwich. I don't want them to enable me, however much it might momentarily make me panic that I've turned them against me. I'd like to say I've grown since then, but I had an experience while writing this book that showed me how nervous I can still be about incurring their wrath.

Secretly, I think many of us have these moments of friendship paranoia. When your friend's voice seems a bit 'off' in a text, for example, or you have a missed call from someone who usually prefers to message. *Are they annoyed with me?* you think as you scroll back through your last few exchanges for clues. And yes, you could pick up the phone and just ask. But that would mean having one of those honest friendship conversations that we're so very bad at.

With old friends, that paranoia can balloon because you might not see one another often. Friendship security thrives on routine, and any silence or uncertainty leaves us scrabbling around for hints about how the other person is feeling about us. Which is when we might very well interpret a perfectly innocent message as a sign our friend no longer likes us.

The journalist Julia Carpenter summed it up for me when she tweeted, 'Very tempted to start a podcast called "Are You Mad at Me?" just so I have a quasi-reasonable excuse to interview every single one of my friends each week, at length, to determine whether or not they are actually in fact mad at me.'

I felt exactly that way when I recently had a missed call from Marie, something that isn't unusual as she lives abroad and we often phone one another. Yet I managed to convince myself that I must have upset her. Before ringing back, I had been online to look at flight prices and how soon I could get to her to make sure my old friendship wasn't ruined because I'd put my foot in it over something. Where was my passport?

Of course, it was pure friendship paranoia and she had actually been calling to ask my advice. I felt ridiculous for going back to that place of distrust with one of my oldest pals. Especially because we're closer now than we've ever been – even in sixth form, when we shared a passion for the English Civil War. We still message one another every 30 January to acknowledge the anniversary of King Charles I's beheading – our version of a friendship landmark, I suppose.

Despite the thousands of miles between us, we have

found a way to be there for one another through grief, illness, success, uncertainty, joy. Life's big milestones. As I sit here writing about her, I've just realized that we have been friends for twenty-five years this year. A quarter of a century; almost the full pearl. How come I hadn't even thought about that until this very second? I could scream.

It is my mission, and I hope it can be yours, too, to at least remember these friendship milestones. To consciously think about our friends – old or new – in the way we do our romantic relationships, placing just as much store by those special moments or years passed.

My first convert is Jane Garvey. 'You've put the idea into my head,' she says. 'I think when we're all sixty, my school friends and I should definitely celebrate it. We should definitely mark it much more than we do.'

In the not-too-distant future, Izzy and I will have been friends for thirty years. If that's not a friendship feat worth marking, I don't know what is. Not least because it might have all come crashing down in my teens. For the best part of two decades, I have lugged around a heavy kettlebell of guilt over my teenage behaviour towards my oldest friend. Because when I moved schools, aged twelve, everything changed. I had to make new friends and slowly dropped my Saturdays with Izzy in favour of tagging along with a group of girls in my class who really couldn't have cared less whether I was there or not. I started dating a boy they knew, in the hope it might win me some cool points. (I mean, he did have blond curtains and a white Kappa tracksuit. I'm only human.)

I basically ditched Izzy and I'm not sure I've ever regretted anything more. I've always considered it my biggest friendship mistake and, over the years, wondered how much hurt I caused her. We've never talked about it: not over any of the pints of ale, walks or dinners we've shared. Not in the Christmas cards where, every year, we write the lyrics to a song we made up on the way home from school more than twenty years ago. And yet, when she replied to a short questionnaire I sent out as part of my research for this book, she told me that ours was her happiest friendship story. That was almost too much for my guilt complex to bear.

So I sat down at my desk, took a deep breath and started writing the words I should have already said.

'The way I took our friendship for granted as a teenager, I feel huge regret over – and I always think I should just apologize to you. But it's quite a weird and hard thing to just bring up. I'm sorry, I should never have let my own insecurities about being at a different school get in the way of our friendship. I should have said this years ago and in person.'

I pressed send and swallowed hard. It was 4.53 p.m. on a Sunday afternoon and I had just lifted the lid off a colossal can of worms. What had I done? Three hours later, my laptop pinged. The screen was almost swimming in front of my eyes, as I opened it and read that confusing last sentence, my brow furrowed as I scrolled up and started from the top.

'That's so unexpected – it's amazing how different perceptions can be. I hadn't realized how hard you'd found it to move schools (which in hindsight, obviously it would have been) but we both had to make new friends. I'm not sure

you've got anything to apologize for, but thank you anyway!'

Sometimes old friends are the ones who hold you to just the right standards and want you to know you're being too hard on yourself. They're the people in your life with whom you have a sort of unspoken shorthand and a level of understanding that transcends any 'So what's your news?' catch-up conversations. They can just let you 'be'.

It might not always be obvious, but when that sort of bond does reveal itself it can offer one of the safest environments in female friendship, I think: the space to be yourself, to learn, to feel loved, secure and seen – or, if you're anything like me, to discover that you always were. And if that's not worth celebrating, I don't know what is.

Definitely Not a Love Letter to My Book Club

There is one WhatsApp group on my phone in which I unfailingly read every message. It's titled 'BC', which stands for Book Club – a group of women I have known for the best part of a decade. Every month, we meet at one member's house. The host cooks, pours the wine and buys new books to add to our impossibly large travelling library – a hessian bag-for-life from which we each choose something new to read. There is no 'set text' because life is too short. Instead, we each review what we've managed to read that month (or, let's be honest, watched on the telly) for the others; that way, really good books eventually get passed round seven sets of hands. Mostly, though, we put the world to rights. Five of us are journalists – what do you expect?

During the pandemic, the BC 'Extras' WhatsApp group was born. There were just four of us on it; the quartet who didn't have children. Circumstances count for so much in times of crisis. The seven wonderful women of Book Club are members because we all live in London, we all enjoy eating cheese as a starter (not even sorry) and we all have a horrified fascination with one current Member of Parliament and what is rumoured to be his astonishingly oversized member.

That four of us have created our own chapter in the BC story is mostly down to the luxury of free time. We found ourselves at home with little to do other than message one another, while our other book clubbers had their hands full with the unimaginable demands of home-schooling. Over those long lockdown months, what was comfortable suddenly became essential. It might be the first time that I've been able to be so totally and utterly relaxed with a group of female friends, after a lifetime of distrust and disappointment.

Maybe you had a similar experience, during a period when many of us felt forced to examine the shape of our friendships: who we could face video-calling regularly and with whom we felt little more than a sense of duty to keep in touch. Who we turned to when seeking an emotional connection and who made us laugh when humour seemed thin on the ground. For me, I suddenly felt confident enough in a shared experience (and maybe a pandemic is the ultimate example of it) to be totally open about how I was feeling. You knew your friends weren't going to misunderstand or judge you, because they could relate, hard, even as we all dealt with our own different struggles, too.

The Extras shared photos of our pets: two cats, one dog and an absolutely enormous rat that Rachel's husband caught in a trap under their kitchen sink. We dissected Harry and Meghan's life in America in such detail that I'm amazed CNN hasn't offered us our own talk show. We chose one another's new trainers and picked out what colours to paint our front doors. When things seemed dark, we coped by mercilessly, relentlessly, poking fun at ourselves, and each other, until life seemed a bit less scary again.

We were there during work disasters and unexplained foul moods. We were there through tragedy. When my aunt, my dad's youngest sister, was diagnosed with lung cancer in November, just before the second lockdown, and died two months later, there were only four friends with whom I felt strong enough to share how I was feeling. Whom I felt able to tell just how heartbreakingly awful it had been to help clear out her flat, filled floor to ceiling with the accumulated possessions of a lifetime, and how it made me want to go home and throw away every single thing I owned.

Throughout the first lockdown we had a video call every week. It's no exaggeration to say that those calls kept me going. The conversations were a lifeline at a time when it felt as though so many personal relationships were drifting. When you suddenly couldn't hug your loved ones and were faced with the prospect of not seeing them for who-knows-how-long.

BC Extras were the antidote. Here were the friends to whom I didn't have to say 'Fine, thanks!' when asked how I was feeling. With whom it was OK to moan, even though I knew that I had no damn right to, given that I had a home, garden, husband, job, my health and enough spare cash to buy 'working from home' Birkenstocks.

We didn't skip a single one of those calls because each of us knew that however doomful the day had seemed, the evening would be brighter and sillier. There's something about group chats with friends that can fizz with energy, wit and the sort of all-consuming back-and-forth that means you have to give yourself up to it. For some people, weekly quizzes played that same role: a chance to laugh, commiserate and check-in virtually. It showed us just how powerful digital communication can be for keeping a friendship connection going and how, fundamentally, it's time and effort that count – however you make that happen.

For the Extras, it meant watching *Married At First Sight Australia* night after night, picking over the details as if our lives depended on it, across several thousand messages. We dropped food at one another's houses and diagnosed each other's strange skin ailments via picture messages. We debated all the important issues, such as whether it's OK to be attracted to one's male gynaecologist as he rummages around down there ('he had such a kind, concerned face though').

We met for socially-distanced walks and celebrated one another's birthdays with homemade cake in rusty Royal Wedding tins, eaten shivering while standing around park benches. When I took part in a virtual women's conference and was told by a fellow speaker, 'Honey, the secret to looking good online is a ring light like the influencers have – you should get one' . . . well, you can guess what the Extras bought for my birthday. Trolls.

We went on a weekend away to Dorset, when

restrictions allowed, where it rained almost non-stop and the dog spent our entire car journey passing foul-smelling gas. Turns out face masks do have other uses. We made like the Famous Five – picking russet apples, walking through fields, messing about with sloe berries, lighting fires. If I wasn't one of us, I'd probably have hated us.

We're not a clique; Book Club has three other members, for starters, all loved dearly and missed when they're not around. We all have other, important female friendships in our lives. But we four have formed a bond that I know will last. Or I hope it will. I'm no fantasist and, realistically, the chances of us sending 265 WhatsApp messages a day forever are slim. Like every group, our interactions will rise and fall. But, for me at least, what we've created is something that can't be taken back. After a lifetime of female-friendship fear, it meant so much more than passing the time, or anything approaching a sense of duty.

It meant that I felt able to be myself, at last. And that, not my ring light, was the greatest gift – and surprise – of all.

Epilogue

Female friendship starts with you. It is not about other people.

That might sound strange after nearly three hundred pages of reading about other people . . . but think about it. In order to have kind, warm, generous, fun, supportive, thoughtful, open, giving friends in your life, you have to be all those things first. More often than not, the kind of friend someone is to you is a direct reflection of the kind of friend you are being to yourself.

Perhaps that seems obvious, but how often do we stop and say it? How often do we take the time to think about what, as we have learned, are the most emotionally intimate and fulfilling relationships in women's lives – and yet which are constantly sidelined in favour of romantic love and the 'happy-ever-after' we're told is the pinnacle of any woman's achievements?

Female friendship is not a fairy tale. It's fucking hard, but the truth is that most good things are. That's why it's time to reject the myths that have been holding us back. The unrealistic Hollywood depictions, the stereotypes and tropes designed to keep us in neat little boxes. We are in the golden age of female friendship, so let's start shouting about it. Because being honest is not only liberating, it's good for your friendships.

What I now know over anything else – and hope you do, too – is that there isn't some know-it-all, fail-safe method to making female friendship work. No secret code or magic wand. It is – as we have heard from so many women in these pages – about shared values and interests, finding the same things funny and emotional. It comes down to time, effort, chemistry, energy, vulnerability, trust. And that means trusting yourself. If you can back yourself to be the best friend you can be (and you won't be perfect all the time), if you can give as much of yourself as possible and treat yourself with compassion, understanding and patience, then others are more likely to do so, too.

There will still be hard bits: friendship gaps to navigate, heartbreaks to recover from, unhealthy dynamics to deal with. But there will also be new friends, old friends, unlikely friends, family friends – and the joy, milestones, laughter, mutual respect and support that all of those can bring to your life. Because when they work, female friendships are among the most defining and precious relationships of our lives. They are the *loves* of our lives.

I hope the stories I have shared, my own and those from other women, have helped you to see your own female friendships in a new light. To understand what more you could be giving, and who could be giving you more. Maybe even to recognize, as one early reader did, that a toxic friendship is lurking in your own life.

Piecing together my own friendship history, I realize just how many of those unrealistic narratives I have bought into over the years and just how many potential friendships they prevented. If I hadn't believed in the myth of the BFF, instead of understanding the power of a portfolio, I might not have spent years chasing a female soulmate and my school friends might not have broken up with me. If I hadn't believed that gaps were terminal, I might not have let an important friendship drift. If I hadn't thought it might be too late to make new friends, I might have found the self-confidence to do it sooner.

If you can uncouple your sense of self-worth from that false image of friendship – from those stifling myths – and make the best of the friends you have? You will have learned to trust yourself at last. You don't have to have a perfect girl squad, a BFF twin, a chosen family, a sister or posse. It's so much more nuanced than that: whether you have one close friend your whole life, a special 'moment' with a friend like the IVF fairy – or a wider social circle, like me.

Now I watch those women on my morning train, the Mum Commute Club, and I feel certain that if my mobile phone were to break, I, too, have friends who would offer me their spare. Who would give me honest but supportive work advice. With whom I can chat rubbish and laugh unselfconsciously.

I'm not the finished article – my female friendships

are still a work in progress – but I know what I'm aiming for now, and how to get there in fifty, ninety or two hundred hours' time. And we can all do it.

Here is the truth about female friendship:

Feel the fear and do it anyway. Being open with your female friends won't scare them off. If you trust them, tell them: the bad news and the good. Having women who won't think you're smug for saying that you had a brilliant day are the ones you want to surround yourself with. The ones who listen. Don't be afraid to give them your Franken-heart.

Make time. Friends are easy to fob off when things seem stressful. We relegate them to the bottom of the hierarchy of love, just below our pets. Don't let them always be the first thing to go.

Tell 'perfect' to piss off. Hopefully, you'll know by now that anything that seems perfect probably isn't, and that includes Dave Grohl (just kidding, he is). The BFF myth, girl squads on social media, the idea that any bumps in the road mean your friendships are fatally flawed – it's all part of a narrative designed to make you feel like female friendships should be non-stop rainbows and unicorns. They shouldn't. Like any emotionally intimate relationship, you have to put in the work to reap the rewards.

Use your voice. Not telling a female friend how you really feel is like drinking poison drip by drip and expecting everything to be fine. It's how friendships end. If you love and respect her, brace yourself and have that tough conversation.

Call them. Sometimes a 'checking in' text is enough. Often, it isn't.

Don't mind the gaps. Friendship gaps can appear at any time, so you're quite possibly experiencing one right now. Don't walk away. Give them space and time if they need it, or ask for it if you do. Talk about how you can bridge the chasm between you. It might be a temporary stretch and not one that has to gape permanently.

Laugh. Hopefully, in the future, you'll all be talking about 'lady bants' as if it's the most normal thing ever (though hopefully with a better name). It's good for you, it will make your friendships closer and you know there's nothing as funny as the Mr Croutons of this world.

Never ghost. It's cruel and cowardly, and you're not a sociopath. Sorry.

Move forward. Friendship heartbreak, which I hope you haven't experienced and never will, is as painful as any other. Let yourself express your feelings, accept them, and then move on.

Treasure your old friends. You didn't become yourself by yourself.

. . . But be open to new ones. It's never too late to make new friends, as those wonderful women in their nineties told you.

Mark your milestones. In any way that you choose. This isn't about 'Galentine's Day', it's personal and with none of the pressure that comes with commercialized celebrations. Card, call, text, pint, cuppa, chips: whatever suits your friendship best.

Do you. Your friends don't want a caricature of the 'good girl' – someone who is playing at being the perfect pal. They know your flaws and love you anyway. Give them what they really want: you.

The only thing left to do is do it. Go forth and multiply your friendships; make your circle as happy and fulfilled as it can be, in the way you want. Because there is no female friendship formula. Only the one that works for you.

Notes

1 https://www.ukonward.com/wp-content/
uploads/2021/09/Age-of-Alienation-Onward.pdf

2 https://www.childrenssociety.org.uk/sites/default/files/
2020-09/good-childhood-report-2020-summary.pdf

3 https://www.sciencedirect.com/science/article/abs/pii/
S1090513812001225

4 https://pubmed.ncbi.nlm.nih.gov/21991328/

5 https://www.pnas.org/content/113/3/578.abstract

6 https://pubmed.ncbi.nlm.nih.gov/16758315/

7 https://pubmed.ncbi.nlm.nih.gov/15564353/

8 https://pubmed.ncbi.nlm.nih.gov/9200634/

9 https://psycnet.apa.org/record/2011-19550-001

10 https://www.jneurosci.org/content/37/25/6125

11 https://www.nature.com/articles/srep25267

12 https://scholar.harvard.edu/marianabockarova/files/
tend-and-befriend.pdf

13 https://www.researchgate.net/
publication/345319031_Sex_Differences_in_Intimacy_
Levels_in_Best_Friendships_and_Romantic_Partnerships

14 https://www.researchgate.net/publication/323783184_How_
many_hours_does_it_take_to_make_a_friend

15 https://tandfonline.com/doi/abs/10.1080/014633798093
70099

16 https://www.milkround.com/advice/why-workplace-friendships-are-worth-the-effort

17 https://www.glassdoor.com/blog/glassdoor-survey-reveals-ten-love-office/

18 https://www.totaljobs.com/media-centre/loneliness-causing-uk-workers-to-quit-their-jobs

19 https://www.researchgate.net/publication/323783184_How_many_hours_does_it_take_to_make_a_friend

20 https://www.ncbi.nlm.nih.gov/pmc/articles/PMC4852646/

21 https://www.researchgate.net/publication/323783184_How_many_hours_does_it_take_to_make_a_friend

22 https://807e0053-e54f-4d86-836f-f42a938cfc4c.filesusr.com/ugd/ca3202_51e49dd36f0f4328935720c4ebb29f02.pdf

23 http://papers.ssm.com/sol3/papers.cfm?abstract_id=1490708

24 https://www.wsj.com/articles/looking-for-a-friend-without-benefits-try-match-bumble-and-tinder-11625675336

25 https://statista.com/statistics/1040236/uk-stress-levels-of-generations/

26 https://academic.oup.com/cardiovascres/advance-article/doi/10.1093/cvr/cvab210/6307454

27 https://www.digitalthirdcoast.com/blog/news-consumption-during-covid-19

28 https://news.ucdenver.edu/study-shows-facebook-unfriending-can-have-offline-consequences/

29 https://www.pnas.org/content/pnas/early/2016/04/05/1524993113.full.pdf?sid=6b4259a2-1494-4ed8-8a76-f76d05f47940

30 https://www.sciencedaily.com/releases/2015/03/150316160747.htm

31 https://static1.squarespace.com/static/58dd82141b10e3ddf316781f/t/591802cbf5e2317b6a318c2f/1494745818158/ICAH-Given-Chosen-Fams-Research-Report-YLC-2013.pdf

32 https://www.researchgate.net/publication/261961408_Unfriending_on_Facebook_Context_Collapse_and_Unfriending_Behaviors

Further Reading, Watching and Listening

Reading

Friends: Understanding the Power of Our Most Important Relationships, Robin Dunbar (Little Brown, 2021)

Why We Love: The Science Behind Our Closest Relationships, Anna Machin (Weidenfeld & Nicolson, 2022)

What Did I Do Wrong? When Women Don't Tell Each Other the Friendship Is Over, Liz Pryor (Simon & Schuster, 2006)

You're the Only One I Can Tell: Inside the Language of Women's Friendships, Deborah Tannen (Virago, 2017)

The Business of Friendship, Shasta Nelson (Harper Collins, 2020)

The Inseparables, Simone de Beauvoir (Penguin Vintage Classics, 2021)

Pride and Prejudice, Jane Austen (1813)

The Neapolitan novels, Elena Ferrante: *My Brilliant Friend* (2012), *The Story of a New Name* (Europa Editions, 2013), *Those Who Leave and Those Who Stay* (Europa Editions, 2014), and *The Story of the Lost Child* (Europa Editions, 2015)

Between the Covers, Jilly Cooper (Bantam Press, 2020)

Are You There God? It's Me, Margaret, Judy Blume (1970)

The Panic Years, Nell Frizzell (Bantam Press, 2021)

Ballet Shoes, Noel Streatfield (1936)

The Sisterhood, Daisy Buchanan (Headline, 2019)

Thirty Things I Love About Myself, Radhika Sanghani (Headline, 2022)

Watching

Girls Trip (2017, dir. Malcolm D. Lee)

Steel Magnolias (1989, dir. Herbert Ross)

Booksmart (2019, dir. Olivia Wilde)

Animals (2019, dir. Sophie Hyde, from the 2014 book written by Emma Jane Unsworth)

Lady Bird (2017, dir. Greta Gerwig)

Waiting to Exhale (1995, dir. Forest Whitaker)

Frances Ha (2012, dir. Noah Baumbach)

Bridget Jones's Diary (2001, dir. Sharon Maguire)

Beaches (1989, dir. Allison Anders)

Broad City (2014–19, five series, written by and starring Ilana Glazer and Abbi Jacobson)

Girls (2012–17, six series, created by and starring Lena Dunham)

Fleabag (2016–19, written by Phoebe Waller-Bridge)

Motherland (2016–present, written by Sharon Horgan, Holly Walsh, Graham Linehan, Helen Serafinowicz and Barunka O'Shaughnessy)

Sex and the City (1998–2004, created by Darren Star)

And Just Like That (2021, created by Michael Patrick King and Darren Star)

Listening

Fortunately . . . with Fi and Jane

'Wannabe', Spice Girls (1996)

'Girl', Destiny's Child (2004)

'You've Got a Friend', Carole King (1971)

The High Low with Pandora Sykes and Dolly Alderton (2017–20)

Acknowledgements

If there's one thing that writing a book about friendship teaches you, it's who your friends are – and to whom you owe a full-throated thank-you.

Firstly, to my pals. More than once, it occurred to me that I might not have any friends left once I came out the back of being a book-writing hermit. Thanks to all of you – the old, the new, the Extras, the Arseholes, Ladies and the Shealing gang – for sticking around while I turned down your invitations, was painfully slow to reply to text messages and forgot to post your birthday cards on time. I'm eternally grateful that you still want to talk to me.

Thank you to my endlessly supportive agent, James Gill, for asking me for a book idea and then refusing to let me get away with not putting pen to paper on a proposal. Like all journalists, I needed a deadline and you provided one.

To everyone at Penguin who has put so much enthusiasm into making *BFF* what it is: particularly my fantastic editor Helena Gonda, who coaxed this book to life with her elegant mix of sensitivity, editing skill and straight-talking advice, Kate Fox, who took the reins so capably, Beci Kelly for making it look beautiful, Sophie Bruce for her marketing prowess, and Alison Barrow, the PR genie every author should be so lucky to work with.

I wouldn't be where I am right now without the generosity, vulnerability and honesty of the women (and the odd man) who agreed to share their friendship experiences with me – sparing the time for interviews, coffees, phone calls, Zooms and wine. There are too many of you to name here, but I know who each and every one of you is, which isn't as ominous as it sounds, and I'm thankful from the bottom of my heart. I only hope I've done your stories justice and I'm sorry for those I couldn't include.

For those friends not mentioned by name, know that you still helped me to write this book more than you'll ever know. Ditto my ex-friends, without whom I might never have understood the impact that female-friendship myths can have on all our lives.

But the biggest thank-yous are for my wonderful parents, Jane and Howard, who always believed in me and offered endless support, love, generosity, and never failed to take an interest.

To my darling sisters, Rosanna and Felicity, for whom this will probably be like reading my ultimate diary.

And my husband, Tim – my unwavering champion, who read every word of every draft, made me endless cups of tea and bought me a shiny rose-gold laptop that made me want to sit down and type every day. You're the closest thing I have to a (male) BFF. I couldn't have done this without you.

Claire Cohen is an award-winning journalist, named Women's Editor of the Year by the prestigious British Society of Magazine Editors for her agenda-setting articles and campaigning. She presents the 'BFF? with Claire Cohen' podcast, interviewing high profile women about their female friendships and was the host of the Imposters podcast, in which she spoke to high-profile women, including Priyanka Chopra and Samantha Cameron, about how they turned self-doubt into success.

Claire writes for publications including *The Times, Telegraph, Vogue, Grazia, Guardian* and the *Evening Standard* – and appears as a commentator on the BBC and national radio, as well as being an experienced public speaker.

In 2021, she was listed as one of Britain's Top 50 trailblazers for gender equality and is a proud founder member of the Ginsburg Women's Health Board. She lives in South London with her husband and tiny cat. *BFF? is* her first book.